Peregrinations

Walking in American Literature

AMY T. HAMILTON

UNIVERSITY OF NEVADA PRESS *Reno & Las Vegas*

University of Nevada Press | Reno, Nevada 89557 USA
www.unpress.nevada.edu

Jacket design by Teresa Wingfield

Library of Congress Cataloging-in-Publication Data
Names: Hamilton, Amy T., author.
Title: Peregrinations : walking in American literature / by Amy T. Hamilton.
Description: Reno : University of Nevada Press, [2017] | Includes bibliographical references and index.
Identifiers: ISBN 978-1-943859-64-1 (cloth : alk. paper) | ISBN 978-1-943859-65-8 (e-book)
LCCN 2017038765 (print) | LCCN 2017057836 (e-book)
Subjects: LCSH: Walking in literature. | American literature—History and criticism.
Classification: LCC PS169.W25 H36 2017 (print) | LCC PS169.W25 (e-book) |
DDC 810.9/35873—dc23
LC record available at https://lccn.loc.gov/2017038765

The paper used in this book meets the requirements of American National Standard for Information Sciences—Permanence of Paper for Printed Library Materials, ANSI/NISO Z39.48-1992 (R2002).

First Printing

Manufactured in the United States of America

For Stephen and Andrea Hamilton

Contents

Acknowledgments

This project has been under construction for more than ten years and has benefited from the insight and generosity of many people along the way. I began thinking about walking and literature at the University of Arizona while I prepared for my comprehensive PhD exams. At UA Daniel Cooper Alarcón, Larry Evers, Judy Temple, Edgar Dryden, Luci Tapahonso, and Annette Kolodny were exceptional teachers, mentors, and readers. Their guidance in the early stages of the project was invaluable. To Annette, especially, your intelligence and meticulous attention to detail have made me a better scholar, and your warmth and friendship have made me a better teacher and mentor. I look forward to our next Proustian tea!

Northern Michigan University (NMU) has supported this project with several much-appreciated research and travel grants and, most significantly, a yearlong sabbatical. Former College of Arts and Sciences dean Michael Broadway has been a staunch advocate for my scholarship, as was the late head of the English Department Ray Ventre. We miss you, Ray. Our current department head, Lynn Domina, has sustained NMU's tradition of supporting research and continues to look for ways to champion faculty. Thank you, Lynn. I am also deeply grateful for the English Department's administrative assistants, Lori Rintala and Angela Rasmussen, whose patience and professionalism are second to none.

NMU has provided me with an outstanding community of smart, accomplished, and kind colleagues. My thanks to all of them, in particular Lisa Eckert, Alisa Hummell, Lupe Arenillas, David Wood, Jon Billman, April Lindala, Rebecca Ulland, Grace Chaillier, Alex Ruuska, Shirley Brozzo, Wendy Farkas, Jacquie Medina, Elizabeth Monske, Chet Defonso, Russ Prather, Jim McCommons, Patricia Killelea, Sandy Burr, Jaspal Singh, and Rob Whalen. Thank you to Faith Kirk and Nels Olson for keeping an eye on the home front and for many years of friendship. I am grateful for the opportunity to teach so many bright and engaged NMU students. My special thanks to my former students Kyle Bladow, Ashley Goedker, and Tyler Dettloff. You continue to teach me so much.

I am also deeply indebted to my intellectual communities in the Western Literature Association, the Association for the Study of Literature and Environment, and the Association for the Study of American Indian Literature. My colleagues in those organizations have listened to multiple conference papers about walking and offered much-appreciated feedback and inspiration. P. Jane Hafen encouraged me to think about walking in Louise Erdrich's novels, a casual hallway conversation that eventually led to chapter 5 of this book. Michael Branch, Joni Adamson, and Melody Graulich have been kind and encouraging mentors and role models. My conference pals have become true friends and colleagues. Special acknowledgment is due to Jennifer Ladino, Erin James, Chadwick Allen, Lisa Tatonetti, Joanna Hearne, Christina Roberts, Susan Bernardin, Amanda Gradisek, Nicolas Witschi, Suzanne Roberts, Jim Bishop, John David Miles, Kyhl Lyndgaard, and Rebecca Lush.

Also essential to the development of this project were the contributions of incredibly gifted and generous readers over the years. My neverending gratitude to Brianna Burke, Tom Hillard, Eric Chilton, and Matt Burkhart for their insightful and careful reading, their unflagging support, and their friendship. Thank you, too, to my writing-accountability partner Caroline Krzakowski for keeping me on task and inspired. To my *comadre* Kim Hensley Owens: how amazing that a summer-camp friendship has turned into a lifelong personal and professional collaboration. Thank you, Kim, for the thousands of letters, mix tapes, phone calls, emails, texts, Facebook posts, video calls, and, best of all, visits over the years. Special thanks and recognition are due to my dear friend and colleague Lesley Larkin, who has read every word of this book more than once and is an unfailingly compassionate, intelligent, and supportive presence in my life.

Randi Tanglen, Susan Hardy Aiken, Martin Reinhardt, Chuck Hannaford, Alex Mendes, Talitha Arnold, and Margaret Noodin all offered valuable insights at crucial moments in the drafting process. Thank you.

I was lucky enough to spend my sabbatical year in Santa Fe, researching, writing, and reconnecting with old friends and making new ones. My love and thanks to Lucy Ranney, Darren Smith, Kate Reynolds, Greg Smith,

Devi Schmidt, Jenny and Justin Kaufman, Erica Micander, Allison Monson, Nina Bunker Ruiz, Ari Gilder, Jenny Ramo, Orit Tamir, Kevin Brennan, Kate Noble, Aaron Boland, Karles McQuade, Kathleen Nakamura, Barbara Hansen, Tannis Eberts, the members of my brilliant Santa Fe book club (Johanna, Ruti, Lily, Brooke, Gabby, English, Liza, Sarah, Meghan, Veree, Alana, Rebecca, and Tereza), and so many others.

The staff at the University of Nevada Press has been a joy to work with. Former director Joanne O'Hare offered instrumental feedback and guidance for this project and others. And my sincere appreciation to the current director, Justin Race, for his interest in and enthusiasm for this book and for responding to my emails faster than just about anyone I know. Thank you, too, to editorial manager Jinni Fontana and to my eagle-eyed copy editor, Annette Wenda. And many thanks to my two anonymous reviewers. Your comments and suggestions made this a stronger and smarter book.

Finally, thank you to my family. To my sister and brother-in-law, Maria Hamilton and Ville Sneck, who are wonderful friends and the world's best *tia* and uncle. To my mother-in-law, Sandy Uchytil, whose love and support have been such a blessing. And to my smart and witty aunt, Karin Tompkins (Karen Pettee, in the introduction), who wrote the thoughtful and loving letter that provides a frame to this book. Most of all, thank you to my parents, Stephen and Andrea Hamilton, to whom this book is dedicated. There is not space enough here to express my profound gratitude for your unfaltering support. Thank you for your love of the more-than-human world and for taking me walking. Thank you for housing my family during my sabbatical and for providing me with a room of my own to write this book.

Above all, thank you to Chris, James, and Sammy Uchytil. It is all for you.

Peregrinations

Introduction

Walking at the Intersection of Literature and Materiality

THE STORY OF THIS BOOK begins with a walk. On March 15, 1976, the year of the US bicentennial, George Hormell and Scott King departed Portland, Maine, and began a four-month 3,281-mile walk to Santa Monica, California. Along the way, the two young men established a new record for long-distance walking and collected money for the American Cancer Society. They also carried with them a handwritten letter from kindergarten teacher Karen Pettee to her infant niece—me. My aunt had read about Hormell and King in her local newspaper and contacted them before they embarked on their walk. At the time, my aunt and her family lived near Portland and I lived with my parents in Santa Monica. In her letter, my aunt explains the significance of the walk and of her writing:

> There are several reasons why all this is so special for you. First, your mother's birthday is the Fourth of July and, this year, that is *the* big day to celebrate our nation's bicentennial. Secondly, the men who are bringing this letter to you just happened to plan to leave from a point very near our home and complete their trip very near where you now live. Last, but not least, any money donated during the long walk will be given to the American Cancer Society. That means a lot to your mother and me because we lost our mother (your grandmother) to cancer, two years ago.
>
> So, Amy, I hope this letter arrives safely and that, someday, you will enjoy it as a special symbol of the year 1976. (2)

Over the years, I have revisited this letter many times. I have always viewed it as a meaningful item that connected me—no matter how peripherally—to something as grand as a cross-country walk. It also functioned as a vital tie to the grandmother I never knew. How amazing, I thought, that this letter traversed the span of the United States in someone's pocket and in so doing linked me with members of my family who lived at a remove or were no longer living at all. Reading the letter now, as a scholar of American literature and ecocriticism, I am intrigued by its role as a reminder of my individual connection to walking in American history and literature and by the ways it encapsulates so much about how walking is woven into the fabric of the country. My aunt offers three points for the future Amy to contemplate: the intersection between America's founding and our family, the intersection between Hormell and King's walk and our family, and the intersection between Hormell and King's cause and our family. These intersections speak to the long history of walking in the United States, a history in which walking has generally been framed in terms of physical endurance, masculine identity, and national identity. However, if this story is about movement across the North America continent, it is also bound to myriad other walkers, both men and women, European and Euroamerican, Indigenous, African and African American, Mexican and Chicanx, Asian and Asian American, and more.[1]

The stories of my own family, like those of many American families, are filled with movement: from my many-times-great grandfather who traveled from New York to California in search of his fortune in 1847 and later served in California's seventh legislature, to my great-grandparents who immigrated from Hungary to the United States in 1902, to my mother who moved from Maine to California and later took a solo motorcycle trip across the United States and back, to my parents who moved from California to New Mexico when I was eighteen months old, and to my own story of living in New Mexico, Washington, Arizona, and now Michigan.

I have not always thought of myself as possessing a legacy of movement. In fact, as a person who grew up in the American Southwest, I have more frequently understood my relationship to land to be about a particular place, a particular landscape. Memories of the high New Mexico desert are visual, of course, but they are also always material. When I close my eyes I can feel the desert sand under my feet and smell *petrichor*, the sweet aroma of desert rain. I am *of* the desert in a way that is emotional, intellectual, and physical. However, the American Southwest is not an empty landscape available for a white woman like myself to claim, no matter what personal connections I experience. For me, being attached to the desert also means a responsibility to recognize and engage with the natural and cultural histories that shape it and to consider how those histories and cultures are tied to human interaction with nonhuman nature.[2] That human interaction, both my own and that of the many peoples who walked this land before me, is an engagement rooted in physical movement, in peregrination.

Peregrination has a long list of definitions. According to the *Oxford English Dictionary*, the term is chiefly theological and can mean "the course of a person's life viewed originally as a temporary sojourn on earth and hence as a spiritual journey, esp. to heaven"; "a pilgrimage"; "an act of traveling or going from place to place; a course of travel; a journey, esp. on foot. Also occas.: an account of a journey"; or "a comprehensive or systematic investigation of study; a discourse. In later use: a literary wandering or digression." These definitions demonstrate the multiple ways of understanding walking. Peregrination is a metaphor for the "course of a person's life," a spiritual journey, the physical act of travel, an account of travel, and a scholarly investigation. Thus, this project is a peregrination about peregrinations. In *On Foot: A History of Walking*, an examination of walking in Western traditions, Joseph Amato asserts, "Walking is talking. It can be understood as a language, having its own vernacular, dialects, and idioms. Expressing intentionality, walking conveys a wealth of information about the walker's identity, importance, condition, and destination.... [W]alking is a clear revelation of identity" (4). The language of walking is written in the American trails and paths left by the feet of generations upon generations of walkers, and it is traced into the literatures of the United States. Walking in American literature, as "peregrination" suggests, offers us a way to recognize the links between discursive practices and the physical reality of land and bodies, links that broaden our understanding about how meaning is created.

Rather than understanding walking as a means to an end, simply the way to get somewhere else, this book considers walking as a worthy site of investigation itself. Rebecca Solnit states, "Like eating or breathing, [walking] can be invested with wildly different cultural meanings, from the erotic to the spiritual, from the revolutionary to the artistic" (3). While she does go on to suggest that "imagination has both shaped and been shaped by the spaces it passes through on two feet" (4), Solnit understands meaning as something that is created by human minds. So although I concur with Solnit's contention that walking is meaningful, I argue that what walking means arises not simply out of a human investment or interpretation, but out of the very act of walking itself, both the physical experience of the walker and the relationship between the walker and the more-than-human world they walk. If walking has meaning, that meaning is tied to something more than human imagination. In this book, I examine walking in terms of both cultural tropes and stories and the physical interaction between human bodies and the land itself, looking particularly at those walkers whose journeys have been ignored or dismissed and how walking creates meaning at the nexus of narrative and experience.

A BRIEF AND PARTIAL HISTORY OF WALKING IN THE UNITED STATES

Walking across the land of what is now the United States has always informed how people experience the land and the sorts of stories that they create. Indigenous oral traditions are filled with stories of walking, movement that reflects migration, spiritual identity, and trade. And the land itself is crisscrossed with trade routes and migration paths, physical signs of human narratives. For example, in her collection of essays, *The West Pole*, author Diane Glancy (Cherokee) suggests that for the Cherokee, "the agency of travel was renewal" (2). Storytelling, she contends, "says that we began in chaos and forever make cover for the waters over which we exist. And that migration trails still have to be walked. Because in migration one becomes strong. That is the point of migration" (32). Migration and storytelling work together, Glancy suggests, to strengthen community and to participate in the remembering and continual remaking of culture.

Many American Indigenous creation stories involve movement. In the Laguna Pueblo creation story, which Native American studies scholars have grouped with similar stories as "emergence" narratives, the people move through several lower worlds before climbing through a hole in the earth into the present world, where they migrate south until arriving in their traditional homelands (Marmon and Corbett 2). Another common Indigenous origin-story trope is the "earth-diver" narrative, which also reflects movement. In the Haudenosaunee earth-diver story, Sky Woman falls from the sky to a world of water, and animals devise a plan to dive to the bottom of the sea to find mud to build her land on which to live. But each animal returns empty-handed until at last the muskrat returns with a handful of mud that grows to create a vast land on the back of the turtle (Brooks 2).

The Cherokee origin story is also a story of migration and movement, and, as is the case for many Indigenous origin narratives from oral traditions, it exists in many forms. In a version of the Cherokee origin story originally recounted by an unnamed Cherokee to an Englishman named Alexander Longe in 1717, the storyteller relates:

> [We] belonged to another land far distant from here, and the people increased and multiplied so fast that the land could not hold them, so that they were forced to separate and travel to look out for another country. They traveled so far that they came to another country that was so cold.... Yet going still on, they came to mountains of snow and ice.... [We] passed on our journey and at last found [ourselves] so far gone over these mountains till we lost sight of the same and went through darkness for a good space, and then [saw] the sun again, and going on we came to a country that could be inhabited. (qtd. in Conley 2)[3]

In this story, movement marks the beginning of the Cherokee as a discrete people. Noting that migrations like the one in this narrative are precipitated by separation and grief, Daniel Heath Justice (Cherokee) contends that while much was lost in these stories, the accounts "provid[e] a possibility for community healing through the principles of peoplehood: an engaged relationship with their new homeland, a rededication to the ceremonial history of the People, [and] the renewal of kinship and familial ties" (52). The stories themselves offer these healing principles. "In [the Cherokee] tradition," Glancy argues, "people do not simply speak about the world, they speak the world into being. What we say is intricately intertwined with what we are and can be. To the Cherokee people, all things in the world have a voice—and that voice carries life. Storying gives shape to meaning" (*West Pole* 66). Glancy suggests that storytelling is both making and remaking the world in each telling *and* that the different pieces of the world themselves "have a voice" and take part in their own creation.

These origin stories reveal and create the vital links between the people, the land, language, and movement. As ecocritic Joni Adamson argues, stories and experiences of walking reflect thousands of years of human engagement with and movement across the land and "should be brought to bear on understandings of place and sense of place" ("Ancient Future" 8). The sheer volume of Indigenous stories that involve walking suggests that movement serves a vital function for these communities, conveying a model of living in adherence with the teachings of the land, moving with the seasons and with the flow of animals.

Later, Indigenous walkers were joined by French trappers, Spanish conquistadores, Puritan settlers, western pioneers, Chinese railroad workers, African American slaves, and scores of others moving across the American land. Their footsteps multiplied and broadened the paths pressed into the earth, and their stories were filled with their own walking bodies. Solnit writes, "Walking has created paths, roads, trade routes; generated local and cross-continental senses of place; shaped cities, parks; generated maps, guidebooks, gear, and, further afield, a vast library of walking stories and poems, of pilgrimages, mountaineering expeditions, meanders, and summer picnics" (4). Yet even as the kinds of walking and the footsteps themselves increased, the movement of Euroamerican settler-colonists quickly pushed other walkers off the path of American literature and history. Walking in America became associated primarily with white men.

In interviews given around the time of their walk, Hormell and King aligned themselves with the tradition of masculine Euroamerican long-distance walking, a history with roots in exploration and the frontier. In a *Los Angeles Times* article printed soon after their arrival in Santa Monica, Hormell says, "We want to bring a message of pride to the American people.... The true meaning of our bicentennial has been lost in commercialism and our purpose is to make everyone aware of the hard work of the settlers who paved the way for all of us to enjoy the freedoms we have" (qtd. in Smith). Hormell's statement repeats the tenets of Manifest Destiny and a long history of imagining the origin story of America as the struggle of rugged Euroamerican men claiming and taming the American land, a narrative that is complicated by the experiences of women and people of color. A contemporaneous article that appeared in the *Portland Press Herald* also links Hormell and King to the triumphant settling of the West by relating the physical troubles the men encountered and their determination to persevere. Though King's "feet became badly infected while they were walking through Pennsylvania" and he had to ride in a car for a few days as Hormell walked on alone, King told the reporter, "We'd been bragging so much about the trip that there was no way we could have turned back" (qtd. in Gevalt).

Hormell and King express sentiments identified by Wallace Stegner eleven years after their walk: "The interior West was not a place but a way, a trail to the Promised Land, an adventurous, dangerous rite of passage." Like Hormell and King, Stegner is interested in the experience of Euroamerican explorers and pioneers crossing the plains to find a new home in the mythical land of plenty. When he argues that the West is "largely a civilization in motion, driven by dreams," he evokes visions of frontiersmen compelled to walk into a threatening wilderness by a powerful myth, just as Hormell and King overcome the difficulties of walking in order to live up to the image they had created for themselves (21). Walking is framed in this story as the means by which Euroamerican men surveyed the land in their quest for self-definition; in pacing off the American land, Euroamerican men placed survey stakes around their own identities and the identity of the nascent nation.

The story of American walking as a masculine tradition of conquest and domination of the American land is a compelling national origin narrative, filled with adventure and triumph over the odds. Stories of Euroamerican exploration and movement on the frontier often include descriptions of men on foot, braving the dangerous land with nothing but their own fortitude. In *Regeneration Through Violence*, Richard Slotkin locates this narrative in the nineteenth century, embodied enthrallingly in representations of Daniel Boone crossing the Cumberland Gap, as one of the foundational American stories. Slotkin traces the development of archetypal American men walking out to confront the dangers hidden in the American land: "the rogues, adventurers, and land-boomers; the Indian fighters, traders, missionaries, explorers, and hunters who killed and were killed until they had mastered the wilderness; the settlers who came after, suffering hardship and Indian warfare for the sake of a sacred mission or a simple desire for land" (4). The story of male prowess on the frontier was popular throughout the nineteenth century as Euroamericans pushed ever westward and sought to develop a particularly *American* story, one distinct from and superior to narratives of European masculinity.

Nineteenth-century American philosophers and poets connected intrepid American male walking to a rich tradition that extends back in time through Jean-Jacques Rousseau and the European romantics all the way to the Greek philosophers, and links walking to reason and inspiration. In 1851 Henry David Thoreau wrote in his journal, "Methinks that the moment my legs begin to move, my thoughts begin to flow, as if I had given vent to the stream at the lower end and consequently new fountains flowed into it at the upper" (165–66). A renowned walker (Emerson even used Thoreau's "endless walks" as the structuring image in the eulogy he published about Thoreau in the *Atlantic* in 1862 [399]), Thoreau understood thought and movement as entwined and strode out across the American land in his quest to develop ideas about what life, particularly life in the United States, should strive to be. In a similar way, Walt Whitman celebrated American walking as a tool for creating and understanding American identity and land throughout his writing life. For example, in the 1892 edition of *Leaves of Grass*, he proclaims:

> I tramp a perpetual journey, (come listen all!)
> My signs are a rain-proof coat, good shoes, and a staff cut from the
> woods,
> . . . .
> [E]ach man and each woman I lead upon a knoll,
> My left arm hooking you round the waist,
> My right hand pointing to landscapes of continents and the public
> road.
> Not I, not any one else can travel that road for you,
> You must travel it for yourself. (91)

Whitman presents the story of the United States and the story of each individual American as a triumphant journey, one that must be embraced for life to be fully realized. "The public road" functions as the structure of travel and the primary means for each individual to learn both more about themselves and more about the nation. And while he sometimes mentions women and nonwhite walkers, he casts the ideal rambler in his own image, a Euroamerican man.

Not coincidentally, alongside nineteenth-century representations of walking men, competitive walking arose as one of the first popular spectator sports in the United States, and it attracted huge crowds to watch men walk in circles for days at a time. In fact, in 1879 the first major event scheduled in the new Madison Square Garden was a pedestrian race. The race, called the Astley Belt, lasted six days and ended with the winner covering 530 miles (Algeo 183). While some women competed in pedestrian races, notably Bertha von Hillern and Ada Anderson, they were generally thought to be less suited to athletic walking feats. Reflecting prevailing opinion, Dr. J. H. Kellogg noted in 1881:

> A woman walks less gracefully than a man, owing to the greater relative breadth of her hips, requiring a motion of the body together with that of the limbs. In consequence of this peculiarity, a woman is less fitted for walking long distances.... The ancient Greeks and Romans amused themselves with witnessing the gladiatorial contests of their male slaves; but it was left for civilized America to introduce woman into the "ring" and make her show her paces on the race-course. An ungraceful figure she cuts, and a repulsive spectacle she presents; and worst of all is the havoc which she makes with her health.

For Euroamerican men in the nineteenth century, walking was a particularly male activity because of both stereotypical masculine personality traits of determination and grit as well as misperceptions (like Kellogg's) of physical strength and anatomical design. In the guise of care and concern, Euroamerican men staked an unambiguous claim to walking. Walking, an activity that prompted muscular creative thinking and innovation, also provided a medium for the performance of masculine physical stamina, joining inspiration with exertion.

In the introduction to *Desert, Margin, Garden, Range: Literature on the American Frontier*, Eric Heyne argues, "Crossing the frontier is a quintessentially American act, our national (male) rite of passage (as when Deerslayer follows Hurry Harry into 'the deep shadows of the forest,' Melville's Ishmael sails out of sight of land, or Faulkner's Isaac leaves behind his compass and rifle)" (7). Yet movement over the American land has a much longer and much richer story in the Americas than this masculine narrative allows. Looking back at the letter, photographs, and newspaper articles pasted in my baby book, what strikes me now is how walking traverses national and cultural stories, belief systems, and the materiality of place, concerns that extend far beyond the narrow confines of Euroamerican male experience. Indeed, it is through these concerns that my own story joins the stories of countless other readers and walkers.

Framing American walking as a site for masculine expression promoted Euroamerican male movement and obscured the experiences of other walkers. Since Europeans first arrived in the Americas, travel has often been traumatic and coerced for nonwhite, nonmale walkers. Instructively, as the most popular genre in the United States for nearly two hundred years, so-called Indian captivity narratives about Euroamerican women's experience as captives nearly always involve long passages chronicling the pain the women endured as they were forced to walk.[4] Further, the labor required to "open" the American West to Euroamerican settler-colonists depended on the physical movement of thousands of Chinese and Mexican migrant workers to build the railroads and, later, to cultivate crops. The slave trade demanded the transportation of millions of African men, women, and children, first across the Atlantic and then along roads in the Americas. And American Indian nations were systematically uprooted from their homelands and forced along deadly marches to reservations, marches that Diné writer Laura Tohe calls "part of America's holocaust" ("Hwéeldi Bééhániih" 82). Where walking opened up possibilities for exploration, physical triumph, and intellectual growth for white men, it was often physically, culturally, and mentally devastating for other groups.

When these diverse perspectives are taken into consideration, it becomes clear that stories of the American land have always been stories of movement. From narratives of Indigenous emergence and migration to accounts of Spanish exploration and conquest to chronicles of Euroamerican frontiersmen to pieces by contemporary American authors and artists, walking has been a way of expressing the reality of human experience on the American land. Too often dismissed by literary critics as empty or utilitarian transitional passages or read only through European traditions of the romantic sojourner, representations of walking offer readers moments of rich and complex meaning, where cultural stories and histories join human relationships with the material environment. Walking bodies alert readers to the ways the physical world—more-than-human animals, trees, rocks, wind, sunlight, and, yes, human bodies—has a hand in creating experience and meaning. Focusing on walking in American literatures clarifies the wide variety of stories about human relationships with the land and the ethical implications of how we understand the embeddedness of human beings in the more-than-human world.

MATERIAL ECOCRITICISM

In *American Indian Literature, Environmental Justice, and Ecocriticism*, Joni Adamson calls our attention to the reality that the natural world is not composed simply of "'wilderness areas' celebrated by many American environmentalists and nature writers," but in fact is filled with "contested terrains where increasing numbers of poor and marginalized people are organizing around interrelated social and environmental problems" (xvii). In attending to the complexity of these conditions and relationships, Adamson and ecocritic Salma Monani advocate the importance of "Indigenous 'cosmovisions'—conceptions of entangled human relations with more-than-human worlds" (3). Such an approach demands that scholars recognize the importance of examining literature through the interrelated lenses of cultures, histories, and landscapes, with an eye to how humans and nonhumans interact materially and discursively.

The material connection between humans and the more-than-human is located in movement. As human bodies walk, they move through crosscurrents of air, through pollen particles, through dust motes. Their feet press into the earth, disrupting grains of sand, intervening in the paths of insects. Their presence is noted by more-than-human animals who might hide or scurry out of the way. This physical engagement enacts the entanglement between human and more-than-human matter and forces. Diane Glancy's *Pushing the Bear: A Novel of the Trail of Tears* (1996) illustrates this intimate melding of body, land, and story in the narrators' recollection of the violent removal of the Cherokee from their traditional homelands in the 1830s and their forced march to Oklahoma along the deadly Trail of Tears. One of the narrators, Maritole, remembers, "We walked across a huge land. It had entered us. Along with the cornfields we left. I was full of trees. Full of corn. Full of walking. My feet churned inside me at night as if they entered my body when I slept" (176). Maritole captures the human intermeshment with the more-than-human through corn and through walking. By means of walking, Maritole's bodily relation with the land is made manifest. Acknowledging the physical, material interconnections between human and nonhuman points to the ways human and land are linked to other systems—environmental, political, economic, social—thereby underscoring the importance of recognizing the ethical implications of how humans and land are represented and defined. Adamson argues that Maritole highlights the connection between the Cherokee and their seed corn. She explains that the novel illuminates issues of food sovereignty and the close connection between humans and corn: "The earth regenerates the human body when people eat corn and, when they die, humans return to the earth and the cycle continues" ("Seeking the Corn Mother" 228). Movement entangles human bodies with plant and animal bodies, linking them together in continuing cycles. Potawatomi biologist Robin Wall Kimmerer notes that Indigenous scientific knowledge arose from this long relationship: "The land is the real teacher. All we need as students is mindfulness" (222). Tewa scholar Gregory Cajete elaborates on this concept, stating, "[Indigenous] people understood that all entities of nature—plants, animals, stones, trees, mountains, rivers, lakes, and a host of other living entities—embodied relationships that must be honored. Through the seeking, making, sharing, and celebrating of these natural relationships, they came to perceive of themselves as living in a sea of relationships" (178). Indigenous land knowledge emerges through long experience and story, exemplified through material walking bodies. How human bodies move through space both determines and is determined by a complex nexus of cultural systems and stories and the material reality of both bodies and land.

While Indigenous peoples have long understood the vital relationship between human and more-than-human, in recent years a growing number of ecocritics have also begun to recognize the importance of *matter*, the physical reality of the world. Scholars Serenella Iovino and Serpil Opperman describe this "material turn" as an "emerging paradigm [that] elicits not only new nonanthropocentric approaches, but also possible ways to analyze language and reality, human and nonhuman life, mind and matter, without falling into dichotomous patterns of thinking" (2). Material ecocriticism, then, like Indigenous scientific and spiritual knowledge, insists on attention to material land and the physical presence of nonhuman beings and on the fact that human bodies are intimately and inextricably entangled with the substance of the world. Iovino and Opperman contend, "The world's material phenomena are knots in a vast network of agencies, which can be 'read' and interpreted as forming narratives, stories.... All matter, in other words, is a 'storied matter'" (1). Story and meaning arise not out of a purely human discursive action but through *intra-action*, the "*mutual constitution of entangled agencies*" (Barad, *Meeting* 33; emphasis in the original). Intra-action is the dynamic interlacing of human experience and discursive practices with the material agency of nonhuman nature. How and what human and nonhuman experience means arises from this active entanglement. Material ecocriticism considers how intra-action functions and how authors engage the matter of the world. As Iovino and Opperman explain, "A *material* ecocriticism examines material both *in* texts and *as* a text, trying to shed light on the way bodily natures and discursive forces *express* their interaction whether in representations or in their concrete reality" (2; emphasis in the original).

Reading literature from a material ecocritical angle requires an attentiveness to the agential power of the nonhuman material world, whether that world is rendered as fiction or nonfiction. Literary engagement with materiality, how we conceptualize and give meaning to the "stuff" of the world, necessitates framing material forms as symbol, a process that seemingly moves matter away from the reader through this act of translation. "Metaphor emerges as a mode of biological, mental, and textual-semiotic operation," critic Hubert Zapf argues, "that translates these processes into language and cultural discourse" (54). However, rather than privileging a frame that positions this translation as a distancing between human minds and nonhuman matter, it is perhaps more instructive to understand it as the method by which matter is rendered knowable to (and by) the human intellect. Zapf continues, "Literature has been a medium of cultural ecology in the sense that literature has symbolically expressed fundamental interconnectedness between culture and nature in tales of human genesis, of metamorphosis, of symbiotic coevolution between life forms. It has presented human experience as part of a shared world of bodily natures and embodied minds" (57). While metaphors *can* obscure the physical matter of the world when they remove attention from the material in preference for the abstract, metaphors can also function to sharpen our understanding of the material world. Ian Bogost posits that if we accept the premise that "relation takes place not just *like* metaphor but *as* metaphor, then an opportunity suggests itself: what if we deployed *metaphor itself* as a way to grasp alien objects' perceptions of one another" (67; emphasis in the original). Indeed, such a stance opens up the possibilities for understanding literary representations of land and nonhuman nature as sites of relationality, not simply inert renderings but active participants in the continuous making and remaking of the world.

Literary representations of the material world are neither passive descriptions nor solely responsible for constructing meaning. Feminist theorist, physicist, and philosopher Karen Barad argues that matter is "a discursive production in the posthumanist sense that discursive practices are themselves material (re)configurings of the world.... That is, discursive practices as boundary-making practices are fully implicated in the dynamics of intra-activity through which phenomena come to matter" (*Meeting* 151). Rather than suggesting a turn to an essentialist reading of matter *in place of* linguistic or cultural approaches to literary analysis, Barad proposes a kind of reimagining or reprioritizing of theoretical approaches to matter such that it is understood as not secondary to human meaning-making processes but of primary importance. Meaning is achieved not only by human linguistic abstractions but also through the agential power of the material world—including the materiality of human bodies—in dialogue with discursive practices. As Christopher Breu contends, "In order for us to fully attend to the materialities of our bodies, we need to insist on the ways in which the materiality of language (as well as the forms of subjectivity shaped by language) and the materiality of the body not only interpenetrate and merge but also remain importantly distinct and sometimes form in contradiction to each other" (9). Such an approach can be expanded to consider not only the human body but also the nonhuman material world. Metaphor becomes, has always been, material.

The growing field of material ecocriticism has largely been formulated from a European and Euroamerican perspective, relying heavily on fields such as Western philosophy, physics, literary studies, biosemiotics, Western feminism, and ecology. Yet, as Maritole's story shows us, understanding humans as deeply enmeshed in the more-than-human world is certainly not an idea that is unique to modern Western academics. Indigenous nations the world over have long recognized the inseparability of humans from the rest of the world.

Adamson was one of the first scholars to urge ecocritics to include marginalized voices, particularly the work of global Indigenous activists and communities, and her work continues to inform and guide scholars in the importance of Indigenous perspectives and experiences. She calls on ecocritics to "expand the field of their vision and the scope of their studies to include other-than-dominant cultures and multicultural literatures" (*American Indian Literature* 26). Adamson, as have other scholars after her, has demonstrated the importance of centering Indigenous frameworks within the field of ecocriticism. *Peregrinations* strives to meet this call through highlighting the importance of interdisciplinary approaches that draw on Indigenous studies, material ecocriticism, science studies, gender studies, and Chicanx studies. Within this theoretical framework, *Peregrinations* contends that it is in the movement of walking bodies that these connections manifest most clearly. Barad argues that the relationship between human and nonhuman, among all matter, is one of agency and intra-activity, which is "an enactment, not something that someone or something has. Agency is doing/being in its intra-activity" (*Meeting* 235). She explains that agency is an intrinsic part of human and nonhuman matter that is always in the process of becoming. Meaning is not produced by humans alone but constituted at the intersections among humans, nonhumans, and the material land. Attending to walking human bodies as represented by literary texts allows readers to begin to recognize the complex relationships among bodies and land, metaphor and material, meaning and meaning making.

WALKING IN AMERICAN LITERATURE

Peregrinations engages texts that grapple with the relationship between representation and the material world, drawing connections among physical experience, cultural stories, and the land through representations of walking bodies. The following five chapters investigate narratives written by Euroamerican women who were taken captive by Indigenous groups, Navajo family stories passed down through generations about the experience of being forced to walk a deadly removal trail, essays by Euroamerican nature writer Mary Austin, a chronicle of a deadly border crossing in the Sonoran Desert, and three novels by Anishinaabe author Louise Erdrich. Together the texts demonstrate the complexity of human experience in and with the American land. Walking, as the central trope that unites the texts, offers an elasticity that accommodates diverse cultural traditions, including Puritan and Catholic teachings, Navajo (or Diné) and Anishinaabe oral traditions, Chicanx histories, and European literary traditions. However, walking in these texts is never simply allegory or symbol. Through representations of walking, the texts continually assert the materiality of land and bodies, the ways meaning is created through the entanglement of discursive practices and material agency, the "dynamic conception of matter" (Barad, *Meeting* 64). In order to craft literary analyses that are able to contend with the complexity of contexts of these disparate works, I have turned to what might at first appear to be a disparate set of methodologies. Although material ecocriticism forms the backbone of my methodological approach, because it is drawn from a largely Western tradition it alone cannot contend with the variety of cultural frameworks the authors in this book represent. Therefore, I also engage the work of historians, anthropologists, Chicanx studies scholars, Native American studies scholars, and feminist scholars, among others. When read through these lenses, representations of walking offer an opportunity to expose the importance of reading American literatures from multiple cultural and ethical perspectives, rather than isolating them within a single frame. Challenging notions of walking connected to Manifest Destiny, exploration, and masculine power, I examine texts that represent walking as historically and materially different from the movement of rugged male explorers, whether the walker is forced to walk in captivity, working to challenge masculine traditions, or refusing constraints imposed by legal and political decisions made far away from the walking bodies they impact most directly. *Peregrinations* reveals the complex kaleidoscopings of narrative and materiality that are contained in stories of walking human bodies through a material ecocritical reading practice that is attentive to specific historical and ongoing issues of oppression, exclusion, and displacement.

While humans have walked across the land that is now the United States for thousands of years, *Peregrinations* focuses on walks and walking narratives along frontiers, or what Mary Louise Pratt has termed "contact zones," walks that happened *because* two or more cultures came into contact. Annette Kolodny defines the frontier as the site for "the complex intersections of human encounters and human encounters with the physical environment." Such a definition, she continues, "enjoin[s] us to see the ways in which the collision of languages encodes the physical terrain as just as much a player in the drama of contact as the human participants, with the landscape variously enabling, thwarting, or even evoking human actions and desires" ("Letting Go" 3). Focusing on walking narratives on post-contact frontiers creates the opportunity to explore how both the act of walking and the literary representation of walking are shaped by the interaction between human and more-than-human as well as by the stories and experiences of previous walkers. Walking, in this formulation, serves as a hub of swirling experiences and stories. In the texts under consideration, walking is never "just walking."

In order to trace walking in American literature in terms of cultural and material influences, the chapters of *Peregrinations* are organized roughly chronologically, beginning after Indigenous-European contact in North America. Chapter 1 examines two narratives penned by Euroamerican women who were taken captive by Indigenous groups. Part of a genre commonly referred to as "Indian captivity narratives," these texts bridge dominant Euroamerican representations of masculine walking and the actual experiences of Euroamerican women whose walking is directed by Indigenous peoples who are being displaced and dispossessed. Though written nearly two hundred years apart, *The Sovereignty and Goodness of God* (1682) by Mary White Rowlandson and *Six Weeks in the Sioux Tepees* (1864) by Sarah Wakefield are both heavily influenced by European and Euroamerican traditions of female captivity and a dangerous, threatening wilderness. They are also deeply material texts; their experience of captivity is of bodily constraint and redirection. The layering of cultural ideologies, preconceived expectations, and physical experience is further complicated by the material and cultural spread of Euroamerican presence, which directly determines both the women's captivity and the routes on which their captors lead them. In this chapter I analyze the narratives through the lenses of Puritanism, Manifest Destiny, the generic form of the "Indian captivity narrative," and the history of colonialism and the American frontier. When Rowlandson and Wakefield write about their walking bodies, they reveal a complex web that draws together dominant and Indigenous ideologies, religious and cultural mappings, power differentials, and their material enmeshment with the land and with other human and nonhuman beings. These Euroamerican women were compelled to walk into the American land during historical moments when women's bodies were seen as less capable than male bodies, yet their Indigenous captors were facing extreme pressure and violence by the very Euroamerican communities to which the women belonged. Rowlandson and Wakefield, I argue, find space within this fraught context for personal agency and cultural critique in the intra-action between their bodies and the material world around them, both human and nonhuman.

Chapter 2 focuses on forced walking that is historically contemporaneous to Sarah Wakefield's captivity examined in the previous chapter, but is narrated from the perspective of Indigenous peoples who were forcibly pushed off their traditional lands. In this chapter I examine family narratives and poetry recorded and written in response to the Navajo Long Walk, an event that violently removed thousands of Diné from their traditional lands and confined them to a small "reservation" (in reality an internment camp) more than three hundred miles away. The Long Walk, like the scores of other deadly removal trails Indigenous nations were forced to march, continues to reverberate in contemporary Diné narratives. Walking functions in these narratives to signal the trauma of physical pain, death, and land loss as well as the importance of Diné cultural traditions, many of them directly connected to mobility and the material land. Through linking their experiences during the four-year Long Walk era to Diné stories—both recent and traditional—about movement and travel over the land, the storytellers and poets considered in this chapter reconfigure walking as a means of resistance and survival.

In the third chapter I pivot from histories of forced walking to examine another kind of frontier walking narrative, the nature writing of Mary Austin, a Euroamerican author who traveled in the American West when Indigenous peoples had already been confined to reservations and the land was understood as "won" and the frontier "closed." Austin, a midwestern transplant to the California desert, immersed herself in the land and crafted narratives that drew heavily on and challenged Euroamerican nature writing traditions. Her experiences in the desert led her to find these masculine traditions largely developed on the East Coast to be insufficient. In response, she turned to the Shoshone and Paiute peoples living nearby for inspiration. In this chapter, I analyze Austin's most widely read book, *The Land of Little Rain* (1903). This text blends Euroamerican nature writing, Indigenous songs and teachings, and the "reality"—what Iovino and Opperman define as an "intertwined flux of material and discursive forces" (3)—of the land. Through the rhythm of walking, Austin represents the agency of the nonhuman and stresses the necessity of human recognition of the intra-action among human, nonhuman, and land in the creation of meaning. However, it is important to note that she does so in part by incorporating an ethnocentric and problematic understanding of the Indigenous lifeways she encounters.

The walking examined in chapter 4, though very different from Austin's nature rambles, shares with her writing a recognition of the power and agency of the desert and the significance of Indigenous experience. Written one hundred years after *The Land of Little Rain* and invested in addressing the tragedies of the modern US-Mexico border, Luis Alberto Urrea's *The Devil's Highway* (2004) chronicles the story of a group of twenty-nine Mexican men who attempted to cross the Sonoran Desert into the United States in 2001. Fourteen of the twenty-nine died as a result of hyperthermia and exposure. I analyze *The Devil's Highway* through the history and stories of the borderlands, the Catholic tradition of pilgrimage, and the material desert that continually intrudes into the story and upsets narrative conventions used to represent and contain human experience on the border. Urrea blends reportage, testimony, description, and poetry to create a text that attempts to move readers closer to the bodies, experiences, and land he describes. In other words, the blending of literary techniques and cultural contexts serves to foreground the materiality of border crossings.

In the final chapter, I continue to focus on how Indigenous knowledge and settler-colonial policies reverberate in contemporary literatures. Set on a fictional Anishinaabe reservation and in the nearby towns, three of Louise Erdrich's "North Dakota novels"—*Tracks*, *Four Souls*, and *Love Medicine*—trace the lives of several generations of a community impacted by federal treaties and land policies. With attention to Erdrich's remapping of Indigenous land in the context of Anishinaabe storytelling traditions and the history of land theft, in particular the repercussions following the 1887 General Allotment Act, I analyze how the novels represent communal and individual identity in relation to land and movement. Erdrich repositions paths and roads—often considered marginal spaces—as centrally important, thereby drawing readers' attention to how conceptions of space have far-reaching implications for defining and controlling land and human and nonhuman beings. Movement along paths and roads functions in these novels as the primary representation of the relationship between humans and the material world, emphasizing intra-action and reciprocity in the creation of meaning.

The chapters of *Peregrinations* are arranged chronologically to demonstrate the way that walking in American literatures has developed over time in relationship to changing colonial, cultural, and environmental factors. However, this book is not meant to be an exhaustive or comprehensive study of walking in American literature. Rather, *Peregrinations* offers analyses of several select contexts to illustrate that walking in American literature suggests a rich range of cultural histories and worldviews as well as consistently foregrounding attention to the material presence and agency of the American land itself. In writing this book, I take seriously Iovino and Opperman's contention:

> The emerging dynamics of matter and meaning, body and identity, being and knowing, nature and culture, *bios* and society are therefore to be examined and thought not in isolation from each other, but *through* one another, matter being an ongoing process of embodiment that involves and mutually determines cognitions, social constructions, scientific practices, and ethical attitudes. In this perspective, there is no simple juxtaposition or *mirroring* between nature and culture, but a combined "mesh." Here culture and nature become a hybrid compound, congealing, to use Haraway's term, into *naturecultures*. This natural-cultural plexus is the cypher of our world, and therefore the necessary terrain of every critical analysis. (5; emphasis in the original)

Drawing from the language and theoretical concepts of material ecocriticism, *Peregrinations* reads representations of walking in American literature from a cross-cultural perspective. Though the texts under analysis approach walking from a variety of specific cultural contexts, they are linked through an interest in the ways walking intersects with stories of communal and individual identity formation, archetypes of journey and transformation, and a deep engagement with the material land.

In 1976 George Hormell and Scott King, like myriad men and women before and after them, undertook a peregrination. They placed one foot in front of the other. They set a clear goal for themselves—reaching the Pacific Ocean. However, as they quickly discovered, that goal was only a small part of their walk. In fact, it was in each step, in the movement of their bodies across the American land, that the true importance of their walk lay. When walking in American literature is understood as something more than symbol or more than a device for relocating action from one place to another, something profound emerges. Walking reveals humans as material bodies in a matrix of intra-action. The stories we tell about walking are acts of translation, attempts to articulate the fragility of the human body and the agency of the natural world. The dynamic materiality of practice cannot be separated from the meaning-making process. Walking tells profound stories about individual and cultural experiences and about the deeply complex interlacings of nonhuman and human agencies. *What* human experiences mean is intimately linked to *how* they mean.

On the page facing my aunt's letter, there is a picture pasted in my baby book. In it Hormell and King, soaking wet from a triumphant leap into the Pacific Ocean, hand an envelope to my father, who holds me in his arms. For my part, I am laughing and squirming, exuberantly physical. Like the narratives of walking discussed in *Peregrinations*, the photograph is a layered representation, a deceptively simple image. The snapshot, my aunt's letter, the bodies of the walkers, the bodies of my father and me bring together a complexity of meaning: family history, walking and movement in American history, visual and linguistic representation, and the materiality of the human and the nonhuman. *Peregrinations* seeks to follow the literary and material trails of human bodies as they walk across the American land and the multivalent stories these walks participate in, including the ever-changing narratives determined by the land itself. Iovino and Opperman argue that "this natural-cultural plexus is the cypher of our world," a window for interpreting how meaning is created through the collaboration of material and discursive modes (5). To this end, I argue that literary representations of Indigenous, Chicanx, and female walking offer focal points for investigating the ways materiality intra-acts with abstract human epistemological and ontological systems. Walking human bodies are both matter and symbol, intersections that reveal the complex intermeshment of human interpretive systems, human bodies, and more-than-human nature in the ongoing creation of the world.

NOTES

1. See note 1 in chapter 4 for an explanation of my use of the term *Chicanx*.

2. A note on the terms *nonhuman* and *more-than-human*: Serenella Iovino and Serpil Opperman define *nonhuman* as "not only sentient animals or other biological organisms, but also impersonal agents, ranging from electricity to hurricanes, from metals to bacteria, from nuclear plants to information networks" (3–4). They cite David Abram's book *The Spell of the Sensuous* for introducing the term *more-than-human*, which is meant to "overcome the nature-culture bifurcation, suggesting that the human world should be considered a subset of the more-than-human world, as a subset of a material collective that contains, yet exceeds, all our human designs" (16n4). In other words, *nonhuman* simply identifies agentic entities outside of the human, while *more-than-human* places the human as only one part within a matrix of complex forces. Throughout my book, I largely follow these definitions, using *nonhuman* in places where I am defining a difference between the human and the surrounding world and *more-than-human* in places where I am highlighting the agency and vibrancy of a world that includes, but does not privilege, the human.

3. Daniel Heath Justice discusses another account of the Cherokee origin story found in *Cherokee Vision of Elohi*. Originally recorded in *Vinita Indian Chieftain* by Nighthawk Keetoowah Sakiya Sanders in 1896, the story was reprinted as *Cherokee Vision of Elohi* in 1997. In many respects, this version mirrors the version recorded by Alexander Longe. However, it is much more detailed, refers to an early form of writing (predating Sequoyah's syllabary), and includes conflicts with other communities once the Cherokee have reached their new land (Justice 50–52). James Mooney, writing in the late nineteenth century, references another "lost" version of the origin story: "The Cherokee formerly had a long migration legend, which was already [by 1823] lost, but which, within the memory of the mother of one informant—say about 1750—was still recited by chosen orators on the occasion of the annual green-corn dance.... The tradition recited that they had originated in a land toward the rising sun, where they had been placed by the command of 'the four councils sent from above.'... After this genesis period there began a slow migration" (20).

4. "Indian captivity narrative" is the common name for the genre of narratives written by Euroamericans following captivity among Indigenous nations. The genre is marked by deeply negative and racist conventions, and the term itself is extremely problematic, as it lumps hundreds of distinct Indigenous groups into a monolithic "Indian." Therefore, I use the term cautiously to identify a particular genre of American writing while also acknowledging its problematic history.

1

Paths in the Wilderness

Walking Bodies and Material Agency in Early American Indian Captivity Narratives

WHEN THE FIRST EUROPEAN immigrants set out on their voyage to North America, they did so with pen in hand, recording their experiences of travel and movement as they went. These first narratives were crafted by explorers such as Captain John Smith of Virginia and settlers such as William Bradford of Plymouth; men who were interested in promoting stories of male conquest of the physical and symbolic wilderness. Women's stories were often minimized or left out entirely.[1] One place to uncover accounts of female movement across and engagement with the land that is now the United States is in the vast collection of "Indian captivity narratives" written by Euroamerican women.[2] On the surface, these narratives chronicle women's victimization in the wilderness and thus maintain travel as a male pursuit; however, within the framework of their stories, Euroamerican women made a space to narrate their own adventures of physical movement in the American land.

Captivity narratives, whether "true" or fictionalized, fascinated Euroamerican audiences from the late seventeenth century to the end of the nineteenth century, a two-hundred-year period when they were the most popular genre in America. According to Gary Ebersole, "A modern checklist of American Indian captivity narratives compiled by the Newberry Library of items either based on fact or presented as factual accounts lists almost two thousand items published before 1880" (9).[3] As the genre developed over time, the narratives began to assume a common outline: "The author or the protagonist is snatched from his or her home and forcibly carried off into an alien culture, into the world of the Other. There the captive undergoes a series of ordeals or adventures while living among the Indians and later escapes or is ransomed and returned to civilization" (Ebersole 10). Kathryn Derounian-Stodola and James Levernier assert that this basic outline is fleshed out with stereotypical scenes and characters, such as "a *mother*, at least one male *Indian*, and a *child*, usually held by the *heels*, whose *brains* (or *head*) are *dashed* against a *tree*" (148; emphasis in the original). These common elements contributed to the popularity of the genre that Billy Stratton explains was valued for its "inherent iterability" that allows for an "endlessly reproducible master narrativ[e]" (10–11).

By the nineteenth century, the motifs and outline of the captivity narrative had been retold hundreds of times and came to shape how Euroamericans experienced life on the frontier. Glenda Riley suggests that nineteenth-century women in particular "were so thoroughly convinced that they were about to come face to face with the fiendish visages of creatures who were little more than consorts of the devil that they transformed every sight and sound into an avenging native" (83). Indian captivity narratives with their stock scenes and characters offered a skewed and simplified vision of the complex and conflicted relationship among Euroamericans, Indigenous peoples, and the land. Yet the crush of formulaic scenes also allowed the writers an opportunity to express the multifaceted and contradictory experiences of captive movement.

Among the most compelling and elastic tropes that developed in Indian captivity narratives written by Euroamerican women are representations of the captives' physical movement, especially walking. Former women captives frequently illustrate their experiences of forced walking through descriptions of their painful, blistered feet and their exhausted bodies. For example, in her narrative of captivity among the Dakota, Helen Tarble recalls that her "feet were torn and bleeding" and that she longed for "a pair of shoes badly, for my feet were in a terrible condition from bruises and thorns" (40, 36). Similarly, in a narrative recorded by the Reverend Royal B. Stratton, Olive Oatman relates the first night of her captivity among the Apache: "I had no strength to walk. . . . I crept, snail-like" (319).[4] Later, when her Apache captors traded her to the Mohave, she recollects: "This trail to a second captivity was not improvement on the first. . . . Our feet soon became sore, and we were unable on the second day to keep up with their rapid pace" (329). Walking through pain and crawling when walking becomes impossible are tropes that appear repeatedly in Indian captivity narratives written by women.

These episodes complicate the division between the material and the metaphoric. Such descriptions record the very real pain women felt when forced to walk for long distances and across terrain for which their Euroamerican clothing and lifestyle had ill-prepared them, yet descriptions of painful walking also reflect the deep fear and emotional trauma the captives experienced as they moved away from their familiar homes into the wilderness known to them only through other narratives and stories. Further complicating these deceptively simple images is that even as captives locate their suffering in representations of forced walking, recording these moments also allows many formerly captive Euroamerican women to claim a degree of agency. Walking, whether coerced or voluntary, always requires the effort and agency of the walker. As opposed to a passive body carried away on horseback or in a wagon, the captive who walks is intensely aware of her embodiment, as she must purposefully place one painful step after another. In narratives written months and even years after their actual captivity, the writers use representations of themselves walking in captivity to express not only physical and emotional pain, but also a degree of agency and resilience. In captivity narratives, from Mary White Rowlandson's 1682 account of her captivity with the Naragansetts and Wampanoags through Sarah Wakefield's narrative of captivity among the Dakota in 1864, walking is so central to the experience of captivity that it even influences the form and structure of the narratives themselves, pairing physical movement with narrative movement.

Rowlandson's and Wakefield's narratives bookend the nearly two-hundred-year period when Indian captivity narratives enjoyed incredible popularity. Rowlandson's narrative, *The Sovereignty and Goodness of God*, a text that Christopher Castiglia calls the "first distinctly American best-seller" (1), was an instant success, second in popularity among American readers only to the Bible (Derounian-Stodola and Levernier 14).[5] Her narrative helped shape the tropes and structure that Wakefield's narrative, *Six Weeks in the Sioux Tepees*, both adopts and resists. While Rowlandson links her walking to the larger Puritan "errand into the wilderness,"[6] punctuating her narrative with biblical passages and pious observations, Wakefield ties her walking to nineteenth-century narratives of hunter heroes and explorers, even as she maintains a foothold in the usually sedentary story of the domestic sphere reflected and reinforced in nineteenth-century American domestic fiction.[7] Alongside these cultural stories, Rowlandson and Wakefield also repeatedly describe the physical reality of walking and the material impact of the land on their bodies. In the introduction to *Material Ecocriticism*, Serenella Iovino and Serpil Opperman write, "This world... is far from being 'pure exterior.'... It is through all these natures, agencies, and bodies that 'the world we inhabit,' with all its stories, is 'alive'" (1). The materiality of the world contains its own power and is not simply an inert background or setting upon which the action takes place. The stories that Rowlandson and Wakefield tell are actively informed and shaped by the stories of the world around them: the narratives and preconceptions the writers carry with them, the stories of the Indigenous peoples they walk with, and the stories created by interaction with the land itself. "Agency assumes many forms," Iovino and Opperman argue, "all of which are characterized by an important feature: they are *material*, and the meanings they produce influence in various ways the existence of both human and nonhuman natures.... [R]eality emerges as an intertwined flux of material and discursive forces, rather than as [a] complex of hierarchically organized individual players" (3). Through their captivity narratives, Rowlandson and Wakefield claim a space in which to write their personal experiences as well as the complicated ways those experiences, and the narratives relating them, are influenced and formed by the stories of the people who have captured them and the land in which they move. They emphasize the materiality of their experiences even as they use them to structure and lend symbolic weight to their stories.

MARY WHITE ROWLANDSON'S PILGRIMAGE THROUGH CAPTIVITY

In the early morning hours of February 10, 1676, Mary White Rowlandson awoke to chaos when a group of allied Nipmucs, Wampanoags, and Narragansetts attacked the small Puritan settlement of Lancaster. Daughter of the town's wealthiest citizen and wife of its resident minister, Rowlandson was taken captive along with her three children, including her mortally wounded six-year-old daughter, Sarah. Stumbling in terror, losing blood from a gunshot wound to her side, and separated from her two older children, Rowlandson carried Sarah for a week until the child died in her arms. For eleven weeks and five days, Rowlandson lived and traveled with a group of Narragansetts and Wampanoags before being redeemed for twenty pounds (Lang 18). Published six years after the events it chronicles, Rowlandson's story of her captivity went on to be the most influential and widely read Indian captivity narrative of all time, shaping popular conceptions of Indians, wilderness, and captivity for generations of Euroamericans.

The attack on Lancaster was part of a larger conflict known as Metacom's (or King Phillip's) War. According to critic Neal Salisbury, in proportion to total population, Metacom's War was the bloodiest and most destructive war in American history. The conflict, which lasted a little more than a year, took the lives of approximately five thousand Indians and twenty-five hundred settlers, roughly 40 and 5 percent, respectively, of the two area populations (Salisbury 1). Over the previous decades the Indigenous peoples in the Massachusetts area had established a strong trading relationship with the early colonists in Lancaster. The English demand for furs and the Native demand for English goods had led Indigenous and European trappers to procure as many pelts as possible, driving southern New England beaver, otter, marten, and mink populations to the brink of extinction (Salisbury 18). These decreases in fur-bearing species exacerbated fractures in trade relationships that were further compounded by European-introduced diseases and ever-increasing numbers of settler-colonists. The Wampanoag leader Metacom told Rhode Island governor John Eaton that English "cheating, discrimination, and pressures to sell land, submit to Plymouth colony's authority, convert to Christianity, and consume alcohol had undermined a half-century of friendship and driven the Wampanoags of Pokanoket to the point of war" (Salisbury 19). Similar sentiments were expressed by the Narragansetts, Nianics, and Nipmucs.

Amid these growing tensions, the murder of John Sassamon in 1674 pushed the tenuous peace to a breaking point and precipitated violent confrontations (Lang 16). According to reports, Sassamon, a "praying Indian" (Christian convert), was acting as an informant for the English. When he was found murdered, the colonists assumed that his people had killed him after discovering his perfidy. Three Wampanoags were arrested and executed (Salisbury 21). Following the executions, Metacom led an attack on Swansea, Massachusetts, burning several houses on June 20, 1675. The English retaliated, and over the next six months hostilities continued to escalate. In November of that year, the United Colonies of Massachusetts, Rhode Island, Plymouth, and Connecticut attacked and massacred an encampment of Narragansetts in their winter home in the swamps of central Rhode Island, killing an estimated six hundred Narragansett men, women, and children. The attack on Lancaster was part of a continuing Indigenous offensive started after this massacre. Of the thirty-seven people occupying the garrison in Lancaster that February morning, twelve were killed, one escaped, and twenty-four were taken captive, among them Mary White Rowlandson (Lang 17).

Apparently written around 1677, Rowlandson's narrative attempts to erase the complicated colonial history surrounding her captivity in order to recast her experience as a pilgrim's journey through a spiritual wasteland.[8] As a result, Rowlandson's captivity has most often been understood through the lens of the Puritan errand to the wilderness. Rowlandson and her family were among the thousands of Puritans who crossed the Atlantic in the seventeenth century to settle in America. They understood themselves to be the spiritual successors of the biblical Hebrews with a special covenant with God, and they imagined their mission in the American wilderness mirrored and extended the exodus of Israel from Egypt. The Puritans believed their temporary exile from an idolatrous land (England) and the subsequent period of travail in the wilderness would purify their community and bring it to a more valid worship of God, just as it had for the Hebrews (Slotkin 37–42). Movement into and through the wilderness was vital to their sense of themselves as the chosen people, as it suggested a literal manifestation of their inner spiritual journey to closer communion with God. As David Jacobson contends, the Puritans saw themselves "journeying to the Promised Land, metaphorically, in the sense of some Edenic future. But that Edenic future is also located physically...where the future will be realized" (32). Wandering through the actual wilderness encouraged the Puritans to imagine themselves drawing closer to the nonmaterial Promised Land.

In this context, Rowlandson constructs her story to follow the traditional pilgrim's journey, beginning with her separation from what is known and familiar, followed by a long journey filled with hardship, and culminating in an enlightened return.[9] Cultural anthropologists Victor Turner and Edith Turner define pilgrimage as a "*rite de passage*... marked by three phases: separation, limen or margin, and aggregation." Following a detachment of the individual or group from a "relatively stable set of cultural conditions," pilgrims pass through "a realm or dimension that has few or none of the attributes of the past or coming state" and seek to return to a classified and stable social life (2). Like a pilgrim, Rowlandson identifies the second phase, the journey, as the most important.

Although Rowlandson's story is focused on her individual experience, in writing herself as a pilgrim she aligns herself with her community. Pilgrimage, Turner and Turner explain, is essentially about communion with similars. Pilgrimage—like all religious ritual—binds pilgrims together: "Likeness of lot and intention is converted into commonness of feeling, into 'communitas'" (13). In *Pilgrims to the Wild*, John P. O'Grady writes that the word *pilgrim* is "[d]erived from an Indo-European root (*ghedh-*) meaning 'to unite, join, fit,' it flourishes in modern English as the words *good*, *gad*, *gather*, and *together*.... [T]hus even when conducted alone, pilgrimage always embodies the notion of the pilgrim's community" (5). The Puritans' conceptualization of their exile in the wilderness fits these parameters of pilgrimage as a sojourn, a temporary state of disconnection on the path to reintegration. Their errand to the wilderness was a vital mark of their difference from the European world they left behind and a central trope that bound them together as a community. Notably, within this structure Rowlandson's fellow pilgrims are her fellow Euroamerican captives and her fellow Puritan settlers and emphatically *not* the Wampanoag and Narragansett people she walks alongside.

Within the Puritan errand, captive white women serve as examples to the larger Puritan community, exemplifying piety, patience, and subservience to God's will. Sacvan Bercovitch contends that the Hebrews' captivity in Babylon followed by their "flight from Babylon under Nehemiah" functioned as "one of the central motifs in early Protestant sermons." "Spiritually," Bercovitch argues, "it signifies Christ's deliverance of his beloved from the bondage of sin" (58). Puritan clergy such as Cotton Mather recognized the force and implications of casting captive women as *Judea Capta*, "the image of Israel suffering in Babylonian captivity" (Kolodny, *Land Before Her* 19). Mather describes this figure on a Roman coin as "*A Silent Woman sitting upon the Ground, leaning against a Palm-tree, with this inscription* JUDAEA CAPTA" (qtd. in *Kolodny, Land Before Her* 21; emphasis in the original). The silent and passive body of the captive woman provided a space for performing the Puritan errand. As Rebecca Blevins Faery indicates, in "the war for territorial dominance... the captive woman was made into a metaphor: she was herself the emblematic territory for control of which the two sides fought" (41). The body of the captive white woman who waits patiently for rescue and redemption was a passive boundary between cultures and between male captors and male rescuers. Her physical body was remade as a symbol, which allowed Puritan leaders to imagine themselves as descendants of Nehemiah, redeeming the white woman and the land from captivity to the Indians.

Rowlandson's identity as a Puritan woman, held captive in the threatening wilderness, waiting for redemption and rescue, is supported by many of the claims and statements in her narrative. For example, in recounting the harrowing death of her youngest daughter, Rowlandson remembers the nine days she "sat upon my knees with my babe in my lap... even ready to depart this sorrowful world." Reflecting on this time, she emphasizes her passive waiting: "I have thought since of the wonderful goodness of God to me, in preserving me so in the use of my reason and senses in that distressed time, that I did not use wicked and violent means to end my own miserable life" (36). Later she writes that the "principal ground" for writing her narrative is to "declare the works of the Lord, and his wonderful power in carrying us along, preserving us in the Wilderness, while under the Enemies hand, and returning of us in safety again." Shortly after this statement, she quotes from Psalm 137: "*By the rivers of* Babylon, *there we sate down, yea we wept when we remembered Zion*," directly linking her experience with *Judea Capta* (42; emphasis in the original). Rowlandson repeatedly and overtly underscores her adherence to God's will, stating that she "was not willing to run away, but desired to wait God's time, that I might go home quietly, and without fear" (61). Rowlandson strives to be the voice of the Puritan faithful, recognizing her subservience to God's will and waiting for rescue, through policing herself to be both mentally patient and physically still.

As a devout Puritan, Rowlandson frequently turns to the Bible for ways of contextualizing and understanding her experience of captivity in the wilderness. Critic Dawn Henwood argues that scriptural passages "furnish

Rowlandson with a public, liturgical language that centers her experience in the communal sphere of meaning" (171).[10] Many of the biblical passages Rowlandson includes in her narrative explicitly tie her movement in captivity to symbolic walking in scripture. The first reference she makes to scriptural walking is with a passage from Psalm 81: "*Oh that my people had hearkened to me, and Israel had walked in my ways, I should soon have subdued their Enemies, and turned my hand against their Adversaries*" (40; emphasis in the original). Rowlandson includes references to Israel's failure to walk in the ways of God and their subsequent time in the wilderness as a way of understanding her own captivity. She, like the Hebrews, is guilty of backsliding, and her journey, like a pilgrimage, is her penance and her redemption. She has not walked in God's ways, and her captivity is the result of that failure as well as an opportunity to return to "*walk humbly with [her] God*" (Mic. 6:8, qtd. in Rowlandson 51; emphasis in the original). In these passages, Rowlandson adheres to the Puritan errand by emphasizing the need for redemption through bodily immersion in a wilderness state.

Rowlandson deploys scriptural passages about movement and walking not only to contextualize her larger experience, but also to give meaning to the more immediate, material walking she endures. The materiality of walking is particularly evident in the passages where Rowlandson links biblical walking with moments when she is exceptionally physically challenged. Early in the narrative she pairs a "very wearisome and tedious day" of forced marching with the comment, "I then remembered how careless I had been...and how evilly I had walked in God's sight" (35). She struggles to contextualize her physical and emotional suffering and pain by noting that she, like the Hebrews, has walked "evilly," making sense of her painful physical walking by connecting it to her spiritual walk with God. Although, as Annette Kolodny points out, she never learns to navigate the physical wilderness on her own (*Land Before Her* 18), she does begin to understand her experience by placing the physical landscape alongside the scriptural one. Later in the narrative, Rowlandson writes, "After many weary steps, I saw Wachusets hills, but many miles off.... Being almost spent, I thought I should have sunk down at last, and never got out; but I may say, as in *Psal.* xciv. 18, *When my foot slipped, thy mercy, O Lord, held me up*" (53; emphasis in the original). Rowlandson describes her physical pain and exhaustion with a biblical passage that employs a physical stumble as a metaphor for a spiritual stumble. Her physical suffering, then, does not mean that God has abandoned her, just as her spiritual backsliding does not negate her place among the chosen. Instead, her movement in captivity aligns her with the larger Puritan errand, a pilgrimage that purifies her as she wanders in the wilderness. In essence, her wandering and her stumbling prove her status as one of God's chosen.

In addition to connecting her captivity to scriptural language and meaning, Rowlandson's representation of her physical walking also provides a structuring rhythm for her narrative. Rowlandson organizes her narrative to emphasize her physical movement across the material land. Beginning with the moment of attack and ending with a brief recounting of her return to the Puritan community, she centers attention on the journey itself, "the several Removes we had up and down the Wilderness" (33), and the 150 miles she traveled as a captive of the allied Narragansetts and Wampanoags. This structural choice disregards the orderly sequencing of a diary or chronicle that breaks up experience in terms of time (what happened on a particular day or during a particular week), which Marilyn C. Wesley defines as "the available Puritan forms for the organization of private and public experience" (23). Instead, she marks the passage of time by *spatial* passages into the wilderness, "removes" from one place to another.[11] John David Miles argues that while her Puritan readers would recognize the numbered removes as a structuring device because they "hark back to the lengthy nested lists of Puritan sermons... Rowlandson's narrative connects scripture to geography, writing text onto land in a way different from the scripturally focused jeremiad" (111). Bodily movement determines the form of her narrative *and* determines the scriptural references. In other words, movement is the primary structuring force.

This movement provides a consistent narrative thread of self-reliance and agency that challenges Rowlandson's repeatedly offered image of herself as a passive *Judea Capta*. Rowlandson injects subjectivity and will into her representation of the captive white woman. Hers is "the voice of a woman whose experience has given her evident authority outside the fold of the Puritan community" (Faery 32). Faery argues that for Puritan women like Rowlandson, "Indian captivity [paradoxically] represented... an expansion of experience rather than what we might ordinarily think would be a contraction or restriction of experience" (31). Her narrative belies the passivity of the captive woman's body. Although Rowlandson constructs her narrative in accordance with the Puritan worldview, her experience in captivity and her decision to write and publish her experiences place her "out-of-doors," in an unarticulated space (Faery 28).[12]

Through representations of walking, Rowlandson defines herself as an explorer, charting her course through her narrative. With each remove, Rowlandson finds herself psychically and physically farther away from what is known and familiar and further immersed in the wilderness. For a Puritan woman in the seventeenth century, the wilderness represented the threatening unknown, yet Rowlandson frequently challenges this representation through structural signposts she uses to reorient her narrative after digressions. These phrases stress a sense of control over her movement: "But to return to my own Journey"; "But, to Return: we traveled"; "But to return again to my going home" (39, 42, 61). Rowlandson actively maps the movement of her story and the movement of her physical body. Movement is more than a convenient structuring device or a way of emphasizing a spiritual journey. As she walks into and through the wilderness, she becomes more knowledgeable about and familiar with what was once unknown. Rowlandson defines herself not as a passive captive but as an active and interested pilgrim who is entangled with the material world as well as the spiritual world.[13]

The materiality of Rowlandson's experience is further emphasized through her deployment of one of the common tropes in captivity narratives: painful walking. She frequently writes of "all those wearisome steps" (45) that make her mind "reel" (51) and her "knees tremble" (63). Walking is difficult and exhausting. It demands Rowlandson's total attention. Following a particularly difficult remove, she wonders when "the *Indians* sate down in a Wigwam discoursing, but I was almost spent, and could scarcely speak" (52; emphasis in the original). Her identity as a captive is delineated by walking, which focuses attention on the very real, physical experience of Rowlandson's body in captivity. While the Narragansetts and Wampanoags seem to easily shoulder their burdens and walk miles across the land, Rowlandson struggles, even "creep[ing] upon [her] knees" when her strength gives out (45). Physical walking not only reflects her psychological experience of captivity, but also shapes that experience and insists on attention to her bodily agency.

Although she is an unwilling captive, forced to march alongside her captors, agency rather than passivity defines Rowlandson's experience in captivity. Near the beginning of her narrative she emphasizes her agency, declaring, "I had often before this said, that if the *Indians* should come, I should chuse rather to be killed by them than taken alive; but when it came to the trial my mind changed; their glittering weapons so daunted my Spirit, that I chose rather to go along with those (as I may say) ravenous Bears, than that moment to end my dais" (33; emphasis in the original). Rowlandson's language here stresses that even though she was under duress, she "chose" captivity over death. Similarly, in writing of a river crossing in the sixteenth remove, Rowlandson recalls that, even in the face of physical pain and humiliation, she retains a degree of control over her body: "Then I sate down to put on my stockings and shoes, with the tears running down my eyes, and many sorrowful thoughts in my heart, but I gat up to go along with them" (51). The *but* in this sentence signals that against expectations and in a state of pain and fear, Rowlandson still finds the power to keep walking. As the Israelites found their home in the wilderness through constant wandering, so too does Rowlandson move through the wilderness on her own two feet.

Rowlandson's agency is predicated on her physical body moving through space, but that space itself (the "Wilderness") is material with its own agency and power. In her introduction to Rowlandson's narrative, Amy Schrager Lang asserts, "Rowlandson makes no mention of the scenery. She finds no beauty in untamed nature, only terror" (23).[14] Lang's contention implies that because Rowlandson did not write of the *beauty* of her surroundings, she was thus uninterested in or oblivious to the material world around her. Such a reading reasserts the primacy of the symbolic reading of Rowlandson's text. However, Rowlandson is not simply imagining a symbolic or spiritual wilderness; she is walking through a very real wilderness with her very real body. Miles argues that far from ignoring the material land, Rowlandson's narrative is marked by an *attention* to the physical wilderness. This attention, he suggests, signals a departure from Puritan conceptions of the wilderness that it was primarily a "spiritual state... not a physical space" (105).

Rowlandson's direct descriptions of the material world in which she walks are, admittedly, infrequent and brief. Often they do seem more illuminating of her spiritual journey instead of her physical journey. For example, early in her narrative she writes, "I must turn my back on the town and travel with them into the vast and desolate wilderness" (34). Later she emphasizes the "vast and howling Wilderness" and immediately connects it to biblical stories (41). However, she also includes many brief references to the physical landscape and how it impacts her mentally and materially. She writes of climbing hills "so steep, that I was fain to creep upon my knees; and to hold by the twigs and bushes to keep myself from falling backward. My head also was so light that I usually reeled as I went" (45). Later she describes walking in "a great Swamp; through which we travelled up to the knees in mud and water; which was heavy going to one tired before" (53). These episodes, while highlighting the terrible difficulty of her ordeal and thereby emphasizing God's grace in saving her, also serve to shift her experience from the spiritual to the material. Rowlandson's body is materially impacted by the physical and agentic nonhuman nature. Theorist Karen Barad explains that physical matter and meaning are "inextricably fused together, and no event, no matter how energetic, can tear them asunder.... Mattering is simultaneously a matter of substance and significance" (*Meeting* 3). Rowlandson's narrative can only have meaning, can only *matter*, when the material world is present. In fact, the meaning of her narrative depends utterly on the materiality of her time in captivity. And that materiality is experienced in and expressed by representations of her walking body.

Rowlandson's material walking body is not isolated from the world around her; rather, it is deeply connected to and even determined by that world. In *Bodily Natures* Stacey Alaimo uses the term *trans-corporality* to explain how "the human is always intermeshed with the more-than-human world, underlin[ing] the extent to which the substance of the human is ultimately inseparable from 'the environment'" (2). Rowlandson's captivity brings her intermeshment, her trans-corporality, into stark relief. Her experience of the world through her walking body, through her psychological anguish, through her religious devotion, is delineated by her physical relation to the more-than-human world around her. When she "reels" from the experience of a river crossing (51) or admires the ability of her captors to find nourishment in the seemingly barren wilderness around them (60), Rowlandson is experiencing her trans-corporeality, her physical relation to the world. That she interprets that intermeshment through a biblical framework is, of course, predictable for a Puritan woman steeped in a particular worldview. However, the material world's agentic capacity and her own bodily reality cannot be separated from her narrative.

The physicality of walking in the wilderness brings Rowlandson into contact not only with her own material agency as a walking body and the agency of the land she walks through, but also with the agency of the people with whom she walks. Rowlandson's experience in captivity, shaped by her bodily agency and the agency of the material world, is undeniably directed by her captors. As a captive, Rowlandson struggles to understand her own experience in part by attempting to read the activity of those around her. This attempt is visible in her endeavors to create retrospective order by formatting her captivity around physical removes. But this movement is not easily organized, and the removes are uneven. Some removes involve day-long walks, and others do not cover any literal ground at all. Additionally, the removes do not follow Rowlandson's expectations. As Wesley argues, "If Mary is expecting to go to Albany, her captors unexpectedly remove to another destination. If she desires to go 'toward the Bay,' they arbitrarily change direction and proceed 'five or six miles down the River into a mighty Thicket of Brush'" (28). Seemingly "unaware that [the] twists and turns are not random, but are dictated by a survival strategy...[to] evade armed pursuit" (Chedgzoy 183), Rowlandson presents this erratic travel as indicative of her captors' confusing and seemingly pointless movement. She records them "hopping up and down one after another" at a "Powaw" (58), and, in apparent panic at seeing an English scout, "some of the *Indians* ran one way, and some another" (42). In her experience, Rowlandson and everything around her keep "moving at a dizzying and indescribable velocity" (Breitwieser 157). These descriptions suggest that even though Rowlandson's physical movement affords her a degree of agency, as a captive she is ultimately dependent on the movements of others whom she cannot always understand. In choosing to format her narrative around the rhythms of the removes, Rowlandson creates a structure that reveals her experience of the often frustratingly opaque movements of her captors.

Further complicating Rowlandson's relationship to movement, it is not only the Narragansett and Wampanoag's movements that are confusing; Rowlandson also comments on the confounding movement of the English army. She observes that the "*Indians* derided the slowness and dulness of the *English* Army in its setting out" (59; emphasis in the original). Even encumbered as they are with their heavy loads and their children and elders, her captors still manage to outpace the English army, a situation she strives to account for as proof of God's providential plan: "The *English* Army with new supplies were sent forth to pursue after the Enemy, and they understanding it; fled before them till they came to Baquang River, where they forthwith went over safely: that that River should be impassable to the *English,* I cannot but admire to see the wonderful providence of God in preserving the Heathen for farther affliction to our poor Country. They could go in great numbers over, but the *English* must stop" (59; emphasis in the original). If her own walking allows Rowlandson a physical and symbolic space in which to claim agency, the confusing movements of the Naragansetts and Wampanoags and of the English Army threaten to destabilize that agency. Crafting her narrative permits her a certain degree of retrospective control: through the act of writing *her* pilgrimage, she can attempt to incorporate the inexplicable movements of others into a larger providential plan. However, the unknowable bodies of other walkers and the strangeness of the landscape are never fully erased or accounted for.

Walking marks Rowlandson's entry into liminality, the space outside of what is known. Alaimo writes that "our most basic sense of the material world is that it is self-evident, apparent, substantial, and visible" (*Bodily Natures* 71). However, Rowlandson repeatedly experiences the world as opaque, confusing, and elusive. Kate Chedgzoy argues that Rowlandson is thrown into confusion by a "spatial disarrangement" paired with "a rejection of what [she] sees as chronologically appropriate behaviour, turning night into day and a Massachusetts hillside into hell" (179). Rowlandson's walking across an unfamiliar land makes the margin between Puritan communities and the wilderness real and immediate. For example, when she finds that her son is camped a mile away with another allied Indigenous group, she is given permission to walk through the wilderness alone to visit him. As she walks, she "quickly lost myself, traveling over Hills and through Swamps, and could not find the way" (44). Lacking familiar markers, Rowlandson has "lost [her]self" in a material world that she cannot interpret fully. Alone in the woods, Rowlandson physically confronts the liminal space of the wilderness. She is lost in the unfamiliar landscape of hills and swamps, disrupting her understanding of herself and her experience.

The sense of liminality and its attendant rhythms permeate her experience not only during the daily walking, but also in the stillness at the end of the day. Rowlandson describes her inability to be still; she is constantly in motion. In spite of the deep fatigue and emotional anguish that she often mentions, Rowlandson continues to walk. She writes that following her youngest daughter's death, she "could not sit still...but kept walking from one place to another.... I was going up and down, mourning and lamenting" (37). Later, when she was unable to find her way to visit her son, she again "went up and down moaning and lamenting" (44). Rowlandson pairs her pacing with unhappiness and agitation; grieving over her child, unfamiliar with her situation, and unsure of her fate, Rowlandson walks. Unlike the purposeful walk of the pilgrim, however, pacing has no beginning and no end. Rowlandson often reminds herself that she should be patient and "*Wait on the Lord*" (38; emphasis in the original), yet her pacing indicates her spiritual and physical unrest. Walking, even without a purpose, holds the potential of a destination, of movement out of the liminal state.

When Rowlandson chooses captivity over death, she chooses motion. Movement, whether it is haphazard, forced, or repetitious, is the power to survive. When she is not traveling with her captors or pacing in the camp, she is still in constant motion: she visits with fellow captives, exchanges her sewing for food, and goes from wigwam to wigwam in search of food and shelter. "Throughout her captivity," Wesley argues, "[Rowlandson] understands that the more dangerous course is stasis" (Wesley 29). Stasis represents surrender, while survival requires adaptation. In the twelfth remove, Rowlandson writes that after traveling only a short way, "my Mistress [Weetamoo, the female leader of the Pocassets, allies of the Narragansetts] gives out she would go no further, but turn back again, and said I must go with her." On being told she must turn back without explanation, Rowlandson's "Spirit" was "very impatient and almost outrageous. I thought I could as well have died as went back" (45). But as a captive she must go with her "Mistress." Once back in the original camp, Rowlandson turns to her Bible for comfort and reads from Psalm 46: "*Be still, and know that I am God.*" However, her attempt to follow this command fails. "Down I sat," she writes, "with my Heart as full as it could hold, and yet so hungry, that I could sit neither." Instead, she chooses to go "walking among the Trees" and gathers "six Acorns and two Chestnuts" (46; emphasis in the original). Rowlandson clearly links survival and movement in this episode, noting that when she walks, she is able to find food, shelter, and the possibility of reaching the end of her captivity.

Toward the end of her captivity and interspersed with moments when walking is physically and emotionally draining, Rowlandson writes, "The thoughts of my going homeward (for so we bent our course) much cheared my Spirit, and made my burden seem light, and almost nothing at all" (45), and later, "I went on cheerfully, (with thoughts of going homeward) having my burden more on my back than on my spirit" (51). To survive her pilgrimage Rowlandson must arrive somewhere; she must return home, in fulfillment of God's promise to "appoint a Place for my people Israel, and I will PLANT them that they may dwell in a place of their OWN, and MOVE NO MORE" (2 Sam. 7:10, qtd. in Jacobson 34). However, it is also noteworthy that Rowlandson comments that her "burden" is more "on my back than on my spirit." Attributable, at least in part, to the nearing end of captivity, the shift of her "burden" from the spiritual to the physical realm reinforces the material reality of Rowlandson's time in captivity and reminds readers that her narrative has an important physical dimension.

Even when she is redeemed and settled back in her home, Rowlandson remains physically and psychologically restless and in motion. After her release she and her husband head eastward, with no clear destination, in search of their still-captive children (Wesley 29). Later yet, when her children have been recovered and the family is reunited, Rowlandson remains agitated. Even though she ends her narrative with a passage from Exodus that instructs, "*Stand still, and see the salvation of the* Lord," she cannot be still (Exod. 14:13, qtd. in Rowlandson 65). She writes that at night, "when all are fast about me, and no eye open but His who ever waketh, my thoughts are upon things past.... [W]hen others are sleeping mine eyes are weeping" (64–65). Her troubled thoughts mirror the aimless pacing of her body in captivity; she is still the captive who understands that only movement can secure survival. Through her material experience of captivity—a materiality grounded in her walking body—Rowlandson has experienced a different way of being in the world. As a woman who has learned to depend on her walking body as a means of agency and survival, Rowlandson is at odds with the Puritan teachings of passive white womanhood. Yet her faith in Puritan teachings is profound, causing a cognitive dissonance between scriptural interpretations and material experiences. Her narrative captures this doubleness, mapping two journeys: one is a symbolic pilgrimage toward spiritual redemption and the other a physical trek necessitating interaction with other material bodies and the material land of colonial Massachusetts.

ADVENTURE AND SOCIAL CRITIQUE IN SARAH WAKEFIELD'S CAPTIVITY NARRATIVE

Almost two hundred years after Mary White Rowlandson's captivity among the Narragansetts and Wampanoags and more than twelve hundred miles to the west, Sarah Wakefield was taken captive by the Dakota, an experience she recounts in *Six Weeks in the Sioux Tepees: A Narrative of Indian Captivity*. Unlike Rowlandson, who begins her narrative at the moment of attack, Wakefield begins with her family's migration west a year before her captivity. "Although I was nervous [about moving 'out of civilization']," she writes, "I enjoyed that ride, for a more beautiful sight than that prairie, I never have seen" (55). When they approached their new home in the Upper Sioux Agency, she declares, "We found we were to cross this river, and ascend a hill 600 feet high, made it seem as if we were going up to some great castle, for we could see the tops of the buildings in the distance and we all remarked that we enjoyed this as much as pleasure-seekers did their visits to the old castles and scenery on the Rhine" (56). She asserts, "We soon knew we could be very happy, although so far away from civilization," and recalls her comfort and pleasure in "rid[ing] through those woods… unprotected." She recounts ascending to Mr. Riggs's Mission, "a delightful spot" with "enormous hills" that would make "a person at the top and commenc[ing] [to] descen[d]…tremble with fear for a while, but at last they would entirely forget all danger, while looking at the beauty of the scene." In these early pages, Wakefield presents herself as an adventurer who enjoys the beauty of the landscape and the "very kind and pleasant" Indigenous peoples she encounters (58). As an immigrant to the Minnesota frontier, Wakefield revels in the landscape and her ability to navigate passage. Although her narration of her subsequent captivity is filled with accounts of physical and mental hardships, she continually returns to a celebration of westward movement with herself as the model adventurer. Through her mobility in both freedom and captivity, she is able to comprehend both the initial promise and the devastating effects of Euroamerica's westward impulse.

By 1861, the year Wakefield and her family traveled to the Upper Sioux Agency, Europeans had already crossed the continent, even though the frontier was not "officially" closed until 1890.[15] Now that the land had been surveyed and trails had been blazed, wave after wave of settlers came west, looking for land and a new life. The promises of the frontier had become firmly ensconced in America's idea of itself and its destiny. The alluring mythos of the West has long attracted Euroamerican writers and adventurers. Eric Heyne explains that the dominant Euroamerican belief holds that "anything is possible out there, including, as so many utopian colonizers have gambled, human perfectibility" (9). The nineteenth-century frontier was imagined in deeply mythic terms as "the margin of the known opened to the possibility of wonders in the unknown.... [T]he line beyond which beckoned freedom from existing social and political restraints" (Mogen, Busby, and Bryant 5–6). Bolstering the fantasy of the frontier were the dual images of Thomas Jefferson's yeoman farmer with his "natural" desire to seek land to cultivate and the hunter-hero, whom R. W. B. Lewis describes "standing alone, self-reliant and self-propelling, ready to confront whatever awaited him with the aid of his own unique and inherent resources" (Slotkin 213; Lewis 5). These figures and the wide-open landscape they yearned for fueled an "irrepressible American urge to travel in mind and body" (Heyne 11). The western frontier, Wallace Stegner writes, "was not a place but a way, a trail to the Promised Land, an adventurous, dangerous rite of passage" (21). The American rite of passage replaced the Puritan pilgrim with the largely secular adventurer, seeking land and excitement.

Like the Puritan errand, the basic parameters for the classic western adventure narrative closely mirror the elements Turner and Turner set forth for the pilgrimage. The hero (pilgrim) departs the everyday and familiar world to seek power and knowledge and then returns triumphantly (Slotkin 10–11). Richard Slotkin argues that the Euroamerican incarnation of the heroic quest involves an attempt to "get back to the primary source of blood-knowledge of the wilderness, the 'Indian' mind" (17). The Euroamerican hero's search for this "blood-knowledge," Slotkin argues, is paired with a sense of exile, "the psychological anxieties attendant on the tearing up of home roots for wide wandering outward in space" (18). The space that this hero wandered was the frontier, which "has meant both the border one crossed to reach new places and the places themselves" (Heyne 6). As a border to be crossed, the frontier in American imagination is continually on the move, a boundary that shimmers and fluctuates in the distance. The Euroamerican hero, like the pilgrim, finds himself cast out, whether voluntarily or not, and must travel and face physical and mental tests before returning with hard-won knowledge and experience to be integrated into the community, even if the hero himself can never be fully reintegrated.

Yet the values of the frontier myth—mobility, versatility, self-reliance, solitude, individuality—were the characteristics of the *male* hunter-hero, not the nineteenth-century woman. Martha J. Cutter contends that while men's lives were often defined through "autonomous, external goals such as the search for fame, career, gold, or a wife," nineteenth-century women's lives were defined through "their love for others, and spurred by relational, internal, and selfless goals" (4). Cutter argues that "from 1780 to 1860 Americans were preoccupied with the feminine virtues of purity, piety, submissiveness, and domesticity—a constellation of attributes known as the domestic saint." Women, she continues, were required to be "'passive, submissive responders' since…'submission was perhaps the most feminine virtue expected of women'" (xv). In order to fit into the accepted parameters of virtuous femininity, women in nineteenth-century America were expected to remain confined to the home. The dominant female virtues were largely characterized by stasis and inaction, whereas the dominant male virtues were characterized by movement and action. Susan Stanford Friedman, drawing on the work of James Clifford, describes these contrasting impulses as "roots" and "routes." "Roots and routes are," she argues, "two sides of the same coin: roots, signifying identity based on stable cores and continuities; routes, suggesting identity based on travel, change, and disruption" (153). For women traveling to the American frontier in the nineteenth century, the expectation that they support "roots" over "routes" meant that to sustain their virtuous femininity, they struggled to retain a sense of stability and place as their literal movement necessitated change and disruption.

In *Six Weeks in the Sioux Tepees*, Sarah Wakefield strives to define and articulate a potentially radical space for white womanhood on the frontier that draws together aspects of the male frontier hero and the idealized Euroamerican mother. The resulting text joins the tropes of captivity, that, by the nineteenth century, were familiar and expected with a pointed critique of accepted gender roles and the racist rhetoric of westward expansion. As in Rowlandson's text nearly two hundred years prior, Wakefield's narrative is structured around movement and walking. Unlike Rowlandson, however, Wakefield's narrative highlights how movement precedes and extends beyond the forced movement of captivity. Wakefield steps past the typical captivity narrative and re-creates herself as an active heroine who embraces the western land she walks across even as she condemns the ideology that has brought her there.

The Minnesota frontier that Wakefield traveled to in 1861 was heavily inscribed with hundreds of years of Euroamerican fantasies and the materialization of these fantasies in policies of Indian removal. Patricia Limerick contends, "From the beginning, the usual justification was that Indians were not using the land properly. Relying on hunting and gathering, savagery neglected the land's true potential and kept out those who could put it to proper use" (190). When Wakefield's husband, John, was appointed physician at the Upper Sioux Agency, the Wakefields joined the settlers who had mushroomed the Euroamerican population in Minnesota territory from six thousand in 1850 to more than two hundred thousand by 1856 (Castiglia 52). The Wakefields, like many of these settlers, lived among the seven thousand Dakota who had farmed the land since a treaty in 1851 that deeded twenty-four million acres to the United States in return for $495,000 and reservation land in western Minnesota (Schultz 9–10).[16] The Dakota and the Euroamerican settlers lived relatively peaceably until 1862, when a poor harvest, broken treaty obligations to provide food and money for the Dakota by area agencies, exorbitant prices and corruption in traders' stores, severe hunger, and the Dakota's continuous loss of territory to the United States led to a confrontation that came to be known as the Minnesota Massacre (Castiglia; Schultz; Anderson and Woolworth; Derounian-Stodola). Internal divisions among the Dakota coupled with a larger number of US troops than the Dakota expected led to their defeat and the conviction of "307 [Dakota] warriors and the utter dispossession" of the Minnesota Dakota people (Castiglia 52).[17]

Wakefield's captivity narrative is one of dozens that came out of the Minnesota Massacre.[18] Wakefield, undoubtedly aware of the outlines and tropes of the generic captivity narrative, infuses her text with these preexisting codes and images to facilitate the deeply critical and even radical charges she levels against Euroamerican westward expansion, making her narrative stand out among the many captivity narratives from the conflict that follow a more expected narrative of Indian atrocities.[19] Ostensibly writing "to vindicate myself, as I have been grievously abused by many, who are ignorant of my captivity and release by the Indians" (53), Wakefield melds the conventions of the captivity narrative with elements of the frontier hero and the domestic saint to complicate Euroamerican visions of women, Native Americans, and the frontier itself.

Mobility shapes her narrative, from the initial home-founding journey through her weeks in captivity to the wandering of the Dakota at the close of the narrative. Though Wakefield's narrative is not organized around successive "removes," like Rowlandson's, she describes herself as always in motion. Whether moving west with the tide of Euroamerican immigrants, marching as a captive with the Dakota, fleeing into the woods to hide from the threat from "bad Indians," critiquing the army's slow pace, or praising the Dakota's stamina, Wakefield's narrative is never still. She depicts herself as a western traveler who "walk[s] as a mode of making the world as well as being in it" (Solnit 29). By beginning her narrative with a home-founding journey and by ending with the wandering and dislocated Dakota, Wakefield reimagines the captivity journey in the context of westward expansion and Indian removal.

Wakefield situates herself within her domestic role at the beginning of her story, clarifying that her movement west was directly tied to her husband's occupation. With the first line of the text, she explains, "My husband was appointed physician for the Upper Sioux Indians at Pajutazee, or Yellow Medicine." She follows this statement with her initial impression of "Indian country": "I could not help exclaiming, 'Is it here where I am to live?' for all I saw was one log hut and about six hundred filthy, nasty, greasy Indians.... When I first arrived at the [lower] Agency I was disheartened, low-spirited, and frightened, for the buildings were situated on a high prairie and as far as the eye could reach was a vacant space." Wakefield recounts that, upon learning that they were to travel thirty miles farther west than this desolate area, "I was alarmed" (55). Her initial reaction to the Indigenous people and the western landscape reveals her anxiety about moving out of "civilization" onto what she sees as a bleak and featureless plain with Indians who seemed to live up to the negative stereotypes with which she was undoubtedly familiar.[20] While Wakefield includes significantly more detailed description of people and land than Rowlandson, her initial descriptions deny actual material reality. By framing her representation almost solely within her preconceptions, she writes over the material reality of the people and the land with a preformed narrative. She is blind to the way that "material forms—bodies, things, elements, toxic substances, chemicals, organic and inorganic matter, landscapes, and biological entities—intra-act with each other and with the human dimension, producing configurations of meanings and discourses that we can interpret as stories" (Iovino and Opperman 7). Her inability to accurately represent the people and the land is directly connected to her anxiety to write herself into the role of the proper domestic woman, desiring safety and "civilized" familiarity.

Still removed from the full material reality of the land, Wakefield's negative impression of the frontier changes quickly when she sees the prairie covered with flowers and tallgrass "waving in the breeze." "It reminded me," she writes, "of a beautiful panorama. It seemed really too beautiful for Nature's picture" (55).[21] When she first glimpses her new home, she remarks that it "resembled a fort," and a few lines later she writes that as she approached the Upper Agency, she imagined "we were going up to some great castle." She has replaced her initial dread of the forbidding wilderness with the fantasy of a strong military and governmental presence. Instead of the earlier "log hut," she imagines a fort and a castle, with flags flying "from many of the buildings in honor of our arrival" (56). For Wakefield, as for many other nineteenth-century frontierswomen, such images "overcame women's initial distrust of the 'dismal prairie.' But even more important, the fantasy of a landscape that might figuratively reconstitute some prior domestic community soothed the sense of irrevocable loss" (Kolodny, *Land Before Her* 97–98). Wakefield pairs her increasing admiration for the "grand" and beautiful scenery with the presence of "a blacksmith, farmer, and doctor[,]...a school[,]...[and] a missionary station." In the same paragraph in which she enumerates these signs of Euroamerican civic settlement, she states, "We soon knew we could be very happy although so far away from civilization" (57). Unlike the hunter-hero's journey *away* from the domestic, Wakefield imagines a journey that retains a sense of Euroamerican community and the trappings of "civilization," which were about material and commercial comfort. Wakefield comes to recognize that rather than moving into "a vacant space," she is part of a larger westward movement, a collective undertaking that she finds initially comforting and eventually deeply problematic.

It is only when she is settled at the Upper Sioux Agency that Wakefield begins to see and experience the material reality of the land, an awareness that she pairs with her increasing comfort moving through the land on her own. "Sometimes," she writes,

> I would go to Mr. Riggs' Mission, which was situated about two miles above Dr. Williamson's [mission], at a place called Hazelwood. It was a delightful spot, and the rides to the place I enjoyed exceedingly. The scenery around Rush Brook was grand. Enormous hills—almost mountains—were on every side of this stream, and when a person was at the top and commenced descending, they would tremble with fear for a while, but at last they would entirely forget all danger, while looking at the beauty of the scene.... I often wondered what an Eastern person would think, to ride through those woods, as we did, unprotected. I usually went with my little boy, alone, to Hazelwood, often returning long after the sun was down, and very often passing through the Indian camp. (58)

In this long passage Wakefield provides a more specific description of the land and establishes the freedom and mobility she enjoyed in the months prior to her captivity. As the wife of a prominent agency employee, Wakefield presents herself traveling easily to visit a neighboring missionary station.[22] She travels to outposts of Euroamerican settlements and observes the mission churches and schools, rather than traveling into the wilderness simply to experience the wilderness for itself. In this way, Wakefield aligns herself with the aspects of the settled frontier that support her role as a domesticating, Christianizing presence. However, while she makes it clear that her movements through the wilderness have appropriate and acceptable destinations, she also relishes her bravery and boldness. She recognizes that her ability to "forget all danger, while looking at the beauty of the scene," and "to ride through those woods...unprotected" would surprise and even shock "an Eastern person." Wakefield connects her freedom of movement with her ability to exceed the constraints of the domestic sphere. By focusing her account of captivity on the story of a woman traveling to and through the Minnesota frontier, Wakefield challenges the gendered ideology of "women's stability that supports the central metaphor of men's travel" (Wesley xiv).

Just over a year after the Wakefields moved to Minnesota, the deplorable treatment of the Dakota reached a boiling point. Annual payments were delayed, and food rotted in the traders' warehouses, in part because they hoped to raise the market value of their already overpriced merchandise. Meanwhile, the Dakota, cut off from their traditional hunting lands, starved (Castiglia 52). Finally, in August 1862, resentments erupted when four young Dakota men fell into a dispute about one another's relative bravery or cowardice and attacked a family of Euroamerican settlers.[23] Following the attack, an angry group of Dakota men determined to fight rather than surrender in the face of the Euroamericans' retaliation (Anderson and Woolworth 13). Inverting the language of Manifest Destiny, Wakefield writes that Little Crow, a prominent Dakota leader, declared the Dakota "must clear the country of all the whites so they might live" (65).[24] News of the uprising was sporadic and incomplete, causing many settlers to mistakenly remain in the path of the Dakota warriors or to run directly toward the fighting when they believed they were running away. As misinformation spread, Wakefield's husband disastrously made arrangements for Wakefield and their two young children to be driven to the Lower Agency—where the attack was centered—by George Gleason, the storekeeper for the Lower Agency's warehouse who had been visiting the Upper Agency (Schultz 61).

Remembering the ride with Gleason, Wakefield claims, "I rode in great fear that afternoon.... I had strong feelings of evil.... I became frightened, tried again to persuade him to return. I was so excited I could not sit still and I endeavored to jump out of the wagon. Then he scolded me" (66–67). Wakefield contends that she sensed something was wrong, and had she been in control, she would have turned the wagon back. As a woman used to traveling alone in the Minnesota land, Wakefield voices her concern about the safety of their venture, but finds herself constrained by a foolish man who accuses her of being "unpleasant" and "'hysterical'" (67). Gleason's inability to imagine that Wakefield might have a valid opinion manifests in his physical control over her body. She cannot leave the wagon and is therefore at the mercy of the driver. Her frustrating helplessness as a passenger is heightened when they are attacked by two Dakota warriors, Gleason is killed, and Wakefield and her children are taken captive. As she is driven away from Gleason's corpse by her captors, Hapa and Chaska, she remarks, "I rode in much agony; I knew not where I was to be taken, or what might eventually be my fate" (69). Her initial fear as a captive is tied to her unknown destination. While Rowlandson was deeply frightened of moving "into the vast and desolate Wilderness" (34), Wakefield is not frightened so much by a wilderness she has come to find beautiful as she is by her lack of agency, her inability to direct her own body.

Once out of the wagon and on her feet, Wakefield, following the traditional contours of captivity narratives, frequently describes the physical pain and fatigue she experienced as a result of forced marching. Michelle Burnham argues that according to the familiar format of the captivity narrative, "the event of captivity is followed by an almost incessant mobility, as the captive must travel with the Indians into and through the wilderness" (*Captivity and Sentiment* 51). For a nineteenth-century woman conditioned to value stability and rootedness, forced movement and unknown destinations caused extreme physical and psychological distress. Recalling one of the first days of enforced movement in captivity, Wakefield writes, "I thought I would be sun-struck, for we were kept on a constant move" (71). She recounts that she "traveled in great distress, barefoot, trotting along in the tall dry prairie grass," until "the skin was all off from one foot" (91). The more she walks, the more her feet become a focus of her concern: "My feet at this time were very bad; proud flesh as large as a silver dollar was eating into my foot" (94). A few days later she writes, "The last few miles we traveled that day I experienced more pain than I ever did in my life before. I might have been tracked by the blood that ran from my feet and legs.... I would certainly die if I had to walk any further" (101–2). In these passages Wakefield aligns herself with the tradition of captivity writers by stressing the physical difficulties she faces in a situation where pressure to travel quickly comes from her Dakota captors, who are themselves compelled forward. Her bleeding and blistered feet are "of interest [to nineteenth-century readers] as the locus of affective responses to external stimuli or as [the body] evokes sympathy or other affective responses in others" (Ebersole 146). Her painful feet signal her feminine weakness and buttress the belief that a woman's proper place is not in the wilderness but in the safety of the domestic space, thus aligning her narrative with the sympathies of her nineteenth-century readers and their expectations.[25] Simultaneously, her bleeding feet also point to her physical immersion in the land. The blood running from her feet suddenly brings into focus her own bodily connection to the land. In these passages the fact is laid bare that "'nature' is always as close as one's own skin—perhaps even closer" (Alaimo, *Bodily Natures* 2).

Linda Nash explains that in the nineteenth century, the predominant understanding of the body involved "a constant exchange between inside and outside, by fluxes and flows, and by its close dependence on the surrounding environment" (qtd. in Alaimo, *Bodily Natures* 90). In this way, descriptions of the physical body were used to understand the environment itself. The nineteenth-century body, unlike the modern body, was not understood to be separate from the surrounding environment (Alaimo, *Bodily Natures* 90). Wakefield's extended descriptions of her bodily experience would be interpreted, as she intended, in relation to her material experience in captivity. Her bloody feet signaled both her struggle and her bravery, her engagement with the wilderness.

Wakefield's painful movement as a captive occurs not only in the periods of forced marching with the Dakota, but also when she must run into the woods to hide from the "bad Indians" who want to kill all of the white captives.[26] The first of these flights occurs early in her captivity, when "Chaska's mother came into her lodge saying that a man was coming to kill me.... She told an old man her story, and he said 'Flee to the woods.'... [W]e ran to a ravine. It was very steep and the banks were like the roof of a house. When we got to the bottom she hid me in the tall grass and underbrush" (72). In this first scare and escape to the woods, Wakefield emphasizes her deep feelings of fear and anxiety. When Chaska's mother is late in coming to retrieve her once the danger has passed, Wakefield represents herself as helplessly waiting for salvation: "I now began to think she had forgotten me and removed.... I knew I could not climb those banks alone, and our bag of crackers would not last long. I now saw starvation as well as other evils staring us in the face. Our situation was truly horrible" (74). She sits fearfully with her "feet in a running brook" (73). As a result, when Chaska's mother finally returns for her, Wakefield "found I could not stand, from the effects of sitting so long in one position, and my limbs in the water had chilled my blood and stopped circulation" (74). She tells a similar story about a second scare, a rumor that Little Crow was coming to camp to "kill us white women" (79). This time she runs with Chaska's grandfather, who hides her in the center of a haystack. She states that once there, "I sat for hours.... I could hear water running but dared not come out of my hiding place." When Chaska's grandfather returns, she finds that once again, "it was some time before I was able to stand, as I had sat in one position eighteen hours" (80). Wakefield's sense of powerlessness is expressed in her lack of mobility. She sits helplessly, recalling earlier images of *Judea Capta* waiting patiently for rescue. In these episodes, Wakefield represents herself as a stereotypical feminine captive whose body is in constant threat, reacting instead of acting.

However, Wakefield emphasizes her physical endurance and strength even in these moments of pain and inaction. After both of these experiences, Wakefield notes that she is able to overcome the physical pain. When Chaska's mother retrieves her from the brook, she writes that when she finds she cannot stand, "the old woman rubbed me and while doing so said...I must try to walk to her tepee." Even though she "was completely prostrated" by her experience and was "shivering with fear and disease," she was still able to walk three miles and ford the Redwood River (74). Further, they "did not go in paths or roads, but through the tallest trees and thickest brush and among all kinds of berry bushes entwined together, with grape vines and ivy. We did not stop to part them, but tore through." When they finally make it back to Chaska's mother's tepee, Wakefield marvels, "I felt comparatively happy" (75). Similarly, when she emerges from the haystack, she writes, "I found I had got to walk several miles. I did not think I could live to walk but strength was given me" (80). Though Wakefield sat helplessly after being forced to run to the woods, her emphasis on her overcoming subsequent painful and difficult movement, with the direct and physical help of her Dakota captors, suggests that she was able to find agency and defy her culturally prescribed helplessness. She revels in her endurance, noting that she found a strength she did not know she had and even felt "comparatively happy."

By the third time Wakefield "fle[es] to the woods," she does not sit fearfully immobile.[27] She "sat awhile, and hearing running water I thought I would follow it, and perhaps I might reach the Minnesota river. I took [my daughter] Nellie on my back (as I had learned to carry her in that fashion) and we followed the brook some ways." Her progress is eventually inhibited by "a large tree which had fallen across [the brook] completely impeding our progress. I was obliged to stop or retrace my steps, and I decided to remain, as it was a very good hiding place" (82). This time when "the old woman" returns to find her, she is the one who is anxious and "much frightened" while Wakefield sits calmly in her "very good hiding place." Once Wakefield has been captured, she is no longer in control of where and when she moves; however, she continues to challenge expectations by presenting herself as strong, resourceful, and practical. She has learned to carry her baby like a Dakota woman and is no longer disoriented in the wilderness. Instead, she carefully considers her situation, observes the world around her, and makes reasonable decisions. In her thoughtful navigation of captivity, Wakefield's narrative joins other captivity narratives that Christopher Castiglia argues "embody women's loss of control but also provide strategies for enduring and altering their powerlessness" (12). Although walking is still so painful that at the end of her third flight to the woods Wakefield remarks that once again "my feet had become so sore I could hardly walk," her movement is directed and purposeful (83).

While Rowlandson gets lost in the wilderness and cannot find her way, Wakefield claims that space, aligning herself not with the pilgrim but with the adventurer building a home in the wilderness. After being reunited with her son, who had been staying at a different camp for a few nights, Wakefield recalls, "This night I was happy. I had my children both in my arms.... I sang for the children that night; we ran around on the prairie, picked flowers, and my spirits were as light as air, although I was a prisoner" (95). Wakefield presents herself at home in the wilderness. Uprooted and captive, she challenges the notion of the frail woman, unable to survive outside of the domestic space of a Euroamerican home. The prairie in this passage is pleasant and inviting. Kolodny argues that by the first decades of the nineteenth century, women began imagining the prairie as "parklike," resembling "the treed lawns and flower beds with which women had always dreamed of surrounding home." Further, "The prairies invited metaphors of intimacy" (*Land Before Her* 8). Wakefield's depiction of the prairie infuses a feeling of freedom and belonging into the unlikely space of captivity. Her happiness is predicated on her comfort in and enjoyment of the "parklike" prairie and her identity as a mother with her "children both in [her] arms." She creates an identity that bridges stability and movement. In the midst of disruptive travel, she establishes a sense of place and belonging.

If Wakefield's depiction of herself as strong and even happy in the wilderness of captivity challenged dominant nineteenth-century conceptions of white womanhood, so did her representation of Dakota women as capable and independent upend Euroamerican conceptions of Indigenous womanhood. Like Rowlandson's portrayal of the physical power of the Narragansetts and Wampanoags, Wakefield marvels at the strength and stamina of the Dakota women. When she is forced to walk barefoot because she asserts "squaws go barefoot when traveling" (87), her feet become blistered and sore; however, the Dakota women walk quickly and easily under the burden of heavy loads. Throughout the narrative she mentions the difficulty she faces in matching the pace of the Dakota women she walks with, having to "run to keep up" (91) with "the other *squaws*" who "will trot as fast as a horse" (91; emphasis in the original), though even the old Dakota women had "eighty pounds to carry" (87). Wakefield's positive depictions of Dakota women walking barefoot through sharp grass carrying heavy loads challenge what Paula Gunn Allen identifies as the Euroamerican "obsession" with "proving that Indians mistreat their women brutally, at every level and in every way—the implication being that civilized people revere women, and savages, who don't revere them, deserve extermination" (5).[28] Although she falls back on Euroamerican comparisons of Indigenous people and animals, not to mention her use of the term *squaw*, Wakefield clearly admires these women's physical strength and presents them as exceeding Euroamerican ideas about the capabilities of women.

Wakefield's portrayal of the movement of Dakota women fuels her critique of the destructive impetus of Euroamerican westward drive. "Poor women!" she writes of the Dakota. "How I pity many of them! driven from their good homes, their families broken up and divided. Many of them are as much to be pitied as the whites, and many of them are no more to blame" (75). Wakefield locates the mistreatment of Dakota women not with Dakota men but with Euroamericans. Further, she links this mistreatment to the basic plot of the Indian captivity narrative. Like the stock white woman captive, the Dakota women are uprooted and their families scattered. Euroamericans disrupt the very domestic image they purport to value. Further, by questioning Euroamericans' hypocritical treatment of Dakota women, Wakefield connects the mistreatment and devastation of the Dakota with Euroamerican society's hypocrisy in claiming to protect white women.

While Wakefield praises the Dakota women's capable and strong walking, she points out that when arrangements have finally been made for the release of Wakefield and her fellow captives, the US Army, under the command of General Henry Hastings Sibley, moves at a snail's pace. "How we looked for Sibley all the next day," Wakefield writes, "but he did not come.... Where could he be? he was only twenty-five miles away." She continues, "The second night we waited for him, an Indian came in saying they had only traveled eight miles, and it was not thirty-six hours since he got our message, and they had camped for the night, spending hours to entrench themselves. An army of over two thousand leaving us, a little handful of persons, with only about one hundred men to protect us!" (108). When they finally arrive, Wakefield comments sardonically, "But I suppose the troops were fatigued, if they marched all the way from St. Paul as fast as they did from Yellow Medicine—taking over fifty hours to travel twenty-five miles" (115). Wakefield invites comparison of the army's slow movement with the efficient, if arduous, movement of the Dakota and of herself while captive. The army's eight miles in one day contrasts sharply with the day Wakefield, barefoot and carrying her two children, walked "without resting even for a drink of water, for sixteen miles" (101). Whereas Rowlandson attempts to rationalize the army's slow movement with arguments about God's larger plan, Wakefield employs the discrepancy between the army's sluggish marching and her own efficient walking alongside the Dakota to critique the army's incompetence.

Wakefield's return to Euroamerican society does not mark the end of her movement; like Rowlandson's, her reintegration is incomplete. Castiglia suggests that Wakefield's critique of US ideology is "bound up in the ironically named 'Camp Release.'... As her experiences in the fort reveal, the project of westward expansion relies not only on an unquestioned discourse of white supremacy; it requires as well a carefully policed system of gender roles in which women are sexually vulnerable, unalterably xenophobic, and physically helpless, requiring the protection and support of white men" (56). In Camp Release, Wakefield finds herself disrespected and unheard. Clearly expecting to hear about rape and other atrocities meted out upon Wakefield's body, Colonel Marshall informs her, "If you have anything of a more private nature to relate, you can communicate it to Mr. Riggs" (113). When she told them she had nothing more to say, "they thought it very strange that I had no complaints to make, but did not appear to believe me" (114). Later, Chaska is wrongfully convicted of Mr. Gleason's murder, and Wakefield is "angry, for it seemed to me as if they considered my testimony of no account; for if they had believed what I said, he would have been acquitted" (116). At Camp Release, Wakefield is back in the realm of entrenched beliefs and assumptions. The men there expect to hear a particular version of captivity and seem unwilling and unable to imagine any other possibility. In response, Wakefield no longer feels the same sort of physical empowerment she experienced even in captivity. She, who used to ride through the wilderness alone with her son and has walked scores of miles in captivity, now does "not wish to walk a quarter of a mile alone" (114). Back in the "safety" of white society, Wakefield feels physically threatened and constrained. She has inverted her understanding of "civilization" and "savagery." Whereas she once saw the Dakota as "filthy, nasty, greasy Indians" (55), she now contends that while in captivity, she "was a vast deal more comfortable with the Indians in every respect than I was during my stay in that soldiers camp, and was treated more respectfully by those savages than I was by those in that camp" (112). Prior to her captivity, she had connected freedom of movement to her standing as the wife of an agency physician; now she imagines freedom of movement with the Dakota, who "proved to be good true friends" (75).

Sarah Wakefield's captivity narrative is not a story of a woman's victimization in the wilderness. She does not sit idly by waiting for rescue, and she resists the binaries of "white and Indian, civilized and savage, masculine and feminine, captivity and liberty," upon which nineteenth-century ideologies depended (Castiglia 57). She ends her narrative not with her joyful reintegration into white society, but with a desolate picture of the fallout from the Minnesota Massacre. After the captives were recovered at Camp Release, the vast majority of the Dakota, both those involved in the uprising and those who were not, were captured. Eventually, those not executed or imprisoned were transferred to a new reservation, Crow Creek, in Missouri (Schultz 282).[29] "The army on the Missouri, under Gen. Sully, has done a good work," Wakefield sarcastically comments, "killing many Indians and destroying their property, while our army has been only enriching the officers, and shielding murderers from justice" (126). She laments, "Now [the Dakota] are wanderers, without home, or even a resting place" (127). By beginning her narrative with her own family's movement to the frontier and ending with the uprooting and dispossession of the Dakota, Wakefield identifies the paradoxical nature of western movement; for Rowlandson movement means survival, but for Wakefield movement represents how the advancement of one community is contingent on the devastation of another.

CAPTIVE BODIES AND TRANS-CORPOREAL ETHICS

As a genre with an "endlessly reproducible master narrative" (B. Stratton 11), Indian captivity narratives offered a seemingly limitless stage for promoting dominant ideologies of incomprehensible and therefore apparently worthless Indigenous claims to land and community as well as divinely given rights for Euroamerican land acquisition. In the process, narratives that give voice to white female interactions with the material land are part of a larger process of creating and supporting "an imperialist cartography—a deterritorialization" of Indigenous land (B. Stratton 38). Writing their narratives in retrospective comfort, former captives inscribe the land with meaning; their narratives both are influenced by the material land and create a narrative framework for understanding the land. By writing into familiar tropes and plot points, former captives reinforce the ideological systems in which they are inextricably bound. Yet somewhere in the matrix of symbol and material reality, Rowlandson's and Wakefield's walking bodies provide both women a means for articulating the complexities of their movement across the land and their captivity among Indigenous peoples, who themselves were enduring policies of removal that complicated their own relationship to movement, land, and walking.

Rowlandson and Wakefield write about walking in their narratives to communicate the physical pain of forced movement, the psychological terror of captivity, and the mental strength to claim agency even in the midst of captivity. Writing within and against a tradition that defines captivity as a simple case of Indian savagery and female persecution, Rowlandson and Wakefield suggest a much more complex and rich story. The unconscious fissures in Rowlandson's narrative and the outright claims in Wakefield's narrative present captive women who exhibit moments of strength and agency within the bonds of captivity. Walking transcends the bounds of symbolic meaning; in moving bodily across the material land with other material bodies, Rowlandson and Wakefield experience to varying degrees a sense of their own intermeshment in the world. In the wretchedness of captivity, walking allows them a certain access to Jane Bennett's conception of materiality: "a rubric that tends to horizontalize the relations between humans, biota, and abiota. It draws human attention sideways, away from an ontologically ranked Great Chain of Being and toward a greater appreciation of the complex entanglements of humans and nonhumans" (112). At the same time that the captives gain a certain amount of agency through their physical movements, their bodies are acted upon by a world "in which the human body can never be disentangled from the material world" (Alaimo, *Bodily Natures* 115). This experience of intermeshment suggests the possibility of what Alaimo terms "trans-corporeal ethics," an ethics that incorporates not only the writing subject (in this case the white female former captive), but also the nonhuman world and, I would add, Indigenous subjects that are similarly intermeshed in a dangerous and unstable colonial system. Rowlandson and Wakefield experienced captivity in large part as a constraint and redirection of their material bodies, a reality that shaped the form and content of their narratives. Yet the very structure and movement of their narratives reveal a much more complex picture of their experiences shaped not by the independent decisions of their captors, but by their captors' responses to the material and cultural incursion of Euroamericans. As surviving witnesses to an ongoing war that is still displacing Indigenous peoples in the United States, Rowlandson and Wakefield are caught in varying degrees between dominant ideologies and the possibility of trans-corporeal ethics experienced in their walking bodies.

NOTES

1. One poignant example is the "missing" story of William Bradford's first wife, Dorothy. Bradford relates the arrival of his ship to Cape Cod in chapters 9 and 10 of *Of Plymouth Plantation*: "Of Their Voyage, and How they Passed the Sea; And of Their Safe Arrival in Cape Cod" and "Showing How They Sought out a Place of Habitation and What Befell Them Thereabout." Yet he fails to mention a significant event. Between first casting anchor in Cape Cod and finally disembarking a month later, his wife died. In "Life of William Bradford," Cotton Mather explains that Dorothy fell overboard and drowned in the harbor. However, in a 1963 introduction to *Of Plymouth Plantation*, Samuel Eliot Morison claims that Dorothy, debilitated from the voyage, likely killed herself rather than face the difficulties of settlement (Wesley xi).

For further discussion of the ways stories of women's movement to and across the American land are often ignored and displaced in accounts and studies of American travel, see Janis P. Stout's *The Journey Narrative in American Literature*, R. W. B. Lewis's *The American Adam*, Henry Nash Smith's *Virgin Land*, and Richard Slotkin's *Regeneration Through Violence*.

2. Please see note 4 in the introduction for a brief discussion of this term.

3. Providing a longer scope for the popularity of Indian captivity narratives, Billy Stratton claims that more than twenty-five hundred captivity narratives were published between 1542 and 1955 (5).

4. Olive Oatman's brother Lorenzo engaged Royal B. Stratton to interview Olive and write a history of the family and an account of the captivity of Olive and her sister. I include this example as Olive's voice, even though I recognize the highly problematic and mediated nature of the narrative.

5. Rowlandson's narrative numbered four editions in its first year in print, twenty-three editions by 1828, and at least forty editions by 1990 (Lang 20–21).

6. See Perry Miller's *Errand into the Wilderness*. The title is taken from a sermon given by the Reverend Samuel Danforth in 1670 (Miller 1).

7. See, for example, the works of Harriet Beecher Stowe, Lydia Maria Child, Catharine Maria Sedgwick, and E. D. E. N. Southworth, among others (Samuels).

8. Scholars have long debated Increase Mather's and Joseph Rowlandson's influence on the writing of Mary White Rowlandson's narrative. Billy Stratton provocatively claims that the similarities between the narrative and Mather's other writings, combined with a distinct lack of other writings from Rowlandson, suggest Mather as the primary author (120). Other critics argue that while it is clear that Mather had a hand in the narrative's publication and is likely the author of the anonymous preface, Rowlandson is still likely the main author

of the narrative itself. While Stratton's argument is compelling, I follow critics such as Toulouse, Burnham, Breitwieser, Kolodny, and Castiglia in recognizing Rowlandson as the primary author of her narrative.

9. It is fitting that the first advertisement for Rowlandson's narrative appeared in the first American edition of Bunyon's *Pilgrim's Progress* (Strong 86; Ebersole 18).

10. Henwood's persuasive larger argument about Rowlandson's use of scripture, specifically the Psalms, is that it empowers her to "speak passionately of her own grief, confusion, and anger. [The Psalms] provide a vital means of self-expression under conditions that threaten to obliterate the captive's identity and even her sanity" (171). The Bay Psalm Book, she contends, "served as one of the first means of giving early American women a voice to be heard" (173).

11. See Slotkin 109; Kolodny, *Land Before Her* 18; Lang 21; Wesley 23; and Chedgzoy 179.

12. See, for example, Slotkin; Derounian-Stodola and Levernier; Ebersole; Lang; Downing; Logan; Henwood; and Burnham. Several contemporary critics, however, consider the contradictions in Rowlandson's narrative—the places where she seems to be in tension with dominant Puritan views. For examples of this approach, see Wesley; and Breitwieser.

13. Many critics have noted the importance of physical movement in Rowlandson's narrative; however, most of them devote only a paragraph or two to physical movement and shift their attention to other aspects of the narrative. See, for example, Slotkin; Kolodny, *Land Before Her*; Andrews et al.; Lang; Derounian-Stodola and Levernier; Ebersole; Logan; Burnham; Breitwieser; Wesley; and Dietrich.

In her article "The Journey Between: Liminality and Dialogism in Mary White Rowlandson's Captivity Narrative," Michelle Burnham looks at Rowlandson's text as a travel narrative in which "personal and spiritual growth become a function of geographic or spatial movement" (71). But Burnham focuses her discussion on the first part of the equation, "personal and spiritual growth," and she uses Rowlandson's physical movement to organize her analysis rather than as the focus of her analysis. Similarly, in his study *American Puritanism and the Defense of Mourning*, Mitchell Robert Breitwieser points several times to the importance of physical movement in Rowlandson's text, noting the many different kinds of movement in the narrative. Like Burnham, Breitwieser focuses on Rowlandson's psychological shifts, and he discusses physical movement mostly as a way to imagine psychic movements. Marilyn C. Wesley makes a similar argument in *Secret Journeys: The Trope of Women's Travel in American Literature*. "For Rowlandson," Wesley writes, "to report on movement is to create the occasion to report on Mary's shifting state of mind" (27). While these perspectives on Rowlandson's movement over the land and her reliance on movement as an organizing principle are instructive, the frequency of Rowlandson's references to movement, in particular to *walking*, necessitates a closer examination of how walking works as a means, not just a metaphor, of spiritual and personal transformation in her text.

14. Kolodny makes a very similar claim: "Never does [Rowlandson] suggest that she perceives any beauty in the landscape" (*Land Before Her* 19).

15. In "The Frontier in American History," Frederick Jackson Turner writes that in 1890, the superintendent of the US Census declared, "Up to and including 1880 the country had a frontier of settlement, but at the present the unsettled area has been so broken into by isolated bodies of settlement that there can hardly be said to be a frontier line."

16. Robert Dodge explains the complex history around the name "Sioux." Scholars agree that the term is a French rendering of the Ojibwe word *nadouissioux* or *nadowe-is-iw-ug* or *na-towe-wa*. However, there is a great deal of disagreement about what the term originally meant. Early definitions of "enemy" or "adder" have been joined with "they are lesser enemies" and even an argument that the term was simply an ethnic designation having nothing to do with snakes or enemies. *Dakota*, like *Lakota* and *Nakota*, translates as "friends" or "allies," with the different spellings indicating dialectical distinctions (Dodge 13–14). In this text, I will use the term *Dakota*, following the people's self-designation.

17. See note 29 of this chapter.

18. See Kathryn Zabelle Derounian-Stodola's *The War in Words: Reading the Dakota Conflict Through the Captivity Literature* for an extensive list of narratives from both Euroamerican and Dakota perspectives.

19. For examples, see the narratives of Mary Schwandt, Jannette E. Skyles de Camp Sweet, and Urania S. Frazer White, available through the Minnesota Historical Society Collections.

20. In her retelling of the first night she spent at the Upper Sioux agency, Wakefield draws attention to the misconceptions that many immigrants brought with them to the frontier:

> The first night passed there was one of horror to all, as we were ignorant of Indian customs any further than what we had learned of them from those who were camped around our town, and this night they were having councils and were talking, shouting, and screaming, all night, and we, poor, ignorant mortals, thought they were singing our death-song, preparatory to destroying us. Towards morning the noise lulled away, and we dropped to sleep, but not to sleep for long, for soon came the tramp and noise of a hundred horsemen close to the

> house. The men all arose, prepared their arms, waited and watched, but no attack was made. What could be the trouble? why did they not make some manifestation? why were they silent—only that terrible tramping? At last one man, braver than the rest, went down, and, behold—it was our own horses which had been turned out. They had come up on the platform to get away from the mosquitoes. This gives, in the beginning, an idea of many Indian scares. (4–5)

21. Mary Louise Pratt writes that, for nineteenth-century travel writers, presenting landscape as a painting was one of three conventional ways for creating "qualitative and quantitative value for the explorer's achievement.... [T]he landscape is *estheticized*" (204; emphasis in the original). Further, the viewer-painting relation implies that the writer "has the power if not to possess, at least to evaluate this scene" (205). Wakefield's adoption of this trope of travel writing further underscores her role as a traveler interested in describing and domesticating the new scenes she encounters.

22. Mona Domosh and Joni Seager argue that mobility, the ability "to move through space," is not only shaped by physical ability but also "deeply intertwined with social status." Mobility, they contend, "is greatest at the extreme ends of the socioeconomic spectrum. The mobility of the destitute is a hardship-induced rootlessness: the homeless, refugees, people of the margins of job markets, and people pushed into migration out of need or crisis are all clustered at this end of the mobility curve. At the opposite end of the spectrum are the high flyers (literally and metaphorically). In contemporary societies, increasing wealth is attended by increasing mobility, and reciprocally, increasing mobility increases privilege" (110). Through the course of their lives, Rowlandson and Wakefield experience both kinds of mobility—the mobility that comes with their higher social status and, later, the movement of the destitute that they experience when they are physically aligned with the Native peoples who are forced to wander by conflicts with encroaching Euroamerican settlers.

23. Kathryn Zabelle Derounian-Stodola provides the following depiction of the incident, based on Big Eagle's account:

> Four hungry young Dakota men went hunting near Acton on 17 August 1862; they found a hen's nest with some eggs, and one wanted to take the eggs, but another said it was a bad idea because the hen belonged to a settler and they might get into trouble. The first man accused the second of cowardice concerning whites; the second man said he was no coward and would prove it by going to the settler's home and killing him.... Finally all four Dakotas went to the house of the settler, Robinson Jones, but he was alarmed and set off for his

> son-in-law's place nearby. The Indians followed and killed three men and two women there.... Thus the war that killed hundreds of people from all backgrounds and led to Dakota death and displacement began as a fight over food. (31–32)

24. Little Crow led one of the nine bands, which together formed the Mdewakanton, one of the four tribes of the Eastern Sioux or Dakota. The Mdewakantons occupied the Mississippi River valley between present-day Prairie du Chien, Wisconsin, and the Falls of St. Anthony in Minneapolis (Anderson and Woolworth 8). Little Crow was a negotiator and signer of the Treaty of Mendota in 1851 and the Treaty of 1858. He also went to Washington, DC, in 1854 to campaign for well-defined boundary lines for the Dakota reservations. Though Little Crow was initially reluctant to join the war, his decision to lead the warriors placed him directly in the thick of the hostilities. When the Dakota were defeated by the American Army, Little Crow and fewer than three hundred people headed for Canada. He held out hope that he would be able to forge an alliance with the Yankton, Yankonais, and Tetons to march south and clear his homeland of Euroamericans. However, his small band eventually broke apart under the stress of exile, and on July 3, 1863, he was shot and killed by Nathan Lamson while he was picking raspberries (Schultz 272).

25. In several places throughout her narrative, Wakefield furthers her identification with the helpless female captive by describing herself as "naturally timid, and afraid of death under any circumstances" (30) and that "surely God gave me strength, or I would have died through fear, for I am by nature a very cowardly woman" (17).

26. One of the common tropes of Indian captivity narratives that Wakefield uses is the juxtaposition of "good" and "bad" Indians. Following dominant ideas about Native Americans, Wakefield imagines "good" Indians, like her captor Chaska, as more "civilized." That is, "good" Indians are Christian and adhere to Euroamerican gender ideologies, whereas "bad" Indians, such as Chaska's brother-in-law Hapa, are essentially "savage"—they are violent and unpredictable and corrupted by alcohol. However, Wakefield stresses the point that if the "bad" Indians are bad, they were encouraged to be so by the Euroamerican presence, in particular the dishonest traders. "All the evil habits that the Indian has acquired," Wakefield writes, "may be laid to the Traders. They first carried the minue-wakan among them. The Traders took their squaws for wives, and would raise several children by them, and then after living with them a number of years would turn them off. It was the Traders who first taught them to swear, for in the Indian language there are no oaths against our God or theirs" (7).

27. The incident that precipitates this flight was a drunken Dakota "in the next tepee" who threatened to "shoot all the white women in our camp" (Wakefield 25).

28. Elsewhere, Wakefield insists, "The Indians were as respectful towards me as any white man would be towards a lady" (86), and even states that Chaska "left me as he found me. My father could not have done differently, or acted more respectfully or honorable.... Very few Indians, or *even white men*, would have treated me in the manner he did" (84; emphasis in the original).

29. After a hasty military commission appointed by Sibley, 303 of the 307 Dakota men initially arrested were sentenced to die. President Abraham Lincoln reduced the execution list to 38 and the rest were imprisoned. The 38 sentenced to death were sent to the gallows on December 26, 1862. It was the largest mass execution in American history (Derounian-Stodola 17, 22).

2

"By This Song I Walk"

Land, Movement, and Memory on the Navajo Long Walk

In 1864, following long years of conflict and struggle over land and resources, the US government enacted a scorched-earth policy against the Navajo (or Diné, their self-appellation).[1] Between eight and ten thousand tribal members were forced at gunpoint to walk a 325-mile route from their traditional lands in the Four Corners area to an internment camp at Fort Sumner along the Pecos River in eastern New Mexico (Tapahonso, *Sáanii* 7; Cheek 41).[2] Four years later, after initiating multiple negotiations with US authorities, the Diné were finally permitted to return to a small reservation on their homeland. By that time, nearly a third of the Diné who walked to Fort Sumner had died; some succumbed to a combination of disease, depression, severe weather, and starvation, and some were murdered outright by US Army troops.

Both the displacement of the Dakota discussed in the previous chapter and the Navajo Long Walk to Fort Sumner belong to a history of contact between Native Americans and Euroamericans, a history Laura Tohe (Diné) calls "America's holocaust" ("Hwéeldi Béého̜ániih" 82). This history is "punctuated by removal after removal in tribe after tribe, by lengthy forced marches upon which dozens and more often hundreds or thousands of people died" (Gould 800). The landscape of the United States is crisscrossed with these violent trails, physical tracings that challenge the myth of triumphant and romantic Euroamerican westering. By the middle of the nineteenth century, such trails proliferated, as removal was legitimized as an official policy of the US government.

With the Euroamerican population growing more and more rapidly in the early nineteenth century, Congress passed the Indian Removal Act in May 1830. The act included legislation that allowed the US president to extinguish Indigenous claims to lands east of the Mississippi in exchange for public domain lands in the West. Although this act did not significantly change existing laws, its approval provided the government with the funds, "$500,000 for the specific purpose of removal" (Banner 217), and, perhaps more important, the political backing to move forward with the forced removal of southeastern Indigenous nations. Following the act's passage, some Indigenous groups relocated on their own, others traveled under the direction of government agents, and some, "deemed hostile for their continuing resistance, traveled in chains" (Marks 90).

The provisions of the Indian Removal Act specifically targeted Indigenous lands east of the Mississippi; however, in providing legal language justifying removal and relocation, the act paved the way for similar violent patterns as Euroamerican settler-colonists continued to push their way into the already contested landscape of the West. When the US-Mexican War ended with the Treaty of Guadalupe Hidalgo in 1848, US territory increased significantly, with Mexico forced to relinquish claims to what now comprises Texas, Arizona, New Mexico, and parts of Utah, Nevada, and Colorado (Gray). Then, in 1862 Abraham Lincoln signed the Homestead Act, which was specifically designed to accelerate settlement of the West by encouraging adult heads of family who had "never borne arms against the United States" to file an application for a federal land grant. Combined with the precepts of the Indian Removal Act, these events dramatically increased Euroamerican settlement and Indigenous dislocation.

The mechanisms of displacement are couched in legal language that obscures the violence and tragedy of wrenching Indigenous peoples from the lands they were connected to for millennia. Indeed, the effects of the violent displacement of Indigenous nations are persistent and reverberate across time. Explaining the centrality of place to Indigenous communal and individual identity, Leslie Marmon Silko (Laguna) argues, "Human identity, imagination and storytelling were inextricably linked to the land, to Mother Earth, just as the strands of the spider's web radiate from the center of the web" (21). Laura Tohe similarly explains, "Since time immemorial the construct of Diné identity is closely associated with the land" ("Grounded" 86). For many Indigenous cultures, including the Diné, emplacement—the connection between individual, community, and land—creates a sense of shared identity that transcends simplistic understandings of home and of self.[3] Larry Evers contends that "by imagining who and what they are in relation to particular landscapes, cultures and individual members of cultures form a close relation with those landscapes.... A sense of place derives from the perception of a culturally imposed symbolic order on a particular physical topography" ("Words and Place" 212). The links that have long joined Native American peoples and particular landscapes form the core of cultural identity and a sense of belonging. Forced removal enacted a violent division of the people from their land that dislocated them in both place and space and threatened to move them away from a coherent identity.

Within Indigenous storytelling traditions, the trauma of dislocation functions on the level of symbol and metaphor, as the land serves to represent the identity and memory of the people. Yet such trauma is also *material*. The removal trails etched across the American landscape interrupted traditional migration routes, hunting paths, and lifeways, creating physical traces of trauma. Diné teacher and writer Grace McNeley explains:

> The Navajo term *kétł'ooł*—derived from *ké*, meaning "feet," and *tł'ooł* meaning "root system"—expresses the concept of having a foundation for one's life in the earth, much as a plant is rooted in the earth.... This webbing of earth, of ancestors, of clan and familiar surroundings all constitute a Navajo home, enabling those within it to flourish, to thrive. (qtd. in Kelley and Francis 43)

Although this concept is not easily translatable from Diné formulations of land and cosmos into Western terms, it speaks to the bodily connection among Diné, land, and more-than-human beings. It is a connection that reaches through time. The removal from land is thus a material removal from *kétł'ooł*, a disruption of a complex relationship between self, land, community, and history.

While "rootedness" suggests a kind of static position, for many Native peoples emplacement is experienced through movement within a sacred land. Prior to the reservation movement, Indigenous peoples possessed freedom of mobility over large tracts of land. Paula Mitchell Marks argues, "The groups we have come to know as tribes did not inhabit a static world before the arrival of Europeans" (xviii); rather, they shifted in response to circumstances such as environmental conditions, seasonal changes, and confrontations and confederations among groups. Gerald Vizenor

(Anishinaabe) links Native American mobility directly to issues of sovereignty. "Native sovereignty," he states, "is the right of motion" (*Fugitive Poses* 182). The ability to move, Vizenor suggests, is intimately connected to self-determination and cultural autonomy.

Movement as an act of sovereignty stands in stark opposition to the forced movement Indigenous peoples suffered on removal trails. In an attempt to control both actual movement and the *meaning* of movement, Euroamericans, who equated fixity with "civilization" and Native mobility with "savagery," forced Indigenous nations along brutal removal trails to then restrict their movement on reservations and further impede sovereignty. Yet Indigenous understandings of movement remained securely embedded in Indigenous worldviews, stories, and ceremonies, even in the face of traumatically forced removal.

Mobility and walking across land inform both the form and the content of many Indigenous storytelling traditions. Vizenor asserts, "Natives have been on the move since the creation of motion in stories; motion is the originary" (*Fugitive Poses* 55). Vizenor links mobility to the very source of Native cultures, suggesting that movement within stories and across land is inseparable from individual and tribal identity. Similarly, Reid Gómez (Diné) writes, "There is no finished story because like the people, it too is always in motion. It is a breathing and changing thing. Like the landscape, it will exist and continue on long after this writing and your reading—in motion, with no final words and no retractions" (159). Vizenor and Gómez trace the strands of story, movement, and identity to a common origin. For many Native American peoples, identity and worldview are intimately bound up in land, story, and physical freedom, all of which are marked by the always present potential for change and movement. Critic Paula Gunn Allen (Laguna/Lakota/Lebanese) articulates this connection when she writes, "Human beings play an intrinsic role in the ongoing creation. This role is largely determined by the place where the tribe lives, and the role changes when the tribe moves" (73). Vizenor's claim that "stories of natives on the move are common" (*Fugitive Poses* 49) reinforces the centrality of motion in many Native American cultures, appearing in both actual physical movement and the fluidity of story.

For the Diné, the Long Walk threatened the meaning and experience of walking and moving within the land. The walking they endured on the journey to Hwééldi (Fort Sumner) broke their bodies and displaced them from Diné Bikéyah (the Navajo homeland). The Long Walk endangered the vital links between movement, land, and identity. Yet despite the physical and mental hardship, walking also offered a vital means of redefining the horrors of forced migration. In Diné accounts of the Long Walk period that have circulated for generations within families and clans, narratives of walking offer a language for expressing pain and renewal, the tragedy of removal, and the power of reclaiming the freedom to walk across Diné Bikéyah. Gómez notes, "Mobility is an act of resistance. Imagination and creativity, practices in an understanding of sovereignty as motion, enact an ideological living and resist physical and spiritual containment" (152). Walking, then, functions as resistance on multiple levels. It informs the shape and content of stories, songs, and memory while also linking them to the material reality of land and bodies. Resistance through movement is structural, thematic, and material. The stories collected in *Navajo Stories of the Long Walk Period*, Tiana Bighorse's retelling of her father's story in *Bighorse the Warrior*, and the Long Walk poems by Diné poets Luci Tapahonso and Laura Tohe reflect the ongoing relevance of the Long Walk through language, repeated tropes, and representations of walking as a means of both wrenching away and reclaiming land and identity. Embedding the Long Walk within a narrative of Diné experiences with land and movement (spanning from deep in Diné history and story cycles to the contemporary moment), these storytellers and writers find room within forced walking for agency and survival.

THE LONG WALK

By the mid-nineteenth century, the Diné's ability to move freely across their homeland was being threatened. Policies set in motion in 1830 with the signing of the Indian Removal Act continued to reverberate as the United States pushed its boundaries westward. The Euroamerican explorers and settlers who imagined themselves embarking on a triumphant westering journey found their progress impeded by the thousands of Native American peoples who had lived on these lands for hundreds and, in some cases, thousands of years. The land was neither empty nor free from conflict. In the American Southwest, Euroamerican settlers found a preexisting struggle for land and resources among the New Mexicans of Spanish descent and mixed Spanish and Indigenous Mexican descent, the Diné, and other neighboring Indigenous nations, including the Pueblos, the Apache, and the allied Ute and Comanche (Blackhawk 36). Among these groups, raids on sheep and cattle were frequent, as were forays to steal women and children to be sold into slavery. Although these attacks were perpetrated both by and against the Diné, other groups in the Southwest singled out the Diné as the main instigators.[4] Diné elder Herbert Zahne explains that while, "of course, there were bands of Navajos who took to raiding...the whole tribe was blamed for their actions," and this "false blame placed on the people brought the white soldiers upon them" (232).

With the signing of the Treaty of Guadalupe Hidalgo in 1848 (which marked the end of the war between the United States and Mexico), the New Mexican territory became part of the United States. In the ensuing years the US government met several times with Diné leaders in an effort to arrange treaties; however, they did not take into account that the Diné did not have a central governing body but were made up of "a series of autonomous groups with highly localized leadership patterns" (Iverson 25). Often these groups were organized around matrilineal kinship clans. Only a fraction of these scattered groups had a voice at the treaty table. It is estimated that there were between twelve and sixteen thousand Diné by 1860 (Roberts n.p.), yet in 1854 Governor David Meriwether proposed a treaty to a gathering of fifteen hundred to two thousand Diné (Bailey 66), only an estimated 9.3 percent to 12.5 percent of the total Diné population at the time. The treaty included "a reservation designated by the President of the United States, annuities, and the protection by the government from New Mexican encroachments" (Bailey 67). On July 18 the treaty was ratified, and the Diné "received the first in a series of reservations that would gradually reduce their lands to but a fraction of what was traditionally theirs, and a continued effort to move [them] westward" (Bailey 70).

In the years that followed, pressures continued to mount, and raids and skirmishes with the US Army persisted. In addition, Euroamerican settler-colonists were beginning to see the potential for great wealth through grazing and mining Diné lands. In 1862 the new military commander of the territory, James Carleton, proposed a policy against the Diné whereby they would be gathered, "little by little, on a reservation, away from their haunts, and hills, and hiding-places of their country, and then…to be kind to them; there teach their children how to read and write; teach them the arts of peace…; the truths of Christianity. Soon they would acquire new habits, new ideas, new modes of life; the old Indians [would]…die off, and carry with them all their latent longings for murdering and robbing" (qtd. in Bailey 148). Carleton's words strikingly foreshadow Captain Richard Pratt's 1892 speech that articulates the philosophy under which he founded and ran the Carlisle Indian School: "Kill the Indian in him, and save the man" (R. Pratt 261). Carleton demonstrates that the US government's interests lie in both the seizure of Navajo land and the devastation of Navajo communities and culture, paired goals that together threaten the continued survival of the Diné.

In an effort to realize Carleton's vision, the campaign against the Diné commenced in July 1863. Because the Diné lived in small groups spread out across a large area, the army could not simply ride from place to place, capturing the people as they went; the Diné could see them coming from miles away. The US Army recruited Kit Carson, former friend turned betrayer and bitter enemy of the Diné, to come up with a solution. Carson realized that while he could not physically gather the people, he could attack their shelters and food supplies. He developed a "scorched-earth" approach, systematically razing Diné fields, orchards, and food storage "within a forty mile radius of Cañon Bonito," the site of Fort Defiance in the southern portion of Navajo country, near Window Rock (Bailey 156). When winter came, the Diné had to contend with both military pressure and starvation. As a result, increasing numbers of Diné traveled to Fort Defiance and surrendered. Once a large group was gathered at Fort Defiance, the army began the process of moving them across New Mexico to Fort Sumner in Bosque Redondo, where a small encampment had been identified, a journey that came to be known as the Long Walk. On March 4, 1864, the US Army forced more than two thousand Navajo to begin the brutal, nearly three-month march to Bosque Redondo in eastern New Mexico. Over the next few years, at least six thousand more followed them.[5]

The conditions the Diné found at Fort Sumner, or Hwéeldi, were deplorable. Because attempts at farming were thwarted by insects and the elements, "the government provided rations which amounted to about twenty ounces a day per person" (Diné of the Eastern Region 8). Wood for cooking was scarce, and the drinking water was alkaline. Clifford Trafzer writes, "Those who survived starvation, disease, and the freezing weather were expected to work, digging canals, building hogans, tilling fields, and building a fort" (194). In short, the reservation at Fort Sumner was little more than a concentration camp. In 1868 prominent Diné leaders traveled to Washington to take up their people's plight with President Andrew Johnson (Trafzer 239). Although Johnson did not commit himself to a course of action, he sent General William Sherman and Samuel Tappen to Fort Sumner to assess the situation (Trafzer 240). Once there, Sherman negotiated an agreement with the Diné: they would be allowed to return to a very small reservation on their homeland.[6] In the middle of June 1868, the first groups of Diné began the long journey home. Yet the trauma of the Long Walk with its violent destruction of Diné families did not end with their return to their land. The people were physically, mentally, and emotionally devastated by the events of the previous years. Further, they had lost access to a significant portion of their homeland. The trauma of the Long Walk continues to impact the people today. Historian Peter Iverson notes, "To the Navajo, the Long Walk happened last week" (qtd. in Bighorse n.p.).

WALKING AND THE DINÉ WORLDVIEW

Diné writer Irwin Morris emphasizes the importance of remembering the Long Walk era by incorporating it into Diné oral traditions. He writes, "I shall tell my children about the horror, and they shall tell their children. We can never forget what happened. In the future, if we survive, we must remember every detail. We must remember that we were made to walk the whole distance in the shadow of their guns. That we were made to bear their contempt in silence. We did not know if we would live from one day to the next. We did not know if we were marching into oblivion" (23). Morris includes stories about the Long Walk in his text *From the Glittering World*, placing them next to stories from the Diné oral tradition and personal and family stories, beginning the text with the Diné creation story. Morris's insistence on remembering the story as resistance to "oblivion" and his linking of the Long Walk with the survival of the people stress the centrality of memory and story to Diné identity and continuance. The Long Walk must be put into the context of the creation stories as well as stories of contemporary Diné experience, because, Morris suggests, they are all part of a larger and ongoing story of Diné people and land. It is crucial, then, to understand the Long Walk through the longer story of Diné migration and walking, both historically and in the way movement suffuses Diné language, story, and ceremony.

The archaeological record indicates that the Diné are relative latecomers to the Southwest, with estimates of their arrival from the North ranging from 1100 to 1400 CE (Iverson 16). Meanwhile, traditional Diné stories of creation maintain that the Diné came into being in the Southwest, in their traditional homeland. In these stories the Diné make their way through four successive worlds before emerging into the fifth world, the current world, as the Diné.[7] Thus, while the archaeological and traditional versions of Diné origins in the Southwest may at first seem at odds, in both explanations it is through *movement* that the Diné became a fully developed people.

The Diné creation story begins in the first world, called Running-Pitch place, or Jahdokonth (Klah 39). The first world is inhabited by spirit people, Nílch'i Dine'é, and the Holy People, Hashch'éééh Dine'é (Morris 3). Different versions of the story include different accounts for why the people left the first world and who they were when they left. For example, in Hasteen Klah's version of the story, First Man and First Woman were in the first world from the beginning, whereas in Irwin Morris's version, they were created from ears of corn in the Fourth World. Regardless of these differences, each version emphasizes the movement from one world into the next and the creation of more animals and geographical features in each world. As the people walk and climb from world to world, they learn how to plant and reap corn and other crops, social guidelines are established, witchcraft is created, and First Man and First Woman people the world. By the time they emerge into the fifth, or glittering, world, which is marked with "four sacred mountains made of soil from the lower worlds" (Morris 12), many Navajo traditions and sacred places have been developed and the people bring with them an extensive collection of stories. In short, through *journey* they become Diné. Morris ends his version of the creation and origin story by writing, "It is said that so long as *Diné* remain within this boundary, we will have the blessings and protection of the Holy People. So long as we remain within these boundaries we will be living in the manner that the Holy People prescribed for us" (15).

Significantly, this remaining in place is not a call to remain motionless; movement, in particular walking, infuses the Diné worldview from the creation story to the present. In their study, *The Anthropology of Space*, Rik Pinxten, Ingrid van Dooren, and Frank Harvey explain that the Diné have a dynamic conception of the world, an idea that is "illustrated in the traditional belief of the creation of the world. After things had been 'placed' on Earth, it is said that First Man and First Woman pulled out a feather from Bald Eagle and blew on it, saying: 'From now on everything is on the move. Nothing will be still, not even water, not even rock'" (16). Movement across Diné Bikéyah is central to Diné identity. Pinxten, van Dooren, and Harvey assert, "Navajo knowledge is strictly action-bound in a way Western knowledge is not. That is, not only do most Navajo notions have a clear meaning in terms of action (as they do in the Western system), but moreover they are most often defined with reference to action" (4). According to Klah, traditional Diné stories capture this understanding of action and movement. "Each Medicine Man travels in search of his knowledge," he contends. "The Gods also are great wanderers.... The country where the hero of myth wanders, or where the believing Navajo now lives, is very full of possibilities of adventure and mystery and power" (18). Larry Evers similarly argues, "The principal theme of [Diné] songs, motion, is a major theme in all of Navajo culture. It is estimated that there are over 350,000 distinct conjugations of the verb 'to go' in Navajo. It is the most common verb in the language, somewhat equivalent to [the English] verb 'to be'" ("By This Song I Walk").[8] The world of the Diné is a world of motion, beginning with the foundations of its very linguistic structure and then flowing into story content, and thus to knowledge itself.

This sense of movement and the importance of walking are reflected in many traditional Diné ceremonial songs and chants that repeat refrains of "walking," "moving," and "wandering." For instance, the song sometimes called "House Made of Dawn," which occurs on the ninth night of the Night Chant, concludes:

> Happily, as they scatter in different directions, they will regard you.
> Happily, as they approach their homes, they will regard you.
> Happily may their roads back home be on the trail of pollen.
> Happily may they all get back.
> In beauty I walk.

With beauty before me, I walk.
With beauty behind me, I walk.
With beauty below me, I walk.
With beauty above me, I walk.
With beauty all around me, I walk.
It is finished in beauty,
It is finished in beauty,
It is finished in beauty,
It is finished in beauty. (Bierhorst 329–30)

This song suggests the power of walking home along the "trail of pollen."[9] The walking of the people within the song is mirrored by the movement of the song itself; the progression and repetition within the Night Chant suggest the rhythm of footsteps as the people journey home.[10] Other Diné ceremonial cycles also draw attention to the repetitive and steady rhythm of footsteps. For example, a section from one of the versions of the Blessingway recorded by Leland Wyman repeats the phrase "I walk out" at the end of each line (535–36), and another version repeats the phrase "as I thereby go about" (561–62). Further, Klah's recording of "The Old Age Spirits" repeats the refrain "From far away they are coming" (154), both of the songs he includes from the "First Puberty Ceremony" end each line with "she moves" (152–53), and his "Song of the White Shell Prayer-Sticks" repeats, "I wander about, I—beautiful—wander about" (157).[11]

The frequency of references to movement and walking in Diné chantways, part of ceremonial healing rituals, reveals the significance of walking in restoring health and balance. Wyman writes that Diné chantways are "the means for bringing dangerous elements under control, exorcising ghosts, restoring harmony, curing disease, and rendering the patient immune to further contamination" (*Mountainway* 5). Evers suggests that in the chantways, it is specifically *movement* that restores balance: "In the chantways themselves the idea of restoration through ritual motion is central." As they near the end of their journey, the hero's supernatural guide instructs him, "'Fear not. Your body is holy. You are holy as you travel.' The very act of traveling sanctifies" ("By This Song I Walk"). Further, Margot Astrov points out that "creation with the Navajo is motion.... [I]n many curing ceremonies the idea of sanctification and restoration through ritually directed movement is paramount. On motion life depends" (qtd. in Worth and Adair 200). The preponderance of images of moving and migrating across land in these songs in addition to the rhythmic movement of the repeated lines indicate that a key method of achieving balance and reconnecting to identity and place is through walking, which means recognizing journey and emplacement concurrently.

The centrality of journey and movement extends beyond formal stories and ceremonies to infuse secular and informal stories as well, indicating the pervasiveness of movement as experience and metaphor. Diné poet and scholar Luci Tapahonso writes that both formal and informal Diné stories "indicate distances over a wide area, mostly desert, sometimes mountain" ("Come" 76). "Distance," she argues, "is perhaps important only in the convenience of renewal, of going back to renew yourself. This philosophy accepts adaptation, and it allows for change. Renewal is possible wherever there is distance, and wherever there is space and land" ("Come" 80). Tapahonso's statement suggests that being "in place" and being in motion are not separate ideas for Navajo people, but rather depend on one another to create a sense of identity and the possibility of renewal. Leland Wyman calls motion "the 'psychological leitmotif' of Navajo life" (*Mountainway* 140). Sol Worth and John Adair argue, "Walking [is] a necessary element to a Navajo telling a story about Navajos.... In reading Navajo myths and stories later we were struck by how, in most Navajo myths, the narrator spends much of his time describing the walking, the landscape, and the places he passes, telling only briefly what to [non-Navajo readers] are plot lines" (146–47). Walking across Diné Bikéyah provides a sense of connection to the landscape and a validation of cultural and personal identity.

Non-Diné readers and audience members may be tempted to treat walking in Diné narratives as simply transportation or transition, or what Worth and Adair describe as "connectives of little consequence" (145). However, such a reading misses walking's centrality to meaning in Diné tradition and, indeed, how walking *connects* the people to place and history. Movement locates the Diné in the land given to them by the Holy Beings, in the stories passed down since the creation of the People, and in their relationships to human and nonhuman relatives. It is within this context, an epistemology that holds movement, specifically walking, as a key component in how human beings find meaning and purpose in the world, that the storytellers and poets discussed below consider the Long Walk. Significantly, as Joni Adamson contends, the connection between Indigenous people and the land is not "timeless"; rather, it is a relationship that takes place in history, takes place in time (*American Indian Literature* 12). "Timelessness" dismisses experience and suggests living *on* place as opposed to living *in* place. Considering the Long Walk alongside and through Diné conceptions of walking, humans, and the nonhuman land allows for a deeper sense of history. Such a reading highlights how walking as a complex undertaking in Diné cosmology functions in the Long Walk, an event firmly connected in place and time.

DINÉ MEMORIES OF THE LONG WALK

Recorded in recent decades and narrated by the descendants of the walkers, Diné accounts of removal and return provide a complex picture of the Long Walk from Navajo country to Bosque Redondo and their return walk four years later. Though diverse in length, focus, and purpose, many of these stories are linked through a recurrence of several key themes that are often tied to portrayals of walking. In sometimes strikingly similar language, storytellers describe the difficult and painful movement the walkers experienced, the added weight of carrying children that parents and grandparents struggled under, and the army's murder of those too weak or too tired to keep up. However, they also recall moments when the walkers reclaimed their agency by singing as they walked and the painful but ultimately triumphant walk home.[12]

In the early 1970s, Ruth Roessel (Diné), director of the Navajo Studies Program at the Navajo Community College (now renamed Diné College), led an effort to collect oral stories of the Long Walk "handed down by the Navajo people themselves and which reflect the Navajos' view of the events described" (xii). All of the stories in the anthology were "collected by Navajos from Navajos and translated by Navajos" (xv). Many of the family stories collected in the resulting text, *Navajo Stories of the Long Walk Period*, describe the Long Walk itself very briefly; however, nearly all of them emphasize that the people walked. For example, in his retelling of his grandparents' account of the Long Walk, Charley Sandoval recalls, "I was never told about the number of people who made the journey, but they traveled on foot" (142). Florence Charley's great-grandmother told her they "walked all the way hundreds of miles" (149). Ernest Nelson's grandmother related a similar account of the journey: "Almost all of them had to walk the whole way—maybe three hundred miles or more" (172). Mose Denejolie's grandparents "told us they helplessly walked the whole way" (242). In these brief statements, descriptions of walking become a means of expressing bodily suffering. Sandoval, Charley, Nelson, and Denejolie emphasize the physical hardship of walking by citing the great distance their relatives were forced to travel away from their homeland. Sandoval points out that although he does not know exactly how many Diné traveled to Hwéeldi, he knows that they walked the whole way, and both Charley and Nelson include the idea that the people walked a very long way. Further, Denejolie's use of the word *helplessly* accentuates the emotional toll of forced walking. The stress the storytellers place on forced walking over a long distance keeps attention on the deep physical and emotional suffering caused by uprooting the Diné. If movement *within* Diné Bikéyah provides a space for healing and renewal, the forced movement of the Diné *away* from Diné Bikéyah disrupted cultural cohesion and threatened to destroy the people on both physical and psychological levels.

Another thread that appears in several Long Walk narratives is the reports of Diné who are killed by the army for failing to walk fast enough. Trafzer argues that the army's murdering of Diné who are too tired or sick to keep up is "one of the most common themes running through the Navajo [stories of the Long Walk]" (193). The Diné storytellers who share these accounts present them as moments of deep inhumanity and tragedy. Howard Gorman shares a story handed down through generations of his family:

> [The Long Walk] was inhuman because the Navajos, as they got tired and couldn't continue to walk farther, were just shot down.... This is how the story was told by my ancestors. It was said that those ancestors were on the Long Walk with their daughter, who was pregnant and about to give birth.... [T]he daughter got tired and weak and couldn't keep up with the others or go any further because of her condition. So my ancestors asked the Army to hold up for a while to let the woman give birth. But the soldiers wouldn't do it.

> They forced my people to move on, saying that they were getting behind the others. The soldiers told the parents that they had to leave their daughter behind. "Your daughter is not going to survive, anyway; sooner or later she is going to die," they said in their own language. "Go ahead," the daughter said to her parents, "things might come out all right with me." But the poor thing was mistaken, my grandparents used to say. Not long after they moved on, they heard a gunshot from where they had been a short time ago. "Maybe we should go back and do something, or at least cover the body with dirt," one of them said. By that time one of the soldiers came riding up from the direction of the sound. He must have shot her to death. That's the way the story goes. (30–31)

Gorman's story exposes the profound physical and emotional struggle faced by the Diné on the Long Walk. The brutal killing of the pregnant woman reveals a larger assault on women, families, and futurity. In *Bighorse the Warrior*, Tiana Bighorse tells a similar story.[13] Narrating in the voice of her father, she states, "People were shot down on the spot if they say they are tired or sick or if they stop to help someone. If a woman is in labor with a baby, she is killed. There is absolutely no mercy" (34). In Gorman's and Bighorse's accounts, the inability to keep moving is met with death; beyond the physical and emotional pain of walking away from Diné Bikéyah, the Diné are forced to walk at a particular pace and in a particular way. In these accounts the people find their subjectivity removed and their survival bound up in their ability to keep walking. Further, people are killed if they stop to help someone who can no longer walk, and women in labor are killed. This practice reveals the concerted attempt to destroy familial and communal bonds through removal. These common anecdotes point to the true horror of the Long Walk, the inhumanity of the US Army, and the deep terror and physical and emotional trauma suffered by the walkers.

In a similar anecdote, Dugal Tsosie Begay relates stories he heard from his grandfather about the Long Walk in which its brutality is communicated through the toll it took on the material bodies of women and children, which he links to alienation from the land. Begay narrates the particular places the walkers passed: "*Ch'ínílí* (Chinle)[,]...*Tséhootsooí* (Fort Defiance), *Na'ní'zhoozhí* (Gallup), *Shash Bitoó* (Fort Wingate)." He mentions that sometimes when the people stopped for the night or to make food, they "left several things.... [R]ocks that were used to make bread are still standing or sitting there. Also left were stones used to grind corn." Following the Diné tradition of linking story to material place, Begay mentions specific locations and suggests that physical items used by the walkers still remain in these places. Also linked to the discarded material items are "our women and children who disappeared" along the way (214). Klara Bonsack Kelley and Harris Francis suggest that the place-names included in Diné oral stories are often sacred sites that are on "cross-regional pilgrimage routes" (47). Begay's use of sacred sites in his narrative ties the Long Walk to the material land by naming specific places that can be visited and that connect to Diné oral traditions and pilgrimage routes. Further, by mentioning the physical items left behind and the possibility of women and children remaining in these places, both bodily and in spirit, Begay reinforces a storied landscape where "places with stories...are integrated into larger living landscapes, just as the stories that go with each place are integrated into larger, living narratives" (Kelley and Francis 2). Movement through these landscapes into places where the land is strange and disconnected from the Diné origin stories separates the people from not only familiar landscapes but also a part of themselves. The broken and murdered bodies of women and children are linked to alienation from the land as both threaten dissolution of community and cultural identity.

In the narratives storytellers tell about imposed walking that disrupts communal identity, they also integrate walking that reclaims and bolsters those damaged connections. One of the common anecdotes that emerges is the story of parents and grandparents carrying their children along the trail. Rita Wheeler's grandfather told her about the "slow process" to Hwéeldi and the "babies and some children being carried by their parents and relatives" (84). Herbert Zahne's grandfather had a brother who "was just a little boy, not old enough to travel on foot; so he carried the boy on his back the whole way" (232). Ernest Nelson relates, "The women folks and the men folks carried most of the children, and when they got tired others would take turns" (172). On one level, carrying children conveys the brutal physical effect of the forced walk as the adults are under increased physical stress. Further, if those who cannot keep up are killed, one can assume that were they not carried, these children would have been killed. However, layered with the physical and emotional toll of the walk, these representations of walking while carrying children also indicate a refusal to accept the destruction of communal and familial identity, as the people literally bear their future on their backs. Carrying their children heightens the walkers' determination to continue, as the survival of their children and therefore the survival of their people are their physical responsibility. In spite of the horrors of the Long Walk, many of the storytellers redefine even brutal and forced walking to include these descriptions of cooperation, compassion, and love for future generations.

In reimagining the Long Walk as a potential site to redefine experience by refusing the cultural destruction of removal and insisting on communal strength and support, many of the storytellers incorporate memories of the Long Walk within a more complex history of movement in and away from Diné Bikéyah. Hosteen Tso Begay, a seventy-seven-year-old medicine man at the time his story was recorded, places two contexts around his grandmother's stories of the Long Walk. First, he roots the stories in his own memories of moving around Diné Bikéyah with his grandmother and their sheep. Next, he explains how his grandmother would tell "stories of the events that took place prior to the Navajo roundup for *Hwééldi* (Fort Sumner)" (262). These stories included anecdotes of conflicts with Mexicans, remarking on the particular places these events took place. Only then does Begay tell the story of the Long Walk, noting that "our people walked because there were only a few wagons" (263). Similarly, Chahadineli Benally prefaces his story of the Long Walk with a lengthy story about the kidnapping of a young Diné girl, his grandmother, by Mexicans. The girl "walked quite a distance from the camp [near Black Mesa]" to gather potatoes. She is captured by Mexicans and led away from the places she knows into land that is "unfamiliar and strange" (57–58). She escapes with the help of a Mexican woman, fights off a vicious wolf, gives birth to a baby she has to leave behind, and is led in the right direction by an owl. She eventually sees "a familiar mountain" and finds a horse trail she heard about in a story (71). Her story closely mirrors the experiences of the Diné on the Long Walk: connection to place followed by disruption and travel into the unknown, the loss of a child, and finally a return walk and reconnection to place. In telling his grandmother's story, one distinct from yet thematically and experientially connected to the Long Walk, Benally integrates the Long Walk into Diné history in a way that allows the people to understand the experience on their own terms.[14]

Other storytellers link the Long Walk to seasonal movement to secure food, movement closely tied to place and identity. Eli Gorman notes that in the years prior to the Long Walk, "Navajos...were living around *Dziłna'oodiiłii* (Huerfano Mountain) in New Mexico. When we are living at *Dziłna'oodiiłii*, we started moving around, but we never got too far away from the region. We just kept living and moving right around *Dziłna'oodiiłii*" (198). Rita Wheeler similarly emphasizes walking and movement within the boundaries of the four sacred mountains. Remembering stories about a great-uncle, she says, "He used to travel off to a great distance, from here all the way to *Tsébít'í* (Shiprock) and across the *Tooh* (San Juan River) where he hunted such animals as deer, antelope and wild turkeys.... People were constantly on the move in search of food" (76). Gorman and Wheeler note traditional movement as both constant and within a particular area, maintaining a focus on Diné legacies of movement and a clear connection to place. Movement across the land is closely linked with the specifics of the land, thereby fusing metaphorical movement with the material land.

Tiana Bighorse's retelling of her father's stories makes a similar point by starting the narrative not with the Long Walk or even the conflicts that led to it but in her father's voice, recalling his memories of learning lessons about the land, lessons taught through movement and travel: "My father takes me all over the Navajo land to see the place when I am nine years old. We ride mostly every day—four years, summer and winter. We always start from Tsoodził, Mount Taylor, where we live and keep coming back.... We want to know how big the Navajo land is, and we find out. It is big.... I am very happy my father takes me everywhere to look at all these places. By the time I am fifteen years old, I am already taught to be a brave warrior" (3–8). Bighorse links movement over Diné land to the later movement to Fort Sumner, but also always explicitly relates it to Gus Bighorse's identity as a Diné warrior. When Tiana explains what it means to be a Diné warrior, she says, "In Navajo, a warrior says what is in the people's hearts. Talks about what the land means to them. Brings them together to fight for it" (xxiv). Gus's warrior education, the bravery and wisdom he needs to help his people survive the Long Walk era, is intimately connected to land and movement, to an understanding of place and, through place, self. Like

Gorman and Wheeler, Bighorse carefully notes specific places (Big Sheep Mountain, Shiprock, Chinle, Gallup, and others), drawing his audience's attention to the land itself, its material reality and its sacred status, as the land bestowed on the Diné at the time of creation.

Reinforcing these ties between land, walking, and Diné identity, several of the walkers incorporate traditional Diné stories and songs into their narratives. Such inclusions work to reintegrate the experiences along the walk into a larger narrative of the Diné people. Reid Gómez argues, "The stories are alive; we participate in them, along with the ancestors—the spirit beings—and with our enveloping land base. The storyteller has participated in the movement of the people, their travels, and their escapes, all experienced within the context and creation of the stories" (160–61). She continues, "Everything is changing. Everything is remaining the same. The stories do not change but have innumerable versions and allow unlimited possibility in the changing world, countless possibility for making more stories and restoring *hozho* [a Diné term meaning a state of beauty and balance]" (165). By including traditional songs and stories, the Diné walkers and storytellers perform an act of integration and resistance. For example, Tezbah Mitchell relates the story her grandmother told her about running away from Hwééldi. After running into some nearby mountains, the girl saw a brown bear that seemed to motion to her. "This big animal," Mitchell relates, "was her guide and protector for three days as they traveled together" (252). In this story, Mitchell's grandmother aligns herself with stories of Sun and Changing Woman, who often had bears as guardians and protectors (Pavlik 479). By connecting her experience on the Long Walk with those of central figures in traditional Diné story and song, Mitchell's grandmother creates a sense of continuity and strength. Her individual story becomes another version of Sun and Changing Woman and so participates in a larger communal story.

It is not always in a retrospective telling that these connections between experience and story are made clear; the storytellers also remember the walkers' use of song on the trail as a means of integrating the Long Walk into Diné oral tradition and cultural knowledge at the time it was happening. Bighorse states, "Everybody has to know something—maybe a ritual or a song—to be safe from the enemies or starvation or sickness or freezing. They have to remember, to keep it in their mind when the enemies are all around them.... There is a song too. They call it a traveling song, wherever you go it keeps you safe.... This is how lots of Navajos survive [the Long Walk]" (26–27). Safe movement is connected to song through rhythm, land, and language. Reflecting the importance of song and traveling, John Beyale Sr. tells the story passed on to him by his grandfather of the walk back from Hwééldi. His great-grandfather Gish'néétíní "sang the Blessing Way ceremonial song all the way from Fort Sumner to Fort Defiance" (Diné of the Eastern Region 42). Gish'néétíní's singing is an act of reclaiming power and redefining experience. The Navajo trace the origin of the Blessingway to "just after the Emergence at Emergence Place rim itself" (Wyman, *Blessingway* 6). The Blessingway is thus explicitly tied to Diné Bikéyah, and singing the Blessingway while walking links the return home to the journeys within Diné sacred traditions. Discussing his own traveling song, a part of the Nightway, Diné singer and educator Andrew Natonabah explains that "this song is for traveling. When one travels, he should sing this.... The songs were created at White House Ruins. When traveling, one should sing the songs." Traveling songs act as a link between the materiality of walking and spiritual metaphor. Robert McPherson argues that for the Diné, "all of life is a metaphor in which one reenacts the spiritual through the physical. Places, wind and water, seasons and climate, objects, people, and other living things are thought of in terms of qualities important to Navajo values.... For the Diné, the land and its inhabitants form a web of life that is both physical and supernatural" (75). Singing traveling songs, unlike retrospective weaving together of traditional stories and events, connects spiritual belief and communal identity to experience *as it is happening*. In that way, the space between materiality and spirituality is radically collapsed, and physical experience is immediately and forever remembered in the context of Diné oral tradition.

If the movement to Hwééldi was an experience of moving away from sacred land and Diné identity, for many Diné storytellers the return to Diné Bikéyah marked the return to the part of them that exists only in a particular landscape. Laura Tohe explains that throughout their time at Hwééldi, the Diné's connection to their homeland remained: "Even though they were imprisoned hundreds of miles away, the land within the four sacred mountains was still there for them. It held their birth stems. It is a place chosen for them by the Holy People.... I believe it was the mountains that sustained the hearts and spirits of the Diné and helped to bring them back" ("Hwéeldi Béého̗niih" 81–82). Though filled with pain and difficulty, the walk back did not have the same sense of isolation and despair because they were returning to their homeland. Manuelito, one of the Diné leaders, reported, "When we saw the top [of one of our four sacred mountains]...we wondered if it was our mountain, and we felt like talking to the ground we loved it so" (qtd. in Marks 181). Tiana Bighorse's father recalls the reaction of one elderly Diné woman who, when she sees Mount Taylor in the distance, cries out, "'Mountain! We are home!' and she faints. Then she gets really sick, and she dies two days later—dies from being so happy" (56). Tohe recalls a similar story and reflects, "Such is considered a good death" ("Hwéeldi Bééhániih" 82). Harry Pioche's grandfather told him that "after the Navajos returned to their homeland, the condition of the land returned to normal. It was believed that the Navajo land needed THE PEOPLE to inhabit it in order to prosper" (Diné of the Eastern Region 5). Once the journey back to Diné Bikéyah is completed, both the people and the land are able to find *hozho*, even in the face of a very changed world.

Diné leader Barboncito made this connection explicit to William Tecumseh Sherman in 1868 as they brokered a deal to allow the Diné to return to Diné Bikéyah: "It was told to us by our forefathers, that we were never to move east of the Rio Grande or west of the San Juan rivers and I think that our coming here has been the cause of so much death among us and our animals.... Because we were brought here, we have done all that we could possibly do, but found it to be labor in vain.... I think this ground was never intended for us." Barboncito explains the hardships faced in Hwééldi in terms of the material land. In his analysis of this passage, McPherson writes that Barboncito was speaking in metaphorical language, using "geography" to "represen[t] his culture's conscious and subconscious symbols of what was important and unimportant." However, such an explanation, while recognizing the link between material and metaphor, privileges the abstract, or what McPherson terms "intangible roots of belonging" (2). Barboncito's own language, especially when examined alongside the oral histories of the Long Walk, is very clearly and persuasively grounded in the material land. He prefaces his statement that "this ground was never intended for us" with geographical references to the Rio Grande and the San Juan, concrete locations. His reference to the Diné origin story with its admonition to remain between the sacred mountains is likewise materially specific.

These family stories of the Long Walk are more than simple reminiscences; they function on multiple levels to reclaim ignored or denied histories, maintain and develop oral traditions, and underscore personal and communal connections to land and place. The Long Walk interrupted Diné history and threatened to disrupt Diné identity, just as Carleton had intended when he proposed Fort Sumner as a reservation where "the old Indians [would]...die off" (qtd. in Bailey 148). However, in continuing to tell their stories through multiple generations, the Diné have rewritten the meaning of the Long Walk by incorporating it into histories and oral traditions. Simon Ortiz (Acoma) describes this kind of reclaiming as "the creative ability of Indian people to gather in many forms of the socio-political colonizing force which beset them and *make these forms meaningful in their own terms*" (8; emphasis added). In the telling of their family stories, the Diné storytellers enmesh the Long Walk within their particular worldview and locate it within their particular homeland. They "bring about meaning and meaningfulness" (Ortiz 9) through reclaiming and reshaping the narrative, an act of profound cultural resilience.

THE LONG WALK IN CONTEMPORARY DINÉ POETRY

Diné families and communities continue to circulate memories of the Long Walk through sharing oral stories, and in recent decades Diné writers have brought these stories to a larger audience through published novels, essays, and poetry. Diné poet Luci Tapahonso explains that her own writing is an extension of the Diné "love of stories." She writes, "It seems each time a group of more than two gather, the dialogue eventually evolves into sharing stories and memories, laughing, and teaching. To be included in this is a distinct way of showing affection and appreciation for each other. So it is true that daily conversations strengthen us as do the old stories of our ancestors that have been told since the beginning of Navajo time" (*Sáanii* x). Thus, she asserts, "It is with this perspective that I share... stories, poetry, and prayers" (xi). Tapahonso understands her contemporary writing practice to flow out of her Diné identity and family; she argues that her writing is "not 'mine,' but a collection of many voices that range from centuries ago and continue into the future" (xii). Significantly, poets like Tapahonso tell their stories through adopting and adapting Western generic conventions, infusing them with Indigenous structures, tropes, and meanings.

In the introduction to the critical anthology *Speak to Me Words*, Dean Rader argues that Indigenous poets "resist the imperial colonizing thrust of contemporary culture through participation in it." He continues, "Their inventive use of the lyric transforms both public and private discourses and allows them not only to counter prevailing establishments of identity but also to tell who they are in their own words. They resist cultural erasure by attacking those armaments designed to annihilate their ability to speak themselves into being; yet, through the lyric poem they recoup the performative energies of the oral tradition and engage both Anglo and Native discourses" (Rader and Gould). Rader argues that contemporary Indigenous poetry works on multiple fronts, resisting the colonizing effects of the Western genre, while honoring and embodying traditional oral literatures. In this vein, Diné poets Tapahonso and Laura Tohe draw upon Diné oral narratives and their own family stories in their poems about the Long Walk. Their reworking and exploring of these stories through the structure of contemporary poetry continue to keep stories of the Long Walk in the present, as they link back to oral traditions and forward through form and content to Indigenous futures. In connecting the stories structurally and thematically with what precedes and follows them as well as grounding them within the particular physical landscape, Tapahonso and Tohe insist on a narrative coherence that weaves together past and present into a larger story of modern Diné experience and identity.

Tapahonso's poem "In 1864" reflects the living memory of the Long Walk and, in so doing, participates in the ongoing recollection and reclamation of history. Tapahonso builds her poem through an accumulation of stories that reshape the linear structure of time, allowing "the 'past' to intrude into the 'present'" (Gould 799). As the speaker's car passes near Fort Sumner, the speaker recalls a story about a Diné electrician who once put up power lines here, and his story, in turn, reminds her of the story of the Long Walk. The land evokes stories filled with images of walking that bring together the physical journey of the Diné with movement and migration in the Diné tradition. These kaleidoscoping stories and meanings signify a living and continuing people.

Tapahonso begins "In 1864" with motion as the speaker and her daughter drive along the highway near Fort Sumner, New Mexico. As they drive they tell stories and the "stories and highway beneath / became a steady hum. The center lines were a blurred guide" (*Sáanii* 3–4). Tapahonso creates a new way of moving; whereas the cadence in traditional Diné chant may take on the rhythm of footfalls, here the story takes on the steadiness of a car whizzing down the highway. Though the agent of motion is changed, story and movement across the land remain intertwined.

As the two women drive, the speaker is reminded by land and movement of a recent story, one that happened "a few winters ago" (6). In the story, told by the speaker in the third person, an electrician installing power lines in that part of western New Mexico looks out across the plains and notices that "The land was like / he imagined from the old stories—flat and dotted with shrubs" (11–12). Left alone at the campsite one evening, he "heard the cries and moans carried by the wind / and blowing snow. He heard the voices wavering and rising / in the darkness" (18–20). He understands that he is hearing the voices of his ancestors who were forced to Hwéeldi; the land has absorbed their pain. He sings, "humming songs / he remembered from his childhood.... He sang for himself, his family, and the people whose spirits / lingered on the plains, in the arroyos, and in the old windswept plants" (20–24). The electrician seeks to balance the pain and anguish he hears in the voices on the plain through traditional Diné songs. However, the pain of the Long Walk remains linked to the land, and he decides that he must return to Diné Bikéyah to find balance: "The place contained the pain and cries of his relatives, / the confused and battered spirits of his own existence" (30–31). The electrician recognizes the lasting impact of the Long Walk; the horror and tragedy of the forced march to Hwéeldi continue to reverberate in the very land the walkers crossed over. He is reminded of the importance of his own land, his own home.

The electrician's story then triggers the speaker's family stories of the Long Walk, connected by movement through the material land to the electrician and to the speaker and her daughter. The speaker begins the next story with the words of her aunt, shifting perspectives first from the speaker to the aunt and then from the aunt to the great-grandmother. This nesting of perspectives begins with this quotation: "My aunt always started the story saying, 'You are here / because of what happened to your great-grandmother long ago'" (33–34). By quoting her aunt's opening, the speaker recalls the traditional openings of stories that emphasize other storytellers to indicate the larger significance of the story as well as the storyteller's place within a longer tradition, contributing to a sense of continuity and connection. In addition, this opening ties the story, the narrator, and her daughter to their family history. Further, the line break after "'You are here'" emphasizes the connection of the story to the land as well as the speaker's and the speaker's daughter's place in Diné Bikéyah.

The poem moves from the quoted aunt's perspective to the great-grandmother's perspective, drawing the speaker and her daughter and by extension the reader into a personal relationship with the Long Walk. Tapahonso's retelling of the Long Walk echoes the oral family stories discussed earlier in the chapter. She, like them, emphasizes the distance they walked, the children they carried, and the fate of those who fell behind. "The journey began," the speaker tells her daughter in the voice of her great-grandmother,

> and the soldiers were all around us.
> All of us walked, some carried babies. Little children and the
> elderly
> stayed in the middle of the group. We walked steadily each day,
> stopping only when the soldiers wanted to eat or rest.
> We talked among ourselves and cried quietly.
> We didn't know how far it was or even where we were going.
> All that we knew for certain was that we were leaving Dinetah,
> our home.
> . . . .
> We had such a long distance to cover.
> Some old people fell behind, and they wouldn't let us go back
> to help them.
> It was the saddest thing to see—my heart hurts so to remember
> that.
> Two women were near the time of the births of their babies,
> and they had a hard time keeping up with the rest.
> Some army men pulled them behind a huge rock, and we screamed
> out loud
> When we heard the gunshots. (50–66)[15]

The poem creates a sense of community and historical consciousness. The use of the first-person perspective makes the events immediate and real. The first-person voice, Tapahonso writes, "is the stronger voice and truer to the person who originally told the story" (*Sáanii* xi). As the speaker and her daughter drive along the same land, they relive the pain and fear of the Long Walk, and time seems to constrict. Just as the center line of the highway blurs, so too does the line between past and present. The two journeys become one, though one is in a car in the late twentieth century and the other is on foot in the mid-nineteenth century. Even in the recitation of a story of cultural disruption, Tapahonso's poem insists on the strength and endurance of a people with a long history of walking. "We walked steadily," remembers the speaker (51).

In her poem "In Dinétah," Laura Tohe similarly nests the story of the Long Walk in other narratives.[16] Like Irwin Morris and several of the storytellers recorded in *Navajo Stories of the Long Walk Period*, Tohe contextualizes the Long Walk by beginning with a telling of the Diné origin story. She recalls the "perilous journey" of the Twin heroes (10) and the teaching "to dwell within the sacred mountains" (15). She follows the Diné origin story with a story of colonialism that emphasizes the distance between the settler-colonists and the land:

> Did they not know we are
> all created from the same elements?
> Rainclouds for hair,
> fingernails formed from beautiful seashells,
> the rivers flow through our veins, our lifeline,
> from the wind we came to life,
> with thunder voices we speak. (38–44)

Although the Diné origin story and the story of colonialism may seem distinct from Tapahonso's story of a road trip and an electrician, they similarly ground the story of the Long Walk in the land and in Diné experience. This grounding serves multiple functions: First, it integrates the Long Walk into Diné worldviews where place and land are central to identity. Second, it challenges a sense of time that is linear, linking contemporary speaker and past event. Third, it refuses any inclination to abstract the Long Walk and thereby soften its brutality. The Long Walk happened on *this* land, to *these* people.

Like Tapahonso, Tohe chooses to tell the story of the Long Walk with pronouns that make it immediate. Tohe uses the first-person plural to recall:

> When The Long Walk began, we witnessed our women murdered
> and raped
> our children and relatives swept away in the rushing currents of
> the Rio Grande
> We heard explosions that silenced mothers giving birth behind
> rocks.
> We saw the newborn and the elderly left behind. (80–83)

Whereas Tapahonso identifies the first-person narrator of the Long Walk as the speaker's grandmother, Tohe's first-person plural positions the narrator of the Long Walk as the collective voice of the Diné. "We are Diné," the speaker tells us (77). The memory of the Long Walk is realigned from individual to communal memory, from personal to shared experience.

Storytelling is necessary for the psychological, cultural, and *physical* survival of the Navajo. Tiana Bighorse writes in her father's voice, "I want to talk about my tragic story, because if I don't, it will get into my mind and get into my dream and make me crazy.... That is why we warriors have to talk to each other. We wake ourselves up, get out of the shock. And that is why I tell my kids what happened, so it won't be forgot" (81–82). Bighorse stresses that the importance of storytelling goes beyond the preservation of a particular story or event. Similarly, Tapahonso's speaker stresses the centrality of story:

> There were many who died on the way to *Hwééldi*. All the way
> we told each other, "We will be strong as long as we are together."
> I think that was what kept us alive. We believed in ourselves
> and the old stories that the holy people had given us.
> "This is why," she would say to us. "This is why we are here.
> Because our grandparents prayed and grieved for us." (75–80)

The speaker ends the story by returning from her great-grandmother's voice to her aunt's voice. In her aunt's voice the speaker reminds her daughter of the importance of the story itself. Just as the walkers kept themselves alive through their belief in themselves and their stories, the speaker's aunt called on her, as the speaker calls on her own daughter, to continue to believe in the power of stories and in particular the power of the story of the Long Walk. Further, in repeating the words *we* and *us*, the speaker draws attention to Diné identity as connected through time, even with the challenges and changes the community has faced. Tapahonso employs the oral histories of the Long Walk that emphasize the role of story and place in survival. Like the electrician who sings for himself, his family, and the voices of his ancestors, those same ancestors also reach to story and song for strength and renewal.

Tohe, similarly stressing strength and survival, follows her retelling of the Long Walk with twenty-three lines about the lives of the Diné after they returned from Hwééldi, including "We are the Code Talkers who used our language to help save America" (111), "We are teachers, cowboys, lawyers, musicians. / We are artists, soldiers, politicians, architects, farmers" (121–22), and, finally, a repetition of the line that began the story of the Long Walk, "We are Diné" (128). Following the Long Walk section that emphasizes communal identity and communal memory, this section insists on the reader's acknowledgment of the communal *and* individual identities of the Diné by combining *we* with more specific individual experiences while maintaining a commitment to collective experience.

Tohe ends her poem with an overt connection to Diné prayer and chantways, entering the Long Walk into both historical and spiritual contexts. She writes:

> In Beauty it was begun.
> In Beauty it continues.
> In Beauty,
> In Beauty,
> In Beauty,
> In Beauty. (131–36)

Anthony K. Webster argues that Tohe's recollection of the "four repetitions" that ends chantways "gives a sense of 'surrounding,' because of a metonymic linkage with this idea of the four sacred directions" and the four sacred mountains (45). This sense of "surrounding" or, I would argue, "belonging" is reinforced by movement. Repetition opens a sacred space, connecting readers, those walking to Bosque Redondo, and the Diné who came before and those who will come after. Often, as discussed earlier, chantways incorporate movement into their repetition of beauty. In the final four lines of her poem, Tohe echoes the rhythm of the heartbeat or of footfalls in the meter of each "Iň Beáutў." In addition, the structure of these lines enhances the rhythm, with each line indented farther than the previous, suggesting footsteps and forward movement. Framing the Long Walk with the context of Diné origin stories, the history of colonialism, contemporary Diné lives, and sacred ceremonies, Tohe insists upon communal coherence and suggests that even in the face of adversity and pain, the Navajo can draw upon their stories and the land itself to walk with agency and determination.

WALKING AND SURVIVAL IN DINÉ BIKÉYAH

The history of the Long Walk is one of dislocation, trauma, and loss. Yet, as Tapahonso writes, "This is why we are here. / Because our grandparents prayed and grieved for us" (79–80). Similarly, Tiana Bighorse tells us, "These are brave stories, and knowing them can make you brave.... The reservation was fought for" (xxvii). The Long Walk is part of a continuum of experience from creation stories to contemporary life. The nesting of the Long Walk within thousands of years of Diné experience reinforces the entanglement of the Diné and the land. Karen Barad contends, "Existence is not an individual affair. Individuals do not preexist their interactions; rather, individuals emerge through and as a part of their entangled intra-relating.... [S]pace and time, like matter and meaning, come into existence, are iteratively reconfigured through each intra-action, thereby making it impossible to differentiate in any absolute sense between creation and renewal, beginning and returning, continuity and discontinuity, here and there, past and future" (*Meeting* ix). Barad, a Euroamerican theoretical physicist and philosopher, articulates an idea that Indigenous peoples have long understood. Meaning emerges not from attempting to tease the strands of past and present apart or from uncovering a lost sense of authentic experience. Rather, understanding is gleaned from the entanglement itself, the recognition that the Long Walk exists and has meaning within the context of Diné philosophies, histories, bodies, and lands.

What is made clear from an examination of these stories and poems is that one route to making sense of the Long Walk within Diné contexts is through the material act of walking. Motion, as Vizenor says, "is the originary" (*Fugitive Poses* 55). That many of these stories turn to walking to express both cultural fragmentation and cultural continuance suggests the deep connection between imagination and mobility, a connection that creates a sense of self and, therefore, a sense of community. By reimagining and identifying with the significance of walking the Long Walk, Diné storytellers and writers challenge historical "facts" and encourage cultural cohesion and survival. Through their contextualization of walking, the storytellers reassert the humanity and agency of the walkers while also presenting a land that is an "intensely social spac[e]" (Julie Cruikshank qtd. in Adamson, "Source" 261). The Long Walk *cannot* be an isolated or isolating experience because it is tied thematically and materially through movement to Diné story archives and lived experiences. Writing and speaking against a history of the United States that would empty the land and create Indigenous peoples as tragic and doomed figures, these stories of the Long Walk insist upon a complex vision of land and people in which movement suffuses linguistic, symbolic, and material registers.

NOTES

1. In her autobiographical introduction to *No Parole Today*, Diné poet Laura Tohe contextualizes her choice of Diné over Navajo: "Although outsiders gave us the name Navajo, we call ourselves Diné, *The People*. I prefer to call myself the name my ancestors gave us because I am trying to de-colonize myself" (x). Linguist Anthony K. Webster explains that the use of *Diné* is "often political, it is outward facing. It is a claim to a prior placement and knowledge base that rejects being labeled 'Navajo.' It is the Navajo term that references 'the people' and its use indexes a particular stance by the speaker, often a politicized stance. This is the stance of self-naming, of self-determination" (171). I have followed the lead of Laura Tohe and Luci Tapahonso in using *Diné* throughout this chapter. In the few places where I use *Navajo*, it is in quotations, in proper names for institutions, and when common usage retains *Navajo*, as with the term *Navajo Long Walk*.

2. Ostensibly called a "reservation," the camp at Fort Sumner was little more than a concentration camp; indeed, it was one of the camps studied in detail by Adolf Hitler as a model for his extermination camps (LaDuke and Cruz 74).

3. In *American Indian Literature, Environmental Justice, and Ecocriticism*, Joni Adamson, writing about the Shoshone "and other American Indian peoples," explains, "For them, unique geologic features within their homelands

are often alive with the mythic, historic, and sacred meanings of their cultures; these places are expressive of a particular way of life, and when threatened, they become symbols of the threat to distinctive cultural identities" (71).

4. Iverson writes, "The non-Indian and even some of the non-Navajo Indian residents of the Southwest used the Diné as scapegoats for anything that went wrong and identified as Diné any stranger or group of strangers who committed any violent act" (54).

5. Iverson notes that the Long Walk "was not a single event" and that there is documentation of fifty-three different episodes of the Long Walk from 1863 through 1866. "In some instances," he writes, "only a handful of people made the journey; in other cases hundreds of Diné were herded along to Fort Sumner. The trip took several different routes, beginning in the Fort Wingate area, heading toward Albuquerque, and then branching south to the Bosque" (52).

6. In his text *Diné: A History of the Navajos*, Peter Iverson provides the full text of the 1868 treaty. Its articles include provisions for a reservation that drastically reduced from their traditional homeland, the establishment of a permanent agent to the Diné, the option for "heads of family" to select 160 acres to tend themselves as opposed to holding the land in common, the education of all Diné children between six and sixteen by Euroamerican schools, and a railroad right-of-way through the reservation (325–34).

7. Iverson writes, "If the Navajos today are, in part, descended from peoples who migrated to the south and to the east, if they speak a language that bears a resemblance to languages spoken elsewhere, they are, nevertheless, a community that started within this particular environment. All that may have occurred prior to what happened here is prelude. Prior to this place, there were no Navajos. Without this place, there could be no Diné. The traditional stories thus say: This is where we began, and this is where we were meant to be" (6). Iverson's point here is to highlight the Diné version of the creation as the most important version, regardless of what archaeologists might argue about migration. I agree with Iverson's emphasis on place and the idea that while Diné ancestors may have moved into the area from elsewhere, the Diné as a distinct people came into being only in the Navajo homeland. However, I disagree that the migration is simply "prelude"—movement through and interaction with the land were the means by which the Diné came to be Diné.

8. Linguist and anthropologist Harry Hoijer explains in more detail how movement infuses Navajo language:

> [Motion] permeates the Navajo lexicon in the sense that many verbs, not at first sight expressive of movement, proved to be so on more detailed analysis. For example, the theme ha.h "one animate object

> moves (in an unspecified fashion)" is easily recognized in a large number of words, the meanings of which appear to be far distant from any concept of motion. The following examples are typical: oa. -na-...-ha. "be busy, 'preoccupied,'" literally "one moves continuously about with reference to it;"?e.h-...-ha. "one dresses," literally "one moves into clothing;" hO-...ha.h "the ceremony begins," literally "a happening moves;" na-...ha "one lives," literally "one moves about here, and there;" ?ani.-na-...ha "one is young," literally "one moves about newly;" "yisda-...ha.H "one is rescued, saved," literally "one moves to safety." (qtd. in Worth and Adair 201)

9. Wyman writes that for the Diné, pollen is a "symbol of fertility, happiness, and life itself" (*Blessingway* 31).

10. In "Words and Place: A Reading of *House Made of Dawn*," Larry Evers notes that in this song, "a journey metaphor is prominent.... One of its central messages is that ceremonial words are bound efficaciously to place" (225).

11. In her essay "Come into the Shade," Luci Tapahonso relates the story of a contemporary puberty ceremony:

> In the Kinaaldá the girl who is having the puberty ceremony has to run about two miles every morning to the east, dressed in her whole outfit: long skirt, velvet blouse, concho belt and earrings, and a lot of other jewelry. She has to run to the east and run back, and people can run after her. As she is running she has to yell out loud to strengthen her lungs, to give her a good singing voice, so she can be physically strong. People can run after her, but they can't pass her. If they pass her, they will age before she does. And they can run after her and yell, too, because as she is running, she lets off—when people run or move quickly, they let off a breeze—that breeze is a blessing, it's a blessing for them. So that is why people run after her. (83)

12. As in the captivity narratives examined in the previous chapter, stock images highlight both the central themes the writers and storytellers want to emphasize as well as the circulation of the stories within a community. Billy Stratton argues that slave narratives and later Indian boarding-school narratives adopt and subvert the Indian captivity narrative formula (15). Certainly, what might be called the "stock images" of stories from the Navajo Long Walk (in particular, perhaps, the ruthless murdering of women who are pregnant or giving birth) also invert notions about "savagery" and sympathy.

13. *Bighorse the Warrior* is composed of the stories of Tiana's father, Gus Bighorse. Tiana states that when she was small, she eavesdropped on her father's stories. They were "men's stories" and were not intended for women or girls.

When she was discovered, she was at first reprimanded, but later her father realized that she was the only one who was truly listening. He allowed her to listen so that she could keep the stories going. Gus Bighorse's stories are further mediated by the role Noël Bennett plays in the transcription. Tiana Bighorse recited the stories to Bennett, who recorded and edited them. Although Bennett states that "editing was precarious" and she endeavors to "protect the integrity of the Navajo voice" (xxii–xxiii), her role as transcriber and editor impacts the story readers receive.

14. Laura Tohe tells a very similar story. When Tohe asks her grandmother about the Long Walk, her grandmother responds with a story about "a Mexican raider who captured one [of] my great-great-grandmothers, who managed to escape and walk home" ("Hwéeldi Bééhániih" 78).

15. In line 56 Tapahonso refers to "Dinetah," the area "east of the center of the land between the [sacred Navajo] mountains" (Arthur, Bingham, and Bingham 4). Iverson calls Dinetah the "cradle of Navajo civilization, the place of Changing Woman's birth.... Although few Diné live in the area today, Dinetah remains a mecca to Navajos interested in their history and heritage" (20).

16. Anthony K. Webster explains Tohe's choice of *Dinétah* instead of Diné Bikéyah for the Diné homeland: "*Dinétah* is outside the four sacred mountains and not part of the current boundaries of the Navajo Nation. On the other hand, Diné Bikéyah is used for the land between the four sacred mountains and for the current boundaries of the Navajo Nation. In Tohe's poem ["In Dinétah"], Dinétah, the ancestral Navajo homeland, becomes the land between the four sacred mountains. Tohe is linking the current reservation with the ancestral homeland of the Navajos" (163–64).

3

Peripatetic Philosopher

Walking, Rhythm, and Material Nature in Mary Austin's Desert Writing

In 1888 twenty-year-old Mary Hunter Austin moved from Illinois to California, beginning a lifelong engagement with the desert. Austin's experience in the wilderness was defined by movement: walking, riding in coaches and on horseback, and later riding in cars. She rejected the largely sedentary patterns of life for an American woman at the turn of the century and found new patterns of correspondence between the movements of her body and the American land. Early in her life Austin recognized the importance of walking for experiencing and writing about the natural world. She was deeply interested in nature writing and Indigenous cultures, and she envisioned walking as the link between body, land, and writing. As a result, in Austin's writing the descriptions of nonhuman nature, the flow and cadence of narrative, and the actions of her narrators and characters are saturated with the pace of the footfall. Walking provides a rhythm and imagery to express her understanding about connections and relationships among person, place, and writing.

Austin's first encounters with the desert were in California's San Joaquin Valley and Owens Valley. She explored the land and talked with ranch hands, sheepherders, vaqueros (Mexican American cowboys), and Western Shoshone and Southern Paiute peoples who lived and worked in the area (Fink 45–46). Austin's days on the trails and with the inhabitants of San Joaquin and Owens Valleys fueled her imagination and became the basis for later literary works. She describes her experience of riding into the California desert in her autobiography, *Earth Horizon* (1932): "There was something else there besides what you find in books; a lurking, evasive Something, wistful, cruel, ardent; something that rustled and ran, that hung half-remotely, insistent on being noticed.... Even in the first impact, Mary gave back a kindred yearning; it was in her mind that all she needed was to be alone with it for uninterrupted occasions, in which they might come to terms" (187). Austin recalls her early recognition that the land cannot be reduced to a "symbol[l] of the human condition" (Alaimo, *Undomesticated Ground* 81), and that its meaning exceeds the representational power of language. She perceives the agentic properties of the land: the land *acts* in ways that are not always comprehensible or reducible to human needs and desires but offers an engagement of equals between human and nonhuman. This understanding formed a foundation for Austin's desert writings in which human and nonhuman are intimately entangled and the true meaning extends beyond even Austin's attempts to contain it in language.

Austin looked to the rhythms of the land itself to find her inspiration for writing the desert. In *Earth Horizon*, Austin writes that before *The Land of Little Rain* could be completed, she needed to find the correct "key," one she finally discovered "in the rhythm of the twenty-mule teams that creaked in and out of the borax works. The rhythm of the lonely lives blown across the trails" (296). She similarly writes in *The American Rhythm* (1923), "Only a few months ago, I had occasion to turn back to one of my desert books, written eighteen years ago and scarcely looked at since, I discovered the first paragraph striking without intention into the irregular tug and release of the four horse Mojave stage and of the eighteen-mule borax team, from which my association with the scenes described was almost never freed" (14–15). That first paragraph of *The Land of Little Rain* (1903) is made up of a single sentence: "East away from the Sierras, south from Panamint and Amargosa, east and south many an uncounted mile, is the Country of Lost Borders" (9). Each clause suggests the opening of a thought, followed by a clause that arrests the forward motion and begins the process again. In the pattern of these nested clauses, Austin sees the "irregular tug and release of the four horse Mohave stage." Austin suggests that though at the time she wrote *The Land of Little Rain* she had not yet consciously formulated her theories about place and language, the rhythm and stress patterns in her early writing manifest the link between the land, rhythm, and writing.[1]

Critics have long recognized that *The Land of Little Rain* is a text in constant motion; however, their analyses of that movement focus on issues of metaphor and imagery at the expense of materiality. David Wyatt argues that in this text, "strong sentence rhythm serves Austin not only as a counterweight to narrative but as an approximation of the underlying continuity of nature.... We move here through an attempt to describe the form of a motion" (84). Similarly, James Work writes that in reading this text, "we have a sense of watching the author walking through the country, or riding through it, in constant motion," and as "a light trail to follow" the book "presents an almost organic regularity" (298–300). Wyatt and Work grapple with the relationship between physical movement and linguistic movement in Austin's first major work, yet their analyses favor a metaphoric reading of movement as artistic quest, feminine wanderlust, or a "set of moral statements concerning the proper relationship of the human animal to the land in its natural state" (Wyatt 94, 78; Work 297). In her introduction to *Western Trails: A Collection of Short Stories by Mary Austin*, Melody Graulich also reads Austin's inclusion of trails and walking motifs as important metaphors that "always stress connections between places, people, cultures... [and] represent her efforts to create a new American mythology" (4). While all three of these critics recognize the centrality of motion, trails, and walking in *The Land of Little Rain* and their analyses of meaning embedded in these images are instructive, they all sidestep the literal, experiential component of Austin's work. As Corey Lee Lewis contends, Austin "attempts to embody the rhythms and characteristics of the land in her prose, thereby resisting the mediated nature and distancing effects of linguistic representation" (63). Yet her prose is more complex even than Lewis's description. She combines a careful attention to the land with an expertise in crafting English prose; she draws together literary artifice and natural rhythms. To fully appreciate Austin's attempt to join land and language in *The Land of Little Rain*, it is necessary to examine how her treatment of trails and walking expresses physical experiences and the material land as well as metaphoric meaning. Highlighting the cocreative forces of human and nonhuman, Karen Barad argues that "the universe is agential intra-activity in its becoming" ("Posthumanist Performativity" 135). By turning to the rhythms of walking, Austin works to present a vision of an intra-active world where intellectual and corporeal movements of human and nonhuman create meaning.

Combining her early recognition of nonhuman agency with her own ethnocentric interpretation of Indigenous worldviews, Austin began to develop a new philosophy about the land undergirded by rhythm and movement. Intrigued by the rhythms and patterns the Paiute medicine man Tinnemaha helped her to glimpse in the natural world, she turned to Indigenous cosmologies—views Austin imagined to be more "authentic" and closer to the essence of the land itself. She eventually "became convinced... [that] the mold of Amerind verse... is the mold of the American experience shaped by the American environment" (Austin, *American Rhythm* 42). In response to this developing philosophy, Austin rooted her life and her writing in movement: the rhythms of the seasons, the heartbeat, the footfall, and the flow of the natural world around her.

Austin terms the interplay between land, rhythm, and language the "landscape line" (*American Rhythm* 54). She explains that the "landscape line" is "the leap of the running stream of poetic inspiration from level to level, whose course cannot be determined by anything except the nature of the ground traversed.... The length of the leaps, and the sequence of pattern recurrences will be conditioned by the subjectivity coordinated motor rhythms associated with the particular emotional flow" (*American Rhythm* 55–56). Austin argues that the movements of the land itself create a structure and rhythm for life and language. She suggests that critics could use the landscape line as an analytic device: by scrutinizing the rhythms in literature, one could discover the land to which the writer is responding. Indeed, Austin claims that she can do this when listening to recorded Indigenous songs: "I discovered that I could listen to aboriginal verses on the phonograph in unidentified Amerindian languages and securely refer them by their dominant rhythms to the plains, the deserts and woodlands that produced them" (*American Rhythm* 19). Austin attempts to replicate the landscape line in her own prose, and the rhythms and patterns that suffuse her writing flow from the arrangement of the words on the page as well as from the rhythm and meaning within the physical land and the physical body traversing it. Austin imagines an active participation in the rhythms of the land and of American literature. She envisions a harmony between land, animals, human body, and language—a harmony she represents in the rhythms of walking.

Austin's engagement with the nonhuman land and its rhythms presages what Barad posits as a posthumanist notion of performativity that "calls into question the givenness of the differential categories of 'human' and 'nonhuman'" ("Posthumanist Performativity" 126). In this formulation, "things do not have inherently determinate boundaries or properties, and words do not have inherently determinate meanings" ("Posthumanist Performativity" 131). When Austin walks, she is not striding out as a human being who is above and superior to an inert, passive land. The land, filled with agency and movement, requires that its human inhabitants bend to its rhythms.

While Austin did not fully articulate her understanding of these rhythms until later in her writing life, in *The Land of Little Rain* movement in the form of walking informs and determines the rhythms of the text; her language reflects the steady rhythm of the heartbeat and the footfall. Walking serves as what Austin would term a "glyph"—a symbol of a more complex meaning that is not fully expressed ("Non-English Writings II" 627). She uses walking as a glyph that represents the physical movement of the body through space, the motions of thought, the vastness of the land, and the constant and mysterious rhythms that unite human, animal, and land. Drawing on the work of other nature writers, songs and lifeways from Indigenous communities she encounters, and her own bodily ingress in the desert, Austin infuses her writing with a rhythm that underscores the intra-action between human and nonhuman in the desert.

EUROAMERICAN NATURE WRITING AND WALKING

In both physically walking in nature and writing about walking, Austin entered an already well-established tradition of Euroamerican observations of the American land. This largely male tradition stretches back to the first European explorers who reached the shores of America and initiated the convention of linking observations of the land with physical movement. While critics such as Robert Finch and John Elder recognize that "contemporary nature writers characteristically take walks through landscapes of association" (26), these walks are common in American nature writing from at least the late eighteenth century. For example, in *Letters from an*

American Farmer (1782), J. Hector St. John de Crèvecœur repeatedly notes his "constant walks" that afford him the opportunity to observe the land (57). Similarly, William Bartram's eighteenth- and early-nineteenth-century nature writing engages with bodily movement and takes the form of travel literature. Walking also figures prominently in the texts of iconic nature writers such as Henry David Thoreau, John Burroughs, and John Muir, as well as contemporary writers such as Gary Snyder and Terry Tempest Williams. Critic Scott Slovic highlights the physicality of these approaches in *Seeking Awareness in American Nature Writing*, arguing, "Many literary naturalists imitate the notebooks of scientific naturalists, or the logbooks of explorers, or even the journals of non-scientific travelers in order to entrench themselves in the specific moment of experience" (4). These writers engage the generic conventions of explorers, travelers, and scientists in an attempt to achieve an understanding of the natural world that "can only happen by taking the time to enter the natural world, to engage it, to not only run our eyes along its surfaces, but to place ourselves among its things and weathers—to let it exert, at least for intervals in our lives, the ancient influences that once surrounded and formed us" (John Daniel qtd. in Slovic 175). Throughout the tradition of American travel and nature writing, writers have sought this immersion through walking. As Rebecca Solnit notes, "If the body is the register of the real, then reading with one's feet is real in a way that reading with one's eyes is not" (70).

Romantic and transcendental writers understood the rhythm of walking in nature to be intimately connected to the rhythm of thought. Jean-Jacques Rousseau, identified by Joseph Amato as the "father of romantic pedestrianism in Europe and North America," declared in 1770, "I can only meditate when I am walking. When I stop I cease to think; my mind only works with my legs" (qtd. in Amato 108). Although he acknowledged that he walked because he was too poor to travel otherwise, Rousseau celebrated the physical and mental freedom afforded by walking. "There is something about walking," he wrote, "which stimulates and enlivens my thoughts. When I stay in one place I can hardly think at all; my body has to be on the move to set my mind going" (qtd. in Solnit 19). Rousseau and the romantic poets joined walking with thinking and therefore with generating ideas for their writing. For the romantics, walking was "a way to free the captive self from the artificial, urban, and mechanical world and to connect to one's true inheritance," that is, with nature (Amato 104). Celeste Langan argues that walking "is the framing issue of Romantic form and content" (14). For the romantic poet, "freedom *is* walking" (Langan 20; emphasis added). Walking in the natural world represented an avenue to escape the deadening influences of modernity and to reclaim a measure of authenticity and self-determination.

American transcendentalists such as Emerson and Thoreau were influenced by romantic as well as scientific writers and walkers in their conception of the natural world. In the famous "transparent eyeball" passage in *Nature*, Emerson writes, "In the wilderness, I find something more dear and connate than in streets or villages. In the tranquil landscape, and especially in the distant line of the horizon, man beholds somewhat as beautiful as his own nature" (29). Yet while Emerson celebrated the link between the natural world and spiritual experiences, he rarely chose to venture far into the wilderness.[2] Thoreau, on the other hand, saw the connection between engagement in nature and spiritual epiphany as more than a poetic metaphor. While Emerson extolled the importance of immersing oneself in the natural world, Thoreau took to his feet and walked into the wilderness. In his eulogy honoring Thoreau, Emerson described him as one who "would probably out-walk most countrymen in a day's journey.... The length of his walk uniformly made the length of his writing" (402). Emerson suggests that walking for Thoreau not only opens up opportunities for abstract thought, but also has material impact on creativity. For Thoreau, as for the romantic poets, walking, language, and freedom were inseparable. Thoreau wrote in his essay "Walking" that proper saunterers have "no particular home, but [are] equally at home everywhere" (180). Finding "home" everywhere, walking provided the walkers with the comfort and familiarity to move freely.

Further, transcendentalists like Thoreau understood freedom of movement in the natural world to be intimately connected to spirituality. Thoreau contends that "saunterers in the good sense" are always going "to the Holy Land in their walks" (180). They have "a direct dispensation from Heaven to become...walker[s]" and "naturally go to the fields and woods" (181, 183). "I am alarmed," he asserts, "when it happens that I have walked a mile into the woods bodily, without getting there in spirit" (183). Thoreau ties his experience of freedom while walking to the divinity of nature. He contends that the goal of walking is to achieve a sense of freedom that is also a sense of the sacred: bodily movement into the sacred space of nature facilitates mental movement toward divinity and freedom. Thoreau ends "Walking" with the hope that "we saunter toward the Holy Land, till one day the sun shall shine more brightly than ever he has done, shall perchance shine into our minds and hearts, and light up our whole lives with a great awakening light" (205). As Lawrence Buell claims, Thoreau imagined "the whole process of nature rambling as 'sauntering' in the sacred sense—as a kind of pilgrimage" (329). Thoreau, like Emerson, saw a correspondence between the natural and the spiritual; by experiencing nature, Thoreau sought to find unifying patterns and spiritual fulfillment.

Heavily influenced by the transcendentalists and romantics, as well as by naturalists and Christian theology, John Muir developed a more robust understanding of rhythm, the nonhuman world, and walking.[3] If walkers such as Rousseau, Emerson, and Thoreau tied walking to a state of inspiration and spirituality, Muir combined that interest with a more developed emphasis on the materiality of the world and the physicality of walking. In Muir's formulation, supported by his knowledge of Western scientific, literary, and religious teachings, access to the sacred in nature depended on a physical body that was hardy enough to stride into the heart of the wilderness. Even in one of his earliest writings, *A Thousand-Mile Walk to the Gulf*, Muir recognized the value in moving physically into and with the flow of the natural world. As he walked he gained a heightened experience of the landscape. Echoing the language from Emerson's transparent-eyeball passage, Muir notes that in walking, "presently you lose consciousness of your own separate existence: you blend with the landscape and become part and parcel of nature" (*Thousand-Mile Walk* 212). Where Emerson writes, "I am nothing; I see all; the currents of the Universal Being circulate through me; I am part or particle of God," Muir removes God as the referent and refocuses the passage on nature itself (29). Emerson imagines nature as a path to experiencing God, but Muir imagines the rhythms of nature as the goal, as the divine.

Muir believed that there was a deep, if unknowable, meaning and value in the rhythm and flow of the natural world. As Michael P. Cohen argues, Muir "knew that the order of things was deep, and that man was shallow, that the order of things was eternal, and that man was mortal" (42). In *My First Summer in the Sierra* (1911), Muir articulates his vision of the significance of natural rhythms:

> We are reminded that everything is flowing—going somewhere, animals and so called lifeless rocks as well as water. Thus the snow falls fast or slow in grand beauty-making glaciers and avalanches; the air in majestic floods carrying minerals, plant leaves, seeds, spores, with streams of music and fragrance; water streams carrying rocks both in solution and in the form of mud particles, sand, pebbles, and boulders. Rocks flow from volcanoes like water from springs, and animals flock together and flow in currents modified by stepping, leaping, gliding, flying, swimming, etc. While the stars go streaming through space pulsed on and on forever like blood globules in Nature's warm heart. (236)

Muir presents all of nature flowing and moving in similar rhythmic patterns. To fully experience nature, Muir believed that he had to physically enter that flow, to walk, saunter, scramble, and wander in patterns that existed apart from and before human incursion into the wilderness. For Muir, physically experiencing nature's rhythms through walking links scientific and sacred views of nature. Entering the rhythm of the natural world allows him to examine it more clearly; he is able to recognize and study the cyclic and rhythmic patterns that unite the natural world, patterns that hold the key to both science and the sacred.

Like Muir, Austin's perception of the natural world was colored by previous generations of writers and thinkers. However, as a Euroamerican woman, her relationship to the natural world was restricted by societal limits. Beginning her writing career in the late nineteenth century, Austin was familiar with the work of the transcendentalists and nature writers, and their influence is clear in her work, even as her context as a Euroamerican woman necessitates a different approach.[4] John P. O'Grady argues that in part because of the freedom accorded to them as white men, Thoreau and Muir largely "confine[d] themselves to what might sarcastically be called the holiday side of the wild," while Austin was more profoundly aware of the "shadow side" of nature (125). Alaimo similarly characterizes Austin's formulation of the desert as "undomesticated ground ... a lawless place where the landmarks fail, gender unravels, and meanings come undone" ("Trans-corporeal Feminisms" 240). Austin understood that the natural world has its own laws that do not conform to the conventions of human culture; nature holds something more.[5]

As a woman born into a closed-off, protected world, Austin rejected the hierarchical guidelines of both masculinism and humanism that placed men above both women and nonhuman nature. Men were allowed access to wilderness adventure and exploration, while women were confined to the home. As Carolyn Heilbrun points out, "Safety and closure, which have always been held out to women as the ideals of feminine destiny, are not places of adventure, or experience, or life" (20). Similarly, Michelle Campbell Toohey argues that the Euroamerican male nature-writing tradition positioned the (male) nature writer "as a human who has the power to stand outside and name with humanizing superiority" (206). As a female nature writer, Austin refused both the idea that women had no place in the natural world and the notion that nature writing formulated human as superior to nonhuman. Austin's nature writer "is an integral part of the ecosystem as she takes on speaking positions at once distanced from and participating in her surroundings" (Toohey 206). In placing her own body in the desert, Austin acknowledges herself as part of the desert, subject to the desert's rhythms, instead of asserting her own.[6]

Austin moves material rhythms into a place of central importance. For Austin, rhythm is not simply part of the world; it is *the defining feature*. Further, identifying that rhythm is not a key to knowledge so much as a recognition and acceptance of one's place in the universe. Consequently, in Austin's writing walking works on multiple registers as a structuring device and a symbol and perhaps most significantly as the mechanism by which the material human body can be perceived in its state of entanglement with the nonhuman. In her conceptualization of this entanglement, Austin draws not only on Euroamerican traditions but also on her version of Indigenous oral traditions and lifeways. She finds in her interactions with Western Shoshone and Southern Paiute peoples an expression of the connections between human and nonhuman expressed in the rhythm of the footfall that she incorporates into her own philosophy and writing.

INDIGENOUS TRADITIONS AND AUSTIN'S PHILOSOPHY OF RHYTHM

Whereas the genre of Euroamerican nature writing as practiced by men drew on European and occasionally East Asian traditions for inspiration, Austin was captivated early on by the Indigenous cultures she encountered in her wanderings. Her understanding of Shoshone and Paiute culture, while inspired by her relationship with members of those nations, was heavily influenced by her own romantic, ethnocentric beliefs. She believed that Indigenous cultures were naturally in tune with the rhythms of the natural world and that by examining their traditions, Euroamerican writers could find their way to a more "authentic" American literature. As a Euroamerican woman, she longed to access women's "primitive" power, "a power based on the union of mind and body" (Carew-Miller 119). She saw in Indigenous traditions an articulation of power that she understood to be based on intuition and the rhythms of the land. Austin worked to comprehend these rhythms throughout her writing life, but her most complete articulation came in 1923 with the publication of *The American Rhythm*. Part literary theory and part poetic "re-expression" of American Indian verse, *The American Rhythm* posits that the rhythm of the land shapes and determines human experiences and that as humans adjust themselves to the preexisting rhythm of the land, their physical movements, thoughts, and literatures would also be molded.

In *The American Rhythm*, Austin suggests that "Europeanly derived American[s]" are generally too removed from the natural world to grasp the correspondence between bodily rhythms and rhythms generated by the land (31).[7] "All this time," she argues, "there was an American race singing in tune with the beloved environment, to the measures of life-sustaining gestures, taking the material of their songs out of the common human occasions, out of democratic experience and the profound desire of man to assimilate himself to the Allness as it is displayed in all the peacock splendor of the American continent" (19). Austin viewed American Indian ways of thinking as models for creating a uniquely American literary tradition through encouraging connection to "Allness," Austin's version of the transcendental Oversoul that joins all parts of the universe together.

The rhythms of Native American verse, Austin argues, offer Euroamerican writers a path to follow to an authentic and unique American literature, a model that "allows whites to achieve American identity by following Indian examples of living with the land" (Viehmann 11).[8] Yet as Martha L. Viehmann points out, "Ironically, Austin's elevation of Indian culture as a model for the broader American culture lets real Indian people and their contemporary concerns about poverty and the loss of traditions, land, and power slip out of view" (9). Austin's belief that "the homogeneity of the Amerind race makes it possible to detect environmental influences with a precision not possible among the mixed races of Europe" is in line with the belief of the larger Euroamerican society at the time that Native Americans shared a single culture across the United States (Austin, "Non-English Writings II" 630). This view that Indigenous peoples were closer to the rhythms of the natural world was colored by contemporary theories about cultural hierarchies, which speculated that Indigenous cultures were more "childlike" than European cultures and thus more "natural" and in tune with the land.[9] Although Austin attempted to reconfigure this belief so that "natural" was considered the superior state, her generalizations about Indigenous cultures and her romanticization of Indigenous peoples reveal that she is caught in the ideology of her time, even as she tries to challenge it.

Abstracting Indigenous traditions, Austin believed that "all Amerind literature was rhythmic" ("Non-English Writings II" 612). American Indian peoples, she writes, "hit upon the idea of rhythm, vibration, as being the secret harmony, the ululating voice, the cry beaten into rhythm with the hand" ("Non-English Writings II" 617). Going a step further, she contends that the most important aspect of Indigenous songs is rhythm, taking precedence over language. In translating Indigenous songs, she contends, "It is even possible to dispense with words altogether, but the translator will go astray who contents himself with the words and does not put into his work the rhythm pattern and the emotion of the melodic intervals" (Non-English Writings II" 618). Austin believed that meaning in Indigenous song lay primarily in the rhythms of language, not in a word-for-word translation. This focus removes attention from the intellectual capacities of Indigenous singers and places it on the innate bodily connection between body and land, highlighting the nineteenth- and early-twentieth-century belief in Native peoples' natural and unthinking connection to nature.

Ancient and mystical Indigenous connections to the rhythms of the American environment, Austin contends, are reflected not only in the rhythm of Native American verse, but also in their accompanying bodily movements. She argues that through dance and drumbeats, Native Americans are able to more fully access nonhuman rhythms. Imagining an ancient Indigenous "Stone Age Man," she describes him "danc[ing] as the buck dances, and the pelican.... With his bare foot he stroked out on the bare earth the assurance of identity... [and] discovered that, by making rhythmic movements and noises, power comes" (*American Rhythm* 26). She describes this power as the culmination of "coordinat[ing] with his dance the rhythm of sun, wind, or falling water, making himself part of the inextricable pattern of the hour" (*American Rhythm* 31). Shaped by her understanding that Indigenous cultures exist in a more primitive and authentic relationship to place, Austin perceives in Indigenous verse and dance a complex interaction among land, body, and words, dependent on complementary rhythms.

Because Austin viewed Indigenous verse and ceremony as closer to the land and more authentically American than Euroamerican writing of her time, she attempted to use her understanding of these forms as a model for her own writing. In her autobiography, *Earth Horizon*, Austin explains her process of learning to write as a process of coming into contact with the power and "Allness" she imagines in Indigenous traditions, something she refers to as "the Friend-of-the-Soul-of-Man." Narrating this experience in the second person, she writes:

> There is this thing called the Friend-of-the-Soul-of-Man, a reality, an influence which you can call up around you. You wrap yourself in it. You are effective through it. You make use of it through rhythm; the beating of the medicine drum; the pound of feet in the medicine dance. You give way to it through rhythmic utterance. You find it expressing itself in rhythmic movement, the running of quail, the creaking of the twenty-mule team, the sweep of motion in a life-history, in a dance, a chant. You perceive that these patterns made writing; you struggled for them; won, caught, and ensnared them. (289)

Austin sees writing as a way to "ensnare" and translate the rhythms of the natural world. She strives to match the rhythm of her writing voice to the rhythms of the land and the physical movement of animals and humans across that land. Dale Metcalfe connects Austin's representation of the rhythms of written language to her understanding of Indigenous life and verse. Metcalfe argues that "from her first forays into the Paiute camps near Bishop and Lone Pine, California, in the late 1880's, Austin's creative work was profoundly influenced by Native Americans" (66). Metcalfe goes on to suggest that Austin was particularly influenced by what she saw as Native peoples' "propensities to actively participate in, rather than simply observe, nature" (67). Though it was not until the 1920s and '30s that Austin fully developed her theories of writing and rhythm, it is clear that these ideas were nascent in her earlier writings, particularly in her nonfiction desert books *The Land of Little Rain* and *Lost Borders*. In these early texts, the rhythm of walking across the land serves as a means to communicate complex theories of rhythm, movement, and thought development.

Drawing on her assessment of Indigenous views, Austin recognized the land as "polyrhythmic," filled with the "reverberating motions of the universe" (Zolla 192). She writes, "The passing of the perception of rhythmic forms in our environment—as the roll of thunder or the run of wind in tall grass—through the sensorium into the subconscious, is experiential in its nature. It leaves a track, a mold, by which our every mode of expression is shaped" (*American Rhythm* 3). She continues, "The intellectual appreciation of such sequences is not enough. There must be a series of motor impulses started somewhere, before the experience is appreciated as rhythmic" (3–4). She argues that the rhythms of the land and the rhythms of the human body converge in a "wave-like motion" that gives rise to the manner of life lived in the American land and the quality of poetic expression created there (5). In essence, the rhythms of land, body, and thought converge to create a life and literature that are uniquely American.

THE LAND OF LITTLE RAIN'S RHYTHMIC DESERT

In her search for an effective literary rendering of the connection between human and nonhuman rhythms, Austin's prose absorbs and replicates the movements of bodies as they experience the land. In *The American Rhythm*, she illustrates this complex union with an extended account of the Corn Dance as performed by "the Rio Grande Pueblos,"[10] of which I provide only a brief excerpt here: "The dancers will number among the hundreds, according to the population of the community. The natural rhythm of their timing feet will run from the pound of the men's thick soles, through the softer shuffle of the women to the patter of the children tailing out the procession around the plaza, rising and falling and overlapping like a musical round" (46). The physical rhythm of the dancers determines the rhythm and stress patterns of the prose. Here, as in much of her writing, the most common metrical foot is a triple foot, an anapest or dactyl. In *A Prosody Handbook*, Karl Shapiro and Robert Beum write that "anapests tend to produce lightness and speed" and that dactyls, common to nursery rhymes, are "appropriate to such droll and frisky effects" (40, 43). So, for example, when Austin describes the movements of the dancers' bodies, she predominantly uses these triple feet, interspersed with other rhythms for emphasis: "frŏm thĕ póund | ŏf thĕ mén's | thíck sóles, | thrŏugh thĕ sóft | ĕr shúfflĕ | ŏf thĕ | wómĕn | tŏ thĕ | páttĕr | ŏf thĕ | chíldrĕn | táilĭng | oŭt thĕ | prŏcéssiŏn | ăróund | thĕ pláză, | rísĭng ănd | fállĭng ănd | óvĕr | láppĭng | lĭke ă | mús | ĭcăl róund." The sentence begins with two anapests, creating a sense of rhythmic movement. Then Austin inserts a spondee ("thíck sóles"), which slows the rhythm to match the sense of the phrase. From there she returns briefly to an anapest before breaking the pattern again, this time with a pyrrhic, a series of unstressed syllables. The pyrrhic, in contrast to the spondee, hastens the pace, just as the women's shuffle is lighter and faster than the men's pounding step. The use of the pyrrhic continues with the description of the children's quick feet. The passage ends with a return to a more regular pattern, a combination of dactyls and trochees, ending with two anapests: "rísĭng ănd | fállĭng ănd | óvĕr | láppĭng | lĭke ă mús | ĭcăl róund." The return to a more regular pattern of stressed and unstressed syllables recalls the even pattern of the heartbeat and the footstep. The rhythm of the prose, then, mirrors the sense of the passage, as Austin imagines that the rhythms reflect the "heart of the sun beating" and rise from the feet of the dancers through their arms, legs, and torsos and into their rattles and finally are expressed in chanting and singing. Austin stresses that the ceremony's meaning extends beyond the dancers; the rhythm and meaning of the words emerge through a bodily expression of natural rhythms of the human and more-than-human world. To fully appreciate the power and intent of the Corn Dance, she suggests, one must look to the multiplicity of rhythms it incorporates—linguistic, bodily, and those arising from the more-than-human world.

In *Earth Horizon*, Austin writes that even as a child, she "wanted to write books that you could walk around in" (73). In its peripatetic structure, *The Land of Little Rain* reflects this aspiration. As many critics have noted, the trails and paths that structure *The Land of Little Rain* invite readers into the land and the stories.[11] Beginning with the opening sketch, "The Land of Little Rain," Austin walks the reader into the desert of Owens Valley, where "not the law, but the land sets the limit" (9). She mentions her own "twice seven years' wanderings" (17) and encourages her readers to look for "footprint tracings in the sand" (13). Subsequent sketches reinforce bodily movement in their titles, taking the reader through the "Water Trails of the Ceriso," "The Mesa Trail," "The Streets of the Mountains," and along "Water Borders." Elizabeth Ammons argues that these trails are not straightforward but rather rhythmic and even "antilinear." She asserts that *The Land of Little Rain* "constantly reiterates the simple construct of push/pull, ebb/flow, shrink/expand that Austin considered the pulse, the constant, cyclic, unaccented rhythm of the earth itself." Ammons contends that Austin borrowed this formal principle from the Native peoples she encountered, linking this structure to Austin's description in *The American Rhythm* of the "dub-dub, dub-dub, dub-dub" rhythm "commonly heard 'in the plazas of Zuni and Oraibi'" (92). The trails in their ubiquity demonstrate the centrality of movement to life in the desert. They not only signify the way the desert requires living beings to bend to natural rhythms and echo the footsteps of humans and animals who have been there before, but also function to bind together the materiality of the land with the structure of thought and writing as exemplified in the text. Material, symbolic, and structural realities intra-act.

Austin suggests that these paths reflect the "proper" way of entering nature's material rhythm by experiencing it primarily through the body, in contrast to the more intellectually based Euroamerican male traditions of nature writing. She writes in *The Land of Little Rain*, "The manner of the country makes the usage of life there, and the land will not be lived in except in its own fashion" (57).[12] In the case of the desert, the aridity of the land makes the quest for water vital, and this quest for water creates a network of paths and trails. Mark Schlenz contends that Austin presents "a utopian integration of people and place, a harmonious community of humans and nature joined by paths of water" (191). While referring to the country of *The Land of Little Rain* as "utopian" seems to miss the desolation and death lurking in much of Austin's depiction, Schlenz is right in suggesting that the "paths of water" act as a web that binds human and nonhuman. Austin presents trails that emerge naturally from the land, trails that are determined by the land.

In emphasizing the trails "written" with the feet of desert animals, Austin draws attention to how the material intra-action between land and animals creates meaning. She describes "coyotes that are astir in the Ceriso of late afternoons, harrying the rabbits from their shallow forms, and the hawks that sweep and swing above them," waiting for "the small fry" to venture onto the water trails (24). Later she describes a horned toad as "a palm's breadth of the trail [that] gathers itself together and scurries off" (89) and observes a badger with "sharp-clawed, splayey feet" as a "swift trailer." She refers to the fox and the coyote as "split-feet" who are "light treaders" (87). The water trails reflect the rhythm of the desert; they are rubbed into the earth by the walking of animals in search of life-sustaining springs, and they provide routes to those springs. The rhythms of the desert are the rhythms of the footfall. The pace of walking reflects the deeper rhythms of the land and makes these rhythms visible through foot-worn trails and paths. These trails and paths link the rhythms of the land to the manner in which the land must be lived.

Austin's attention to the nonhuman bodies that trace paths on the desert, paths that can be "read" to understand the meanings of the land, powerfully highlights the materiality of the world. Serenella Iovino and Serpil Opperman write, "Bodies, both human and nonhuman, provide an eloquent example of the way matter can be read as a text. Being the 'middle place' where matter enmeshes in the discursive forces of politics, society, technology, biology, bodies are compounds of flesh, elemental properties, and symbolic imaginaries...bodies are living texts that recount *naturalcultural* stories" (6; emphasis in the original). Far from the linguistic turn, where "linguistic structure [is allowed] to shape or determine our understanding of the world, [and we believe] that the subject and predicate structure of language reflects a prior ontological reality of substance and attribute" (Barad, "Posthumanist Performativity" 121), Austin presents readers with a world that is always in the process of "becoming." Influenced by Indigenous ecological knowledge, she presents this process as profoundly material, profoundly intra-active, and profoundly storied. The "story" of the land is not one that is defined and delimited by human language, but one that is created by the land and its inhabitants. "Matter and meaning," as Barad explains, "are mutually articulated" (140).

Rather than determining the meaning of the land through her own prose, Austin "reads" the text of the more-than-human desert's rhythms and mirrors them in her language. Writing about the land of the Carrizo Plain near San Joaquin Valley in Southern California, which she calls "the Ceriso," Austin asserts, "By the end of the dry season the water trails of the Ceriso are worn to a white ribbon in the leaning grass, spread out faint and fanwise toward the homes of gopher and ground rat and squirrel" (*Land of Little Rain* 21). Austin suggests that the animals can only live in the patterns of the land, and therefore their trails signal to humans how to adjust their rhythms to those of the desert. She tells her reader, "I have yet to find the land not scarred by the thin, far roadways of rabbits and what not of furry folks that run in them. Venture to look for some seldom-touched water-hole, and so long as the trails run with your general direction make sure you are right, but if they cross yours at never so slight an angle, to converge toward a point left or right of your objective, no matter what the maps say, or your memory, trust them; they *know*" (22; emphasis in the original). In this passage, Austin echoes the pattern of the land both in her description and in the rhythm of her prose. As with her description of the Puebloan Corn Dancers discussed above, her description of the trails etched by the feet of "furry folks" re-creates physical movement with the movement of her prose. She begins the passage with anapests and iambs, mirroring the rhythm of human steps as she walks into the land. Then, when she encounters the trails of the rabbits, she inserts a spondee: "thín | fár róadwăys," slowing down the pace of her prose as she encourages her readers to slow down and observe the land. She then moves to an irregular series of stressed and unstressed syllables, including a pyrrhic, mirroring the scurrying movement of the rabbits: "róadwăys ŏf | rábbĭts ănd | whát nŏt | ŏf fúrrȳ fólks | thăt rún | ĭn thĕm." The quickness of the rhythm here is underscored by the sound, the alliteration. Shapiro and Beum suggest that alliteration "tends to create a kind of discourse which focuses our attention minutely on the linguistic details of a sequence of words: it makes us *feel* the words" (93; emphasis added). The repetition of *r* sounds in the above phrase further focuses readers' attention on the scurrying movement of the rabbits, emphasizing the meaning of the passage—that to understand how to be in the land correctly, one must observe the movements of the animals. The passage ends with inverted feet, a trochee and an iamb that mirror one another—"trúst thĕm, | thĕy *knów*"—further concentrating readers' attention. In stressing "they *know*," Austin offers readers a different kind of knowing. Austin encourages her readers to trust the wisdom of the animals and the land rather than trusting man-made maps or even their own preexisting knowledge. Like Muir, Austin understands these patterns to be beyond ordinary human modes of knowing; the true power of the land can be accessed only by "reading" nature's wisdom in the network of water trails that act as a visible trace of the rhythm of walking the land.

Further emphasizing the material land and material bodies, Austin submits that to truly access the rhythm of the land, one must shift from a human stride to an animal gait. She suggests that to accurately "read" the patterns of the wilderness, one must get "down to the eye level of rat and squirrel kind." "Man-height," she claims, "is the least fortunate of all heights from which to study trails." In addition to getting down to the level of rats and squirrels, Austin recommends going to the top of a "tall hill," because the paths to water are "mapped out whitely from this level, which is also the level of hawks" (*Land of Little Rain* 21). Later she proposes that the proper rhythm of the mesa trails is not found in a human step, which "carries one too slowly past the units in a decorative scheme that is on a scale with the country round for bigness." Rather, the mesa trails are "meant to be traveled on horseback, at the jigging coyote trot that only western-bred horses have learned successfully" (83). Austin argues that just as the "western-bred horses" have learned to adjust their gait to the jog of the coyote, humans in the desert are called upon to adjust their perspectives to those of nonhuman animals and in so doing adjust their physical movement. Moving with the flow of the land requires new ways of "tak[ing] to the trail," new ways of taking a walk (24).

Austin recognizes that tracing the rhythmic forces at work upon the entirety of the natural world requires time. In the preface to the text, Austin tells her readers that to truly "have such news of the land, of its trails and what is astir in them," they "must summer and winter with the land and wait its occasions. Pine woods that take two and three seasons to the ripening of cones, roots that lie by in the sand seven years awaiting a growing rain, firs that grow fifty years before flowering,—these do not scrape acquaintance" (4). Austin argues that the rhythms of the desert cannot be known through casual observation; they do not give away their secrets easily. The trails and paths that crisscross *The Land of Little Rain* invite readers into a country that is already humming with patterns and rhythms. She writes of the "procession of the pines" and of a seedling that "tip-toe[s] above the gully of a creek" (104, 77). Even the moon "wander[s]," stars "[w]heel in their stations in the sky," storms have "appointed paths," "young rivers swa[y] with the force of their running," and "clouds come walking on the floor of heaven" (24, 17, 133, 106, 134). These rhythms transcend human conceptions of time; they communicate something infinite. Understanding the land means submitting oneself to these rhythms over a long span of time, to give oneself over to rhythms that are larger and older than humanity.

Austin identifies the few human inhabitants in *The Land of Little Rain* who live in the flow of the land and have internalized the landscape line. The patterns of their bodies have been altered, and they have matched the "rhythm of walking [that is] always a recognizable background for our thoughts...to the jog of the wide, unrutted earth" (*American Rhythm* 14). Austin writes that the inhabitants of a fictionalized Euroamerican mining town she calls Jimville "understand the language of the hills.... Somehow the rawness of the land favors the sense of personal relation to the supernatural" (*Land of Little Rain* 71). Despite Jimville's location in Squaw Gulch, "a very sharp, steep, ragged-walled ravine" (67), and "the killing and drunkenness, coveting of women...indifference, blankness, emptiness" that characterize life there, Austin contends that in Jimville, there is also "charity, simplicity...[and] no bread-envy, no brother fervor."[13] The inhabitants of Jimville reflect the loneliness and "rawness" of the land; they represent "the courage to sheer off what is not worth while" (71). In Jimville, she writes, "you have the repose of the perfectly accepted instinct which includes passion and death in its perquisites" (72). The flow of life in Jimville matches the flow of the desert, and the inhabitants' relationship to law, land, life, and death corresponds to a place where "not the law, but the land sets the limits," and the land "may breed like qualities in her human offspring, not tritely to 'try,' but to do" (9, 11).

Though Jimville is a fixed location in the California desert, the inhabitants themselves are not motionless; being settled in Jimville does not mean being stationary. The narrator herself learns the stories of Jimville on the seat of a stagecoach. She writes, "First on the way to Jimville you cross a lonely open land, with a hint in the sky of things going on under the horizon, a palpitant, white, hot land where the wheels gird at the sand and the midday heaven shuts it in breathlessly like a tent" (67). In this romanticizing description, Austin recalls the movements of nomads, traveling with their tents across a land that vibrates with the heat of the sun. The language she employs reflects this swaying movement, with its long sentence structure and commas that create frequent pauses suggestive of the movement of the coach. The passage begins with dactyls and trochees, indicating the jolting, off-kilter coach: "Fírst ŏn thĕ | wáy tŏ | Jímvĭlle." When she turns to her description of the land, however, her rhythm opens up into iambic tetrameter: "yoŭ cróss | ă lóne | lȳ óp | ĕn lánd." Shapiro and Beum argue iambic feet create a rhythm that seems "formal and lofty," an elegance that befits the grandeur of the desert (36). As the coach's uneven, rocking rhythm joggles the body, the eye travels out and is stilled by the expanse of the land.

The inhabitants of Jimville also reflect this back-and-forth rocking. Although their houses are permanent, the people move away from the town into the surrounding hills in search of gold and then return to the town. "Yearly," Austin writes, "the spring fret floats the loose population of Jimville out into the desolate waste hot lands, guiding by peaks and a few rarely touched water-holes, always, always with the golden hope" (71). The miners are controlled by a desire to move into the hills that matches the seasonal flow of the land. In the several stories Austin relates of Jimville's inhabitants, the action tends to take place in the hills around the town, but in the end the characters always return to town. In the paragraph-long story of how Squaw Gulch was named, for example, Jim Calkins twice walks away from Jimville and then "walked back" and "came back" (68).[14] The inhabitants of Jimville, like Austin's prose, intra-act with and echo the pulsing rhythms of the land as they physically move away from and back to Jimville.

Even more than the inhabitants of Jimville, in *The Land of Little Rain* Austin's Shoshone characters embody the rhythms of the land. Austin met members of the Timbisha Tribe of the Western Shoshone in their ancestral homelands that include San Joaquin Valley and Owens Valley. By the time Austin became acquainted with the Timbisha Shoshone, they had signed the Treaty of Ruby Valley (1863), allowing the United States access to their land. However, the Timbisha did not cede their land to the United States and, like the Diné, continued to move through their traditional homeland following the seasons (*Timbisha Shoshone*).[15] Describing their seminomadic lifestyle, Austin tells her readers, "The Shoshones live like their trees, with great spaces between.... Their shelters are lightly built, for they travel much and far, following where deer feed and seeds ripen, but they are not more lonely than other creatures that inhabit there" (57). Austin suggests that like the miners in Jimville, the Shoshone mold their lives to the pulse of the natural world. They live "like their trees" and respond to the shifting seasons with physical movement. Austin imagines that as a hunting-and-gathering people, they recognize the wisdom of the deer and the seeds and match their travel to these cues.

Austin draws connections between the Shoshone and the natural world by suggesting, as many Euroamericans did in the nineteenth and twentieth centuries, that Indigenous peoples possess a deep, romantic, and vanishing sense of kinship with the land. In *The American Rhythm*, Austin writes about the original formation of Native American cultures: "Streams of rhythmic sights and sounds flowed in upon the becoming race of Americans from every natural feature" (14). In *The Land of Little Rain*, Austin expresses this relationship between people and place in her description of the ways in which Shoshone life responds to the rhythms of their world. "Young Shoshone," she contends, "are like young quail, knowing without teaching about feeding and hiding, and learning what civilized children never learn, to be still and to keep being still, at the first hint of danger or strangeness" (58). Similarly, she likens the Shoshone to plants, claiming that "the solitariness of the life breeds in the men, as in the plants, a certain well-roundedness and sufficiency to its own ends" (57). Austin's romantic descriptions of the Shoshone reflect her interpretation of the quality of the land they inhabit. She presents their connection to the land as quail-like and plantlike, reflective of a shared origin and a shared nature. She claims that the Shoshone are so connected to the land that they understand how to survive without being taught. The land, Austin reports, "goes very far by broken ranges, narrow valleys of pure desertness, and huge mesas uplifted to the sky-line, east and east, and no man knows the end of it.... This is the sense of the desert hills, that there is room enough and time enough" (56). Austin experiences the desert as a place of brooding silence and mystery, where "no man" (other than the plant- and animal-like Shoshone) can entirely know the fullness of the land.[16] In Austin's depiction, the Shoshone reflect this quality in their nomadic movements. The rhythm of Shoshone life is not the out-and-back rocking of Jimville, but a quieter and more spacious seasonal rhythm, a rhythm that ranges more widely along the desert's trails.

The connection between Austin's Shoshone characters and the rhythms of the land is echoed and reinforced in her characterization of Seyavi, a Paiute woman she became acquainted with while living near George's Creek in Owens Valley. Seyavi lives at the end of the Mesa Trail, a place Austin contends is the "beginning of other things" (*Land of Little Rain* 90). Austin opens Seyavi's story by describing the land of Owens Valley, reminding her readers that "to understand the fashion of any life, one must know the land it is lived in and the procession of the year" (93). Austin suggests that, like the Shoshone, Seyavi molds her life to the rhythms of the land. Austin observes that "twice a year, in the time of white butterflies and again when young quail run neck in neck in the chaparral, Seyavi cut willows for basketry by the creek where it wound toward the river against the sun and sucking winds" (95–96). Seyavi's life and artistry are determined by the ebb and flow of the seasons, a rhythm that is not constrained by the calendar but is governed by when the rains come and is mirrored in the behavior of desert creatures (96). Though her baskets are "wonders of technical precision," what is truly engaging about them for Austin is their connection to Seyavi and the land. Her baskets, Austin writes, "have a touch beyond cleverness. The weaver and the warp lived next to the earth and were saturated with the same elements" (95). The baskets are more than utilitarian pieces and more even than works of art. They reflect the "golden time" when the willows are cut and "the soul of the weather went into the wood." Austin claims that in owning one of Seyavi's baskets, "you would understand all this without saying anything" (96). In Austin's description, Seyavi's baskets both symbolize and physically embody a whole region and people in their patterns; they demonstrate the intra-action among desert dwellers and the desert itself. Austin imagines that the baskets reflect the Paiutes' seminomadic way of life, writing that their home is not "the wattled hut... but the land, the winds, the hill front, the stream" (97). Graulich argues that Austin "felt the Paiutes showed her how to envision patterns in art, to realize rhythm" (*Western Trails* 8). Indeed, in her autobiography Austin records that in observing Paiute women, she learned that "to get at the meaning of work you must make all its motions, both of body and mind" (*Earth Horizon* 247). Seyavi's baskets are not simply symbols of the rhythms of the land; they *are* the land. In their materials and patterns, Seyavi has captured the rhythms and essence of the desert. In her position at the end of the Mesa Trail, Seyavi exemplifies Austin's belief that if the land's rhythms are seen clearly, one will come to wisdom, an understanding of the land and, through the land, of the sacred.

While Austin presents her Shoshone and Paiute characters as worthy to be emulated in their understanding of the rhythms of the desert, it is the Euroamerican Walking Woman in *Lost Borders*, Austin's next collection of stories of the California desert, who represents Austin's ideal melding of human and nonhuman rhythms.[17] The narrator begins her story of the Walking Woman by recounting her own physical tracking of the Walking Woman's story. The narrator encounters glimpses of the Walking Woman's trail from "sheepherders at whose camps she slept" and "cowboys at rodeos [who] told me as much of her way of life as they could understand.... That was very little" (255). The Walking Woman's identity is mysterious and elusive. She is called Mrs. Walker or the Walking Woman because she never reveals her name. The narrator is convinced that "she lost her name" and "never told it because she did not know it herself" (257). Nameless and enigmatic, the Walking Woman is identified by her behavior: she walks. Wyatt argues that as a character, the Walking Woman "fade[s] into the ground" (76). As she walks her individual identity recedes, and what is left in its place are movement and rhythm. Like the desert in which she walks, the Walking Woman evades complete understanding, and her story refuses to be confined and possessed. She walks in the desert's rhythms and hints at knowledge that she never reveals.

The structure of the story reinforces the back-and-forth rhythm of footsteps. Tara Hart describes this structure as mirroring the "tidal rhythms of surge and withdrawal," as the narrator continually restages her depiction of and meeting with the Walking Woman (93); however, the movement can more appropriately be tied to the rhythm of walking in the desert sand, with each footstep shifting backward slightly. The narrator begins the story by asserting, "The first time of my hearing of her was at Temblor," referring to the Temblor Range that borders the Carrizo Plain in Southern California (255). She follows this assertion not with information about the Walking Woman but only with the fact that she had passed by recently. The narrator continues in this manner, mentioning other times and places she hears of the Walking Woman. In this first paragraph the reader learns very little of the Walking Woman other than her elusiveness, her habit of always being just ahead of the narrator's progress. A few pages further on the narrator tells us she "had met her occasionally at ranch-houses and road-stations," and then later she "came upon her in the heart of a clear afternoon" (257). With each rumor and meeting, the narrator reveals a bit more about the Walking Woman, but her full story always lies just out of reach. The sketch captures the rhythmic movement of the Walking Woman and the desert. Like the sketch of Jimville in *The Land of Little Rain*, the structure of "The Walking Woman" reflects a rocking, back-and-forth motion: with each entry into the story, the narrator moves closer to the Walking Woman and then slides back again. Similarly, each time she "begins" the story is like a step in the desert sand, moving the reader closer to the story's meaning, only to give way slightly and draw the reader back. In this way, the woman and the story of the woman are smoothed into the land itself.

What the narrator does reveal about the Walking Woman is her deviation from expected female behavior, a deviation that is represented by and explicit in her walking. The Walking Woman "had walked off all sense of society-made values" (261). She moves with ease in the male world of the miners, sheepherders, ranchers, and vaqueros who allow her to "pass unarmed and unoffended," a fact that surprises even the men, as "it was not, on the whole, what they expected of themselves." The narrator suggests that Walking Woman is able to walk and work in this male world because "you get no affront so long as your behavior in the estimate of the particular audience invites none" (256). The Walking Woman is able to walk away from "a frame of behavior called ladylike" and thrive (265). However, even though the male desert inhabitants seem to accept her behavior, they see her as somehow deformed. The narrator records that "she had a twist to her face, some said; a hitch to one shoulder; they averred she limped as she walked" (257). But these accounts reflect her divergence from ladylike behavior, not an unevenness in her physical body. "Recollecting suddenly that people called her lame," the narrator sees that to the contrary, "in the bare, hot sand the track of her two feet bore evenly and white" (262).

Faith Jaycox argues that it is in the act of walking itself that the Walking Woman broke "the conventional laws of femininity." The Walking Woman, she contends, "is the precise opposite of a confined woman; the endless mobility—not an escape journey, but simply endless mobility—is a powerful symbolic challenge to the enforced physical restriction of women" (9). Walking is both what the Walking Woman does and what she is. In opposition to cultural ideals of the restricted and restrained woman, her identity is bound up in action.

If walking is the Walking Woman's rejection of societal disapproval of women's movement, it is also what allows her to gain entry into the pulse of the desert. Hart argues that in this story, "access to the land . . . occurs only by traveling/reading across great stretches of space and time" (97). While Austin imagines that the access her Shoshone and Paiute characters have to the rhythms of the land is "natural" and instinctive, the Walking Woman has to learn through experience and exposure to the land. In the tradition of many male sojourners in the West, the Walking Woman "beg[an] by walking off an illness . . . [that] drove her to the open, sobered and healed at last by the large soundness of nature" (*Lost Borders* 257).[18] In the beginning of her wandering, she experienced a "period of worry and loss" before "she began to find herself" in the desert. The Walking Woman tells the narrator that she came to a new understanding of herself in the midst of a sandstorm. During the storm she helps her lover, Filon, round up his sheep. She finds the storm, which made the "whole surface of the ground appea[r] to travel upon it slantwise" (258), not terrifying but exhilarating. She asserts that "until that time I had not known how strong I was, nor how good it is to run when running is worth while." The Walking Woman recognizes that her physical strength is a significant aspect in her experience of nature; however, this strength takes her outside of her accepted gender role and redefines her sense of her own possibilities. When night comes, she and Filon take turns keeping watch, and she begins to recognize her body's intimate link to the rhythm of the desert: "I lay on the ground when my turn was and beat with the storm. I was not more tired than the earth was" (259). The experience of connecting with the "beat" of the storm allows the Walking Woman to heal her "worry and loss," as self-reliance, physical exertion, and the pulse of the storm converge. The rhythms of nature and the motions of the body align, and there is a "sense of the unfolding earth" (*Earth Horizon* 104). The Walking Woman is describing her recognition of trans-corporality, "in which the human is always intermeshed with the more-than-human world" (Alaimo, *Bodily Natures* 2). It is this recognition of entanglement in the rhythmic stream of the desert that changes her and allows her to become herself, to become "the Walking Woman."

While there did seem to be a "real" Walking Woman,[19] the characterization of this figure bears a striking resemblance to Austin herself. Like the Walking Woman, Austin walked away from societal ideas about femininity, and Austin imagined herself as possessing the earth wisdom that her character demonstrates. In her autobiography Austin writes that her sense of the essence of the land developed early, that even as a child she felt that "there is something in Mary which comes out of the land; something in its rhythms, its living compulsions, which dominates... governing her own progressions, coloring her most intimate expression." Further, like the Walking Woman, Austin views this "something" as a "rejection of the male ritual of rationalization in favor of a more direct intuitional attack" (*Earth Horizon* 15). Austin endeavored to detach her writing from rigid and oppressive societal influences in favor of a land-based ethic that allowed her to access the deep rhythms of more-than-human nature.

KNOWING AND LIVING WITH THE LAND

By 1924 Austin had long left behind the deserts of California and was struggling with the politics and values of the New York publishing industry. That spring Austin frequently "had the feeling she was living in a nightmare" (Fink 223). Physically distant from her chosen land, she was struggling to finish her collection of stories set in the southwestern desert, *The Land of Journeys' Ending*, under considerable pressure from her publishers, and she was physically suffering from a bacterial infection. Yet, her biographer asserts, Austin was able to find moments of connection to the desert's familiar rhythms, and in those moments "her spirit soared" (Fink 223). In her textual exploration of the source of artistic creation, *Everyman's Genius* (1925), Austin explains that during this time, she sought to make these connections by turning to her own translation of a portion of the Navajo Nightway as she trudged along the congested thoroughfares of the city. For the Diné, the Nightway, as discussed in the previous chapter, is meant to break the path of an illness and set an individual and their larger community on a course toward spiritual harmony with the natural world (Bierhorst 286). Overwhelmed with the crush of the city, Austin chants to herself:

> As I walk .. as I walk..
> The universe .. is walking with me ..
> Beautifully .. it walks before me ....
> Beautifully .. on every side ....
> As I walk .. I walk with beauty.
>
> (*Everyman's Genius* 223; punctuation in original)

She records that she turns to this invocation as a "release from obsessing preoccupations" and as a "rhythmic formula" intended to allow access to one's "deep-self" (222–23). Austin's use of the Nightway is clearly an act of cultural appropriation, on a par with her claiming in *The American Rhythm* that she had at times "succeeded in being an Indian" (41). Austin wrested the Nightway from its proper cultural context and in so doing emptied it of its traditional meaning.[20] For her part, Austin saw herself turning to a verse that sprang from the southwestern land where it originated, and by reciting it in the unlikely landscape of New York, she believed she could access the far-off deserts and the rhythms that reflected her own "deep-self." She recognized the Nightway's rhythmic healing properties, and combined with her own physical walking Austin sought access to the landscape line that she felt contributed to her own genius, an instinct she saw as "aris[ing] in the natural, aboriginal concern for the conscious unity of all phenomena" (*Earth Horizon* 367).

John P. O'Grady suggests that "we might be inclined to take...as a figure of speech" Austin's claim in *Earth Horizon* that "there is something in Mary which comes out of the land" (129). However, Austin's intense perception of the rhythmic presence of the land is evident even in her earliest writings. In a letter to a botanist friend, Austin writes, "I like to dive into the rhythmic stream like a fish into the gulf current and go where it takes me.... Then I like to repeat some of these experiences by writing books or poems about them" (qtd. in Stineman 127). The "rhythmic stream" is necessary to and generative of her "genius," her writing. Barad contends, "There is an important sense in which practices of knowing cannot be fully claimed as human practices, not simply because we use nonhuman elements in our practices, but because knowing is a matter of part of the world making itself intelligible to another part.... We do not obtain knowledge by standing outside of the world; we know because 'we' are *of* the world" ("Posthumanist Performativity" 147; emphasis in the original). Even though her prose reflects a polished and sophisticated understanding of English prosody, like the Walking Woman and Seyavi, Austin understood herself to be entering nature's agentic rhythms and writing from and through them.

Drawing on Euroamerican nature-writing conventions and Indigenous traditions, Austin sought to access and represent the rhythms of the material world in language while acknowledging that the land always exceeds language. She understood that the nonhuman world was agentic, that it created and contained its own meanings. Through walking, Austin made a bodily connection to the rhythms of the land and through this connection found inspiration. At the core of her writing, then, was not the individual genius of the writer, but rather the agentic power of the desert. Walking away from her expected roles of wife and mother, Austin looked to the natural world for a new pattern for living, a pattern that blended body, mind, language, and land into a polyrhythmic synchronization that allowed for a deeper understanding of self, land, and the sacred.

NOTES

1. William Scheick notes that *The Land of Little Rain* "apparently did not require inordinate attention to style," taking at face value Austin's claim that "nothing was further from [her] mind when writing" (37). Considering the highly structured nature of the text, this claim seems to me to be highly suspect.

2. In 1871 Emerson visited Muir in Yosemite. Emerson brought with him a group of eastern friends who "thought that Muir was an amusing figure, perhaps slightly laughable" (M. Cohen 132). Michael Cohen writes that if Muir

had "hoped that Yosemite would be enough to transform this sophisticated group, he was shocked to discover how little Nature affected them. 'I felt lonely, so sure had I been that Emerson of all men would be the quickest to see the mountains and sing them,' he said later" (132).

3. When Muir set out on a cross-country walk that would take him to the Florida coast—his first extended immersion in more-than-human nature—he packed his bag with a plant press to preserve specimens, Milton's *Paradise Lost*, a copy of the New Testament, a volume of Robert Burns's poetry, and his journal (Buske 4).

4. For discussions of Austin's writing in relation to the transcendentalists, see Blackbird and Nelson; Buell; McKusick; O'Grady; Paes de Barros; and Toohey.

5. Benay Blend asserts that while Austin was not the only woman writing about nature in the late nineteenth and early twentieth centuries, "early female nature writers generally placed familial responsibility before their writing," thereby "uph[olding] orthodox patterns of home and family" (32).

6. Rob Nixon cautions us to read Austin's engagement with the desert with a recognition of the ways such an engagement "has all too often morphed into hostility toward displaced people. Edward Abbey's rants against Mexican immigrants, Mary Austin's anti-Semitism, and the Sierra Club's disastrous referendum on zero immigration all evidence a xenophobic strain running through American ethics-of-place environmentalism" (239).

7. In *The American Rhythm*, Austin singles out Walt Whitman, a fellow walker, as an exception. Whitman, she contends, "had been so shaped to the wilderness track that his every public utterance, his homely anecdotes, even, were haunted by its rhythms" (15). However, while she acknowledges Whitman's sensitivity to the American land and concedes that his "was the first clear and self-recognizing song of the road," she also comments that he regulated his verse to the "rutted pioneer track" and that "his rhythms, more often than not, are mere unpatterned noises of the street" (17).

8. In *West of the Border*, Noreen Grover Lape argues that while Austin may occasionally "f[all] prey to this evolutionary, hierarchizing tendency" to imagine Native Americans as less "advanced" on the evolutionary ladder (161), she eventually "arrives at a theory of cultural relativism that enables her to avoid the hierarchizing tendencies of the unilinear paradigm" (162).

9. Several critics have argued that despite her appropriation of Indigenous traditions, Austin saw value in Native American story and verse that her contemporaries did not. Dale Metcalfe argues that "literary critics embraced what came to be called modernism and were only mildly interested in Austin's theories about the process by which Native American chants worked" (66).

10. While Austin conflates the cultures of all of the Pueblo peoples around the Rio Grande, it is important to note that while Pueblo traditions share

some similarities, they are distinct groups with distinct cultural beliefs and ceremonies.

11. See, for example, Buell; Graulich; Hoyer; and Work.

12. Eighteen years later, Austin echoes this assertion in *The American Rhythm*, stressing the importance of "familiarity with the condition under which a land permits itself to be lived" (38).

13. Austin's "Squaw Gulch" seems to be a disguised or imaginary location; however, there are Squaw Gulches throughout the American West. For example, until very recently there were Squaw Gulches in Northern California, Oregon, Colorado, Arizona, and Montana. In the last twenty years or so, most of these places have been renamed in recognition of the term's offensive history.

14. In this tragic story, a miner made a great deal of money and returned to the East, leaving behind his pregnant Indigenous partner. She turned to alcohol in despair and was found by another miner, Jim Calkins, dying in a ravine with her newborn baby at her breast. After burying her, Calkins took the baby and walked back to Jimville. Later he returned to the newly named Squaw Gulch and discovered a rich vein of gold, which he considered his reward for his kindness (68).

15. The Treaty of Ruby Valley continues to be contested. The treaty was *not* a treaty of relinquishment or cession; indeed, the Western Shoshone have never signed such a treaty. However, the US government has claimed that because of development of the land (through ranching, the railroad, mines, and so on), the Western Shoshone title to the land has been "extinguished" (Newcomb).

16. It is worth noting here, too, her phrasing of *no man*. While she may be using *man* as a generic term for *human*, it also may be that she was indicating that men did not have the same connection to the land as women. Throughout her writing life, Austin created a series of "far-seeing desert women" whose wisdom is connected directly to "the land and the American Indians" (Graulich, "Walking Off" 274).

17. Although she is a Euroamerican wanderer (not unlike Austin herself), what makes the Walking Woman's desert wisdom of particular value, Austin contends, is that it is "as reliable as an Indian's" ("Walking Woman" 257). Throughout her writing, Austin presents the possibility of Euroamericans "becoming like . . . Indian[s]" (Viehmann 11). Although Austin understood herself to be celebrating Indigenous peoples through this transformation, in fact such an act of cultural appropriation displaces actual Native peoples, as "Indian nature [is] extracted and actual Indians [are] left behind" (Viehmann 13).

18. Melody Graulich points out that in *Earth Horizon*, Austin suggests that she, "like the Walking Woman, 'had begun by walking off an illness.' Thus the

West provides space for a new construction of womanhood" ("Walking Off" 268–69).

19. Austin's biographer Augusta Fink references Austin's "encounter with the Walking Woman" during the time she spent on the Tejon Ranch (48).

20. Austin's appropriation of the Nightway could be seen as not simply disrespectful but actually dangerous. John Bierhorst writes that "according to the fundamental principle of incantatory medicine, the chant can maim as well as cure. An improper attitude or simply spiritual weakness on the part of the recipient may cause the remedy to backfire" (288).

4

Crossing the Storied Desert

Bodies on the Border in Luis Alberto Urrea's *The Devil's Highway*

ON MAY 19, 2001, twenty-nine Mexican men walked into a stretch of the Sonoran Desert known as the Devil's Highway. They included twenty-six border crossers and three guides, or coyotes. Some walked with friends, uncles, brothers, fathers, and sons. Some walked alone. Most of the men were from Veracruz, where the years preceding the journey had been difficult, as costs increased and employment opportunities decreased. Veracruz is a verdant, humid state lapped by the waters of the Gulf of Mexico. Most of the men had never seen the desert and could not have imagined let alone understood and prepared for the aridity and heat. By the time border agents from Wellton, Arizona, found them, twelve were suffering from severe hyperthermia, fourteen were dead, and three more had vanished into the desert, never to be heard from again.

In *The Devil's Highway: A True Story*, Luis Alberto Urrea crafts a narrative of the men's journey with help from newspaper accounts, sheriff reports, taped interrogations and confessions, testimonies, trial documents, letters, and interviews. The resulting text combines aspects of reportage and literature, "factual" report and imagined story. Urrea describes the men's walk by drawing on the long history of the border, the story of Aztlán, and the Mexican tradition of *peregrinación*; however, the unrelenting material experience of the crossing continually intrudes into the narrative. Combined with the material effects of political and economic contexts, the agential power of the desert writes the experiences of the men, rather than their experiences giving meaning to the land. The deadly walk across the border becomes a form of translation, a narration of the material desert and the intra-action of nonhuman and human in this space. The stories that emerge trace the lives of Chicanx along the US-Mexico border.[1]

Like Mary Austin's Owens and San Joaquin Valleys, the region of the Devil's Highway is marked with ancient paths determined by water and commerce. Located in the borderlands of the Arizona desert west of Ajo and east of Wellton, the Devil's Highway lies in the traditional homelands of the Hía Ced O'odham (or Sand Papago).[2] Before and in the early years following contact with the Spanish, the Hía Ced O'odham traced the area with desert paths, leading from water hole to water hole. The area was also inscribed by a complex web of trade routes connecting Indigenous peoples throughout North and South Americas and allowing for the diffusion of goods such as copper, shell, turquoise, salt, seeds, gold, and animal hides, as well as ideas, songs, inventions, and innovations.[3] With the arrival of the Spanish, the trade routes and the trails of the Hía Ced O'odham were overlaid by a different history of colonization, migration, and death. Crossed in 1540 by conquistador Melchior Díaz, the Devil's Highway was traversed by a long succession of Spanish explorers and missionaries and later by American pioneers, settlers, and railroad workers. In the nineteenth century, thousands of forty-niners walked the Devil's Highway as they made their way from Mexico to the goldfields of California, and in the middle of the twentieth century the United States imported nearly two million Mexican farmworkers as part of the bracero program (D. Cohen 2). When that program was terminated in 1964, undocumented Mexican migrants desperate for work risked apprehension, deportation, and death along the same stretch of desert (Annerino 10).

In the past fifty years the US-Mexico border has been militarized, pushing migration into ever more dangerous desert landscapes. Patricia Price argues that as border checkpoints and the areas around them have become increasingly "brightened [and] muscle-bound . . . a growing number of would-be migrants prefer to risk the long trek through the desert and arid mountains of south central California through to rural Arizona, or cross the Rio Grande and hike for miles through the desolate South Texan brush land" (115). Similarly, Wayne A. Cornelius asserts that an "indisputable consequence" of the increased attention to concentrated ports of entry such as El Paso and San Diego "has been the spatial redistribution of illegal entry attempts." Since 1994, he contends, "the share of apprehensions occurring in California and Texas, where most of the new Border Patrol resources have been deployed, has dropped, while the percentage of apprehensions occurring in Arizona has soared" (667). He continues, "Another consequence of concentrated border enforcement has been a sharp increase in the number of migrants who die trying to gain entry" (669). In other words, in their attempts to avoid border checkpoints, migrants have sought the less patrolled areas, which are often the least populated with the least access to water, leading to tragic consequences.

Establishing a fixed boundary line between the United States and Mexico not only altered the course of migrants, but also imposed a separation between nations, communities, and families that disrupted a long history of freedom of movement. In "The Chicano Homeland," John Chávez argues, "Because of Mexico's prior possession of the Southwest, Chicanos consider themselves indigenous to the region. Their claims are supported by the fact that their [Spanish] ancestors not only explored and settled parts of the Southwest as early as the sixteenth century, but thousands of years earlier [their Indigenous ancestors] permanently occupied the region or migrated through it on their way south" (11). Contemporary debates about creating a wall to prevent migrants from crossing the border without documentation must be understood within this longer history. Movement through the desert borderlands has "taken place over centuries from pre-Columbian times and persists to the present" (McKenna 10). Chicana theorist Gloria Anzaldúa writes that the Chicanx and Mexican "tradition of migration, a tradition of long walks," is part of "*la migración de los pueblos mexicanos*, the return odyssey to the historical/mythological Aztlán. This time, the traffic is from south to north" (11; emphasis in the original). As the constructed and patrolled contemporary border forces migrants into the desert, they turn to ancient footpaths etched into the earth by generations of walkers, creating links among contemporary border crossings, the larger history of Chicanx and Mexican migration, and the legend of the Aztecs' migration from Aztlán to Tenochtitlán.

Because of the palimpsestic layering of movement in the borderlands over centuries, "crossing the border" suggests a rich myriad of metaphorical meanings. In contemporary Chicanx studies critics variously discuss the borders of sexual identity, gender roles, language, complicated ethnic and cultural sources, and religious traditions. These symbolic borders separate peoples, disciplines, nations, languages, and ideas. In his book, Urrea notes that the Devil's Highway provides American writers with a "great metaphor for the horrors of the trail" (31). Indeed, Urrea uses metaphor throughout his text; however, he persistently returns to the material experience of the migrants. He embeds the specific story of the twenty-six men (often referred to as the Wellton 26 or the Yuma 14, for the fourteen who died) who attempted to cross the Devil's Highway in 2001 in the complicated contexts of the US-Mexico border, highlighting the material, cultural, political, and economic histories of the region.[4] As Urrea's text repeatedly reminds us, when the twenty-six walkers crossed the invisible borderline they were doing more than entering a vast complex of metaphors: they were risking—and in some cases losing—their lives. The question of the significance of bodily experience ceases to be ambiguous. In order to access the physicality of walking, Urrea's narrative is caught in multiple contextual webs and ways of representing material movement through a material world. Paradoxically, in order to access the material, Urrea turns repeatedly to the metaphoric, emphasizing the men's trans-corporeality, their intermeshment with Christian stories, Indigenous histories, and economic contexts.

WALKING IN CHICANX AND MEXICAN CULTURES

Movement and walking suffuse Mexican and Chicanx histories and stories. From the trade routes walked by Indigenous ancestors prior to contact to the violent incursions of the conquistadores and Catholic missionaries to the border crossings of migrant workers, the deadly Sonoran Desert has borne the imprints of millions of footsteps. How that walking is understood and characterized can be, perhaps, most productively described through three interlocking frameworks: pilgrimage, Aztlán, and migration.

In many of his writings and speeches, iconic Chicano movement leader César Chávez highlights these three types of walking, linking them to contemporary social protest.[5] On March 17, 1966, thirty-five years before the Wellton 26 walked into the Sonoran Desert, Chávez led a group of striking grape workers on a three-hundred-mile protest march from Delano, California, to the state capitol in Sacramento. The marchers trudged past vast agricultural fields day after day, harassed by farm owners and detractors. Their goal was communal: to rectify the injustices faced daily by Mexican

American farmworkers. As one part of the larger Chicano movement, the march to Sacramento was considered by César Chávez to be part of the Mexican tradition of *peregrinación*, or pilgrimage. Articulating the significance of the march, Chávez writes, "In the 'March from Delano to Sacramento' there is a meeting of cultures and traditions; the centuries-old religious tradition of Spanish culture conjoins with the very contemporary cultural syndromes of 'demonstration' springing from the spontaneity of the poor, the downtrodden, the rejected, the discriminated-against baring visibly their need and demand for equality and freedom" (15). Chávez suggests that walking in Chicanx and Mexican cultures is intimately linked to religion, culture, and economic injustices. When the marchers walked toward Sacramento, they did so with a clear understanding of themselves as Mexican American, tied to particular religious and cultural traditions, homelands, and economic realities.

Chávez links the religious dimension of the march to the living tradition of pilgrimage in Mexican culture that is manifest in visits to major Mexican shrines. He writes that these trips are "made with sacrifice and hardship as an expression of penance and of commitment... [by pilgrims who] may have long since walked-out the pieces of rubber tire that once served them as soles, and many of whom will walk on their knees the last mile or so of the pilgrimage." Chávez specifically connects the march to Sacramento to the Lenten penitential processions found throughout "the Spanish speaking world." The penitents "march through the streets, often in sack cloth and ashes, some even carrying crosses as a sign of penance for their sins, and as a plea for the mercy of God" (15). What becomes clear through Chávez's descriptions of pilgrimage is the intensely material nature of the experience. In order to attain a kind of religious clarity and devotion, pilgrimage demands a physical ordeal.

Even the liminality so often linked with pilgrimage and understood as distinct from the physical plane is at its core material. Cultural anthropologists Victor Turner and Edith Turner argue that pilgrims enter a liminal space through walking, a space where they are "ambiguous, for they pass through a cultural realm that has few attributes of the past or coming state" (249). As such, the pilgrims are in a "no-place and no-time that resists classification" (250). The "no-place and no-time" of the pilgrimage create a sense of continuity between current and past pilgrimages so that with each step, the marcher-pilgrim is tied to the holiness of this particular walk as well as the holiness of the longer history of pilgrimage. The sense of "no-time" paradoxically connects the pilgrim to past pilgrimages, to history and specific places. Martin Robinson writes that "for most [pilgrims]… the sense of treading ground made holy by past events is crucial…. [T]he pilgrims become one with those who have gone before" (qtd. in Fox 250). In this way, pilgrimage is both a liminal experience outside of the prosaic world and clearly and closely connected to the material land.

Pilgrimage in Mexican and Chicanx culture has clear links to Christian traditions; however, it is also tied to much older stories and traditions. Turner and Turner look to ancient Christianity to find the deep roots of pilgrimage in Mexican culture, contending that "pilgrimage *lives* in Mexico…. [I]t is possible to trace genetic links back through Spanish religious culture into the far past of Judeo-Christian tradition" (40–41; emphasis in the original). Anzaldúa, while acknowledging the Catholic influences on Mexican culture, argues that the tradition of "long walks" precedes contact with Christianity. She connects this tradition to ideas about Aztlán by relating the contested theory that "during the original peopling of the Americas, the first inhabitants migrated across the Bering Straits and walked south across the continent." She argues that "in the Southwest United States archeologists have found 20,000-year-old campsites of the Indians who migrated through, or permanently occupied, the Southwest. Aztlán—land of the herons, land of whiteness, the Edenic place of origin of the Azteca" (4). While retaining Christian imagery through her reference to Eden, Anzaldúa interprets the archaeological record to support the much older framework of Aztlán and the importance of north-to-south migration. John Chávez, while not extending his line quite so far into the past, similarly asserts that "the Mexican view of the [Southwest], as far back as the sixteenth century Aztec chronicles, has been focused on the feature of the homeland" (14).[6] As an interpretive scaffold, Aztlán ties together story, movement, and land, emphasizing the geographical materiality of homeland as well as operating as an origin myth for modern Chicanx.

Aztlán's symbolic power lies in combining ancient and still developing legends with apparent geographical fixity. The materiality of Aztlán serves to legitimize a clearly utopian vision of "a paradisiacal region where injustice, evil, sickness, old age, poverty, and misery do not exist" (Leal 8). In this guise, Aztlán unites Chicanx through the memory of a mythologized past and an idealized future that are free from the prejudice and hardships of the present. The power of such an imagining is underscored with the claim of geographic specificity.[7] In her analysis of the symbolic power of Aztlán, Mary Pat Brady explains this relationship between symbol and material as an "alternative cartographic practice in contrapuntal challenge to dominant representations of space" (139). Aztlán, she argues, "almost automatically poses a challenge to Manifest Destiny by suggesting an alternative destiny" (146). While Manifest Destiny asserts the supposedly God-given directive that Euroamericans extend their authority from the Atlantic to Pacific, Aztlán both reorients movement from an east-west to a north-south axis and stresses prior human claims on the land. The emphasis in this way of framing Aztlán is on the symbolic conceptualization of place in relationship to human habitation and use.

Aztlán, then, is frequently understood in terms of its symbolic power, the ways it offers alternative methods for representing and interpreting place and identity. Such a view of Aztlán privileges the idea over the material, the interpretation over the physical engagement with place. However, insofar as Aztlán is connected with the American Southwest, the intra-action among land, nonhuman, and human beings precedes the modern interpretation of Aztlán. Anzaldúa recognizes that Aztlán is fundamentally about movement, and she links it to the Chicanx "tradition of migration, a tradition of long walks" (11). As a story, Aztlán carries with it potent symbols and meanings, tying people to place. Underpinning those meanings are the material land itself and the rhythm of footsteps crossing temporal and national borders.

The modern definition of Aztlán is intimately tied to the movement of migrant workers, returning to Aztlán from the South because of economic pressures. As a "primary metaphor" for Mexican American experience (McKenna 9), the figure of the migrant is a potent symbol of a long history of living and laboring in the margins, a history of lacking a place, both in the sense of "home" and in the sense of membership in US society. However, the people crossing the US-Mexico border fracture symbolic registers and must be understood materially. Not unlike traditional Diné peoples or the Shoshone and Paiute in Mary Austin's *The Land of Little Rain*, migrant border crossers often follow the seasonally determined harvest, yet this movement is constrained by economic, political, and social realities that make migrant work a necessity. Maria Antònia Oliver-Rotger explains that the migrants' movement "back and forth from the US to Mexico" is "driven by the transnational labor circuit that shapes their lives" (185). The bodily experience of the border crossers is established by the materiality of economic and political forces that cannot be limited to symbolic meanings.

While symbolic meanings provide useful frameworks for understanding the significance of movement and walking in Chicanx literature, to understand the border *only* as metaphor risks missing the material and agential nature of the desert and the ways the movement in the borderlands is ultimately materially determined. Luis Leal argues, "Chicano literary symbolism cannot be separated from Chicano cultural background.... The social and literary symbols... are the same" (6). And certainly *peregrinación*, Aztlán, and migrant workers are potent symbols that call to mind complex meanings. Yet descriptions of physical walking play a crucial role in narratives of Chicanx experience. They exceed the symbolic and they prompt readers to situate these narratives in the complex cultural history of Mexicans and Mexican Americans. In particular, these histories form an important structure for reading narratives of the US-Mexico border, an area with a long and complex history of walking.

In telling the story of the Wellton 26, Urrea draws on these contexts and all of their symbolic power; however, he also stresses the materiality of their journey. The materiality of the walkers' experience is written on the land in the trails, paths, and even mummified corpses the desert preserves. As the men trudge through the desert, the stories of Catholic saints and Aztec homelands may give shape to their experience, but those stories cannot elide the material reality of their failing bodies. As desert walkers, their trans-corporeality—"in which the human is always intermeshed with the more-than-human world" (Alaimo, *Bodily Natures* 2)—cannot be ignored. Urrea presents the walkers' bodies as intimately entangled with the material world, "networks that are simultaneously economic, political, cultural, scientific, and substantial" (Alaimo, *Bodily Natures* 20). In other words, their trans-corporeality, their intermeshment and intra-action with the material world, is layered with the economic and political realities that have pushed them into the desert as well as the cultural contexts through which they interpret the desert.

WALKING IN THE BORDERLANDS IN *THE DEVIL'S HIGHWAY*

In *The Devil's Highway*, walking in the scorching desert functions as the central trope of the text. Throughout his descriptions of the walkers' deadly journey and the history and stories of the border, Urrea repeatedly directs his readers' attention to movement and walking. From the structure and language of the text, to the immigrants' crossing, to the Border Patrol's tracking, the text is filled with the movement of the footfall. While walking serves a symbolic function in defining the stories of the land, the materiality of movement across the desert is not a secondary consideration. Physically walking bodies are in the primary position. The primacy of these walking bodies highlights human and nonhuman intra-action and controls the very language and stories through which the desert is delineated. Urrea's text takes readers through multiple webbings and maps, as the physical act of walking in the material land is contextualized through history and story, concrete experience and symbolic image.

In telling the story of the men's journey, Urrea arranges his text into chapters whose titles often point to physical movement. In chapter titles such as "Jesús Walks Among Us," "El Guía" (The Guide), and "The Long Walk," Urrea accentuates the physical and metaphoric dimensions of walking that permeate the text. Through these titles Urrea prepares his readers to understand walking in religious and historical terms. He also gestures toward both physical and metaphorical interpretations, such as the chapter title "Bad Step at Bluebird," which marks both the turning point in the narrative as well as a literal missed step or wrong turn at Bluebird Pass. By including references to walking in the structure of the text, Urrea alerts his readers to the importance of movement and the material land in the story of the men. Walking, in other words, is not incidental to the experience of the border crossers; rather, it operates on multiple levels and provides a trope through which to read border crossing.

Walking extends into the structure and language of the text beyond the chapter titles, as Urrea incorporates diction that stresses the physical movement of the men. For example, he chooses the term *the walkers* to identify the Wellton 26. Before settling on this identification, Urrea notes other terms used to describe border crossers: "illegals, or smugglers, or narco mules," "wets," and "'tonks'... a name based on the stark sound of a flashlight breaking over a human head" (15–16). In the slang of the border, guides call their charges "*pollos*," or chickens, though, as Urrea observes, "the [Spanish] word for 'chicken' is *gallina*. '*Pollo*' is usually reserved for something else. A *pollo*, as in *arroz con pollo*, has been cooked" (60). These terms serve to dehumanize the migrants; the act of crossing the border is minimized to the activity of criminals or the nonhuman. A "*pollo*" or a "tonk" is not an individual with complicated reasons for wanting or needing to cross the border; it is not a person. After identifying these negative terms, Urrea selects "walkers" as his label for border crossers in general and the group of men walking across the border in May 2001 in particular. Urrea's term reduces identity to one activity, yet "walkers" retain agency; "walkers" remain active and engaged. In contrast with "pilgrim" or "migrant," which limit movement to religious or economic motivations respectively, a "walker" moves their body across space, driven by a multiplicity of potential motivations. Thus, while the term seems to limit complex human identities to one action, at the same time it expands the possible ways that identity is understood.

Urrea further draws readers' attention to the physical experience of the walkers by unexpectedly using poetic structures to present the desert not as abstracted, discursive "borderlands" but as site specific and agonizingly material. Underscoring the agential power of the desert, Urrea organizes the testimony of one of the twelve survivors, Nahum Landa Ortiz, as what he terms "modern poetry" (167). Appearing at the end of a chapter titled "The Trees and the Sun," which chronicles the deaths of fourteen walkers, Ortiz's account represents the bodily reality of his experience:

> By Monday we were all dead.
> I was hiding under that tree.
> Out there, I saw people in despair.
> I saw them without water.
> I don't know why I survived.
> Maybe it's a miracle.
> Some of them just died of desperation.
> Some of them went insane.
> Some of them lost their minds.

> You could hear them screaming.
> Some fell all alone.
> . . . .
> I was going to die this morning. (168)

Ortiz's statement is spare and the language clipped and direct. Each sentence, each line, adds another image, and the bluntness of the expression underscores the horror of Ortiz's memories. From a certain perspective, Urrea's decision to present Ortiz's statement as free verse seems to stage the walker's descent into hyperthermia as bleakly aestheticized. Death, in other words, appears abstracted, an object of contemplation. In particular, the last line of the "poem" gives the reader a kind of delicious shiver because it remains safely in the imagined and avoided past: "I was going to die this morning." However, Ortiz's testimony ends a chapter filled with brutal accounts of death and dying, such as the unnamed walker who "went crazy and started jumping up and down . . . screaming, 'Mama! Mama! I don't want to die!'" (166), and the walker who tore his shirt off and tried to bury himself: "He managed to get the top half of his torso buried in the ground. The relentless heat baked him, literally cooking him in the ground. His face bloated and came loose from the bones, tender as barbecued pork" (166). Following such unflinching and unaestheticized descriptions, Ortiz's poem, rather than appearing as a beautiful reflection, instead emphasizes the raw emotion of his memory and the harsh reality of his physical experience. Readers are allowed to glimpse a hint of beauty and transcendence, but are not allowed to escape the brutality of desert deaths. For example, by breaking off the simple line "Some fell all alone" from a series of more explicit images of the men raving in the desert, Urrea encourages his readers to contemplate the horror and isolation of the men and to remember the dead who remain unnamed and unclaimed.[8] While Urrea's text addresses the deeply flawed policies and debates around the border from a political and ethical perspective, the text's central concern is encouraging readers to grasp the material impact of these policies through inhabiting the lived experience of particular border crossers.

Throughout *The Devil's Highway*, Urrea employs metaphor, imagery, and historical and cultural allusions to encourage his readers to understand or "read" the land in a materialist way. As a writer he is constrained by discursive practices in his representation of the men's material bodies and the material desert they walk across. As Christopher Tilley points out, "Language is, in part, a metaphorical construction of the world" (xiv), and therefore any attempt to convey the materiality of the world in language must always rely to some degree on metaphor. Urrea grapples with this complication by continually allowing the desert to intrude into the text in ways that resist linguistic representation. He describes the "terrible landscape… a vast trickery of sand" that refuses containment in language (4). Urrea describes the walkers' testimony of their experience as narratives that "wander like they wandered, their minds unable to process the details of their torments" (134). Karen Barad articulates a way of theorizing the relationship between representation and materiality that recognizes their dependency on one another in the act of becoming. "Discursive practices and material phenomena do not stand in a relationship of externality to one another," she writes. "Rather, the material and the discursive are mutually implicated in the dynamics of intra-activity.… The relationship between the material and the discursive is one of mutual entailment" ("Posthumanist Performativity" 140). In writing about the experience of the Wellton 26, Urrea presents readers with a text that relies on both literary artifice and the fissures that emerge when material reality cannot be reduced to linguistic representation. As a result, the text is at once aestheticizing and materializing and attempts to move readers closer to the bodies, places, and experiences he describes.

BODILY SUFFERING IN THE MATERIAL DESERT

In his retelling of their excruciatingly physical walking, Urrea highlights the trans-corporeality of the walkers, "the time-space where human corporeality, in all its material fleshiness, is inseparable from 'nature' or 'environment'" (Alaimo, "Trans-corporeal" 238). The walkers' physical pain threatens to arrest their progress, to stop them from finding help and salvation. Urrea's text continually reminds readers of the agential power of the burning desert. In the desert, he writes, "heat sizzled at the edges of things, then slammed into them, instant and profound" (117). Exacerbating the overwhelming heat, "Survivors report that about fifteen of the men had thorns in their feet. They had trouble walking, and they were having trouble dealing with the pain of their injuries" (163). Yet they have to keep going forward: "they walked" (164). The desert, far from a purely metaphoric border, insists on telling its own story. As Barad argues, "We are not outside observers of the world. Neither are we simply located at particular places *in* the world; rather, we are part *of* the world in its ongoing intra-activity" (*Meeting* 184; emphasis in the original). The heat of the desert and the thorns of desert plants force the walkers to confront their intermeshment in the desert. The walkers' experience in the desert is determined and shaped by the desert materially asserting itself.

In unrelenting prose, Urrea chronicles the clinical stages of hyperthermia: "Heat Stress, Heat Fatigue, Heat Syncope, Heat Cramps, Heat Exhaustion, and Heat Stroke" (120). The first stage, entered early on when the walkers still have some water with them and still believe that they are within hours of Ajo, involves feeling "tired, or even dizzy, from walking in the heat…the funny stumbling" (121). As the men move through the stages, their suffering becomes more pronounced. By the time the walkers reach the fourth stage, heat cramps, walking becomes more and more difficult as "muscle cramps kick in. Your legs suddenly ache. You get clumsy. You tumble" (123). Urrea describes the fifth stage, heat exhaustion, through both real and metaphorical images of walking. The walkers continue to literally "fall on the burning ground" while they are metaphorically on the verge of another border crossing, an "abyss" where with "one more step… you cannot return" (125). By the time the walkers reach the final stage, heat stroke, dehydration has reduced the walkers' "inner streams to sluggish mudholes," and they are experiencing "a core meltdown" (128). Urrea's description of heat stroke is unflinching:

> Some walkers at this point strip nude.… [T]he walkers couldn't stand their nerve-endings being chaffed by their clothes.… Once they're naked, they're surely hallucinating. They dig burrows in the soil, apparently thinking they'll escape the sun. Once underground, of course, they bake like a pig at a luau. Some dive into sand, thinking it's water, and they swim in it until they pass out. They choke to death, their throats filled with rocks and dirt.… [Their] muscles, lacking water, feed on themselves. They break down and start to rot.… The system closes down in a series. Your kidneys, your bladder, your heart. They jam shut. Stop. Your brain sparks. Out. You're gone. (128–29)

In this description, as in several others, Urrea slips from third person to second person, encouraging his readers to imagine themselves lost in the desert; the pain and misery of the men's bodies breaking down are rendered clearly and personally for readers, "*your* kidneys, *your* bladder, *your* heart… *[y]our* brain" (emphasis added). His prose becomes progressively bleak as he describes the men as first delirious, then as cooking and rotting meat, and finally as misfiring biological machines. The desert is acting on their bodies, denying them autonomy and bodily integrity and taking away their ultimate agency—life. Walking in the desert cannot be understood here only in terms of metaphor and symbol. The entanglements between reader's body and walker's body and between human body and nonhuman desert environment mercilessly hold the focus on material experience.

As the walkers' bodies deteriorate under the searing desert sun, Urrea switches back to third-person descriptions in depicting the liminality of the men on the border between nations and between life and death, dream and reality. Describing the fifth day of their journey, as many of the walkers were already closing in on heat stroke, Urrea writes that "as they walked, they started to lose themselves. Their accounts…fade into a strange twilight of pain" (108). Drawing together linguistic and bodily experience, Urrea writes of the stage "heat syncope," "*Syncope* is a noun that denotes *contradiction*: in a literary sense, you shorten a word by chopping out letters. Never = ne'er. Ever = e'er. Desolation has begun to edit you. Erase you" (123; emphasis in the original). In this disoriented state, the narratives tell confused stories about teetering on the margins of life and death: "Men stumbled away toward illusions in the brutal light. Men thought they were home, walking into their front doors, hugging their wives, making love. Still, they walked. Men were swimming. Men were killing Mendez [their guide who had abandoned them]. Men were on the beach, collecting shells and watching their children splash…. And they walked" (159). Dazed and addled by the heat, the men imagine themselves walking and moving in different circumstances, all of which highlight borders or limens. The men walk through their front doors, crossing the divide between outside and inside, between the external world and "home." They stand on the beach and look toward the waves, on the border between land and sea. They imagine killing Mendez, pushing him over the border between life and death. Turner and Turner write that as a "threshold" and "ambiguous" state, liminality "has frequently been likened to death; to being in the womb; to invisibility, darkness...and the wilderness" (249). Religious pilgrims attempt to walk into an experience of liminality; their goal is to attain an altered state, a sense of communion with God. The walkers crossing the US-Mexico border experience a similar state, but for them their nearness to death is literal, and many of them actually cross over that threshold and cannot return home at the end of their journey. The almost merciful hallucinations they experience are punctuated by the repeated phrase "they walked." They are in between, neither fully in the realm of the illusion nor fully in the realm of the real. They are on the line, on the limen, yet always moving.

The place of liminality, of being betwixt and between, is described by Turner and Turner as being in a "cultural realm that has few or none of the attributes of the past or coming state" (249). However, the liminality that the walkers experience in Urrea's text is not only cultural but also intensely physical. The borders they are experiencing—between nations, between reality and dream, between life and death—are created by their material circumstances. Barad contends, "There is an important sense in which practices of knowing cannot fully be claimed as human practices, not simply because we use nonhuman elements in our practices but because knowing is a matter of part of the world making itself intelligible to another part" (*Meeting* 185). The brutality of the desert has an agential capacity that intra-acts with the human in the process of knowing or of making meaning. Urrea writes, "The desert, out of focus and suddenly terribly sharp, burst white and yellow in their eyes. It tilted. Elongated. It was an impossible angle! It tipped toward the sun, and if they didn't crawl, they would slide right off it and fall forever. It made noise: THERE WERE ENGINES BENEATH THE DESERT" (159). The desert threatens the walkers, imperils their bodies in a way that they struggle to comprehend. As the desert veers in and out of focus and bucks under the walkers' feet, Urrea breaks into the terror of the unfathomable desert with metaphor in an effort to bridge the space between metaphoric and material. In capitalized letters he imposes a decidedly human image of engines, attempting to create order and clear a place for the human in the nonhuman desert. Yet the use of capitalized letters points to the desperation of the writer to foist discursive practices onto the nonhuman and the inability of those practices to contain and translate the agential capacity of the desert. Matter informs metaphor and meaning; it is agential, outside of or before the discursive scaffoldings that are created to explain it.

PEREGRINACIÓN AS SYMBOL AND EXPERIENCE

In Urrea's text both the walkers and the text itself reach toward images of *peregrinación* as a familiar scaffolding within which to contextualize and manage the terrifyingly physical experience of the desert. The material borderlands are matched with the metaphoric liminality of Christian pilgrimage. The walkers' main guide, or coyote, is often referred to as "Mendez," an alias he provides them, though Urrea discloses that his true name is Jesús Antonio Lopez Ramos. Urrea switches between referring to the guide as Mendez and Jesús, sometimes dropping the accent. When he calls him "Jesús" or "Jesus," he often includes religious references, reinforcing the Christian imagery of the walkers following Jesus into the wilderness. For example, in discussing Jesús and his boss, Don Moises, Urrea comments, "Jesus led the walkers gathered by Moses into the desert called Desolation. Jesus has the inevitable birthday of December 25" (68). Urrea ties the walking of the men in the Sonoran Desert to Moses and the Hebrews' forty-year exile in the deserts of Sinai and Jesus's forty-day fast in the Judean Desert. These stories, central to Christian faith, would have been familiar to the walkers, and Urrea's allusion to them suggests an attempt to fit the men's desperate trek to stories of the journey to the Promised Land and victory over temptation by the devil.

Aligning Moises and Jesús with Moses and Jesus points in two directions at once: On the one hand, the names suggest an affiliation, the possibility that like the Puritans imagined themselves to be, the walkers are a kind of warped version of the Hebrews trying to reach the Holy Land. On the other hand, Moises and Jesús are quite clearly characterized as part of the larger machinery of coyotes and traffickers who prey on poor people who are desperate to cross the border, suggesting that the reference to Moses and Jesus should be read as ironic. What is clear from either reading is that for fourteen of the walkers, there is no salvation at the end of their desert sojourn. They do not reach the Promised Land or defeat the devil. The Devil's Highway wins.

Urrea further emphasizes the walkers' Catholic framework in his descriptions of the walkers praying when they begin to enter heat exhaustion and then heat stroke. Their prayers indicate an attempt to connect to the sacred through the communal devotions that link them to the rituals and traditions of their families and communities as well as a drive to layer their walk with meaning beyond economic necessity. They declare the Apostle's Creed, part of the Catholic catechism: "I believe in God the father, creator of heaven and earth" (159).[9] And they recite part of the Hail Mary, a traditional prayer that forms the basis of the Rosary, significantly, a prayer linked with a physical object: "Blessed Mary, Mother of God, pray for us sinners now and in the hour of our death, amen" (160).[10] In their desperation, the walkers turn to their faith through familiar prayers they would have learned as children. Like pilgrims, they recite these prayers as they stumble forward, connecting sacred with material and seeking strength to continue walking.

While one of the goals of pilgrimage is to cultivate a sense of *communitas*, another central goal is individual "salvation or release from the sins and evil of the structural world in preparation for participation in an afterlife of pure bliss." Pilgrimage, Turner and Turner argue, involves "the inward movement of the heart" (8). In her narrative about an annual pilgrimage to Chimayó, New Mexico, with a group of Chicana Catholics, Paula Elizabeth Holmes-Rodman writes about the pilgrims carrying rosaries and reciting prayers as they walk. When she is having a particularly difficult time walking, one of her fellow pilgrims asks her, "Would you like to carry my rosary for a while? It has been in my family for generations. There's a lot of beautiful prayers and stories on it" (40). The pilgrim hands Holmes-Rodman a rosary, a physical manifestation of prayer where each bead represents a separate supplication. The materiality of the rosary links the physicality of walking with ritualized and familiar prayer. The rosary and its attendant prayers provide the pilgrims with a sense of the sacred and a sense of physical connection across time to other pilgrims. In a similar fashion, the walkers in Urrea's text turn toward traditional prayer at moments of severe physical hardship, seeking a familiar way of framing their experience.

The ritual prayer of pilgrimage is also invoked in Urrea's repeated allusions to the stations of the cross as he describes the walkers' entrance into the final stages of heat stroke. In three places in the text—the Border Patrol's "reading" of the last moments of an unnamed walker (113), the death of a walker named Edgar Martinez (165), and the near-death suffering of Jesús (170)—Urrea describes a walker falling three times before succumbing to heat stroke. With these descriptions, Urrea implicitly draws a connection between the walkers and Catholic pilgrims by alluding to the three times

Jesus fell on his way to Golgotha, commemorated in the stations of the cross. Turner and Turner identify following the path of Jesus as a key theme in Christian pilgrimage. Christian pilgrims, they argue, re-create "the paradigm of the *via crucis* [the stations of the cross], in which Jesus Christ voluntarily submitted his will to the will of God" (9–10). The stations of the cross, believed to have originated in the twelfth and thirteenth centuries with veterans of the Crusades, follow the story of the passion of Christ—the hours prior to and including the trial and Crucifixion of Jesus. Each station of the *via crucis* corresponds to an event in the story of Christ's passion, beginning with the Last Supper in Jerusalem and then following his journey to Gethsemane, his trial, and his walk carrying his own cross through the streets to Golgotha, the site of the Crucifixion.[11] The stations of the cross include Christ falling three times, just as Urrea imagines the unnamed walker, Edgar Martinez, and Jesús each falling three times in the moments before they lapse into comas and, for two of them, death. Urrea's description of Jesús's final moments of walking is particularly striking: "He started to crawl. He was on all fours, and sometimes he went on his knees like a religious penitent. The world of sin and race spin in flaming disks around his head. He fell. He rose. He lay. He crawled. He tried to rise. He sat down" (170). Not only does Jesús fall three times, mimicking the passion of Christ, but he is also described as "a religious penitent," his physical deterioration and inability to walk reframed as religious devotion. The links between pilgrimage and the stations of the cross encourage believers to physically experience Christ's final sufferings. The invocation of the stations of the cross at the moment of deepest crisis for the walkers underscores the agential power of the desert intermeshed with economic, cultural, and political networks to create experiences that the walkers must then interpret through their own, more familiar, stories.

AZTLÁN AND BORDER LEGENDS AS ALTERNATIVE WAYS OF KNOWING

If walking in the desert brings to mind Catholic traditions and biblical stories for the walkers, the starkness of the desert also encourages other stories. Urrea writes that Tohono O'odham poet Ofelia Zepeda "has pointed out that rosaries and Hail Marys don't work out here. 'You need a new kind of prayers,' she says, 'to negotiate this land'" (5–6). Ritualized Christian prayers, Zepeda suggests, are not equipped to handle the trails of the Sonoran Desert, trails that "have always" been traveled by "desert spirits of a dark and mysterious nature" (Urrea 5). If aligning themselves with pilgrims and Christian believers ties their walk to the history of Christian pilgrimage and the *via crucis*, walking in the borderlands also layers their walk with the journeys of Indigenous walkers and stories. They walk across a landscape etched with "ghost roads," paths made in recent decades by border crossers as well as paths that are "old beyond dating… [and] no one knows where they lead." The land retains the history of the area: "Footprints of long dead cowboys.… And beneath these, the prints of the phantom Hohokam themselves" (7). Along the way some of these paths are marked with "old rock piles in the shapes of arrows" that point "at a *tinaja* (water hole) among the crags" (7). The land is haunted by this long history, alive with threatening specters: "Mexico's oldest hoodoo, La Llorona" (11), "the dreaded Chupacabras (the Goat Sucker)" (6), and the Cabeza Prieta (a shining black skull with burning white eyes that emerges from the earth) have all been spotted in the region of the Devil's Highway (14).

The walkers enter into a landscape where the previous intra-action of human and nonhuman has created stories. Barad explains that "the relationship between the material and the discursive is one of mutual entailment. Neither is articulated/articulable in the absence of the other" ("Posthumanist Performativity" 140). In this meeting place between nonhuman desert and human being, stories of border ghosts arise; the ghosts serve as an expression of matter and meaning. The ghosts of the border perform paradoxical roles. On the one hand, their stories serve as a warning to the walkers, suggesting that the desert is deadly and can be home to no one. The desert, they tell the walkers, does not want them there. On the other hand, the presence of these same ghost stories reveals that humans have a long relationship with the border and that generations of walkers have passed through. Mary S. Vásquez calls these ghosts "those other border walkers, border crossers. They populate numerous texts of the Borderlands.… Ghosts of those who perished in the crossing. Ghosts of memory, caught in the barbed wire on the line. Ghosts of desire unmet, of aspirations left somewhere along the way. La Llorona, after all, still walks the *arroyos* of the Borderlands. She is a border walker, the ultimate migrant, for whom there can be no home at all" (190). La Llorona, the wailing woman of Chicanx and Mexican folklore, wanders arroyos and rivers at night, searching for the children she drowned in a jealous rage. "Mis hijos," she cries "My children." Parents in the Southwest warn their children not to stay out past dark for fear La Llorona will mistake them for her drowned children and carry them away. In a more sympathetic vein, Anzaldúa describes La Llorona's wailing as her "only means of protest" (21) and writes that as the "Daughter of Night," La Llorona is forever "traveling the dark terrains of the unknown searching for the lost parts of herself." Her crying, Anzaldúa continues, is for her lost children, all of "*los* Chicanos/*mexicanos*" (38). La Llorona's presence in Urrea's text complicates our reading of unnamed walkers calling out "Mama! Mama! I don't want to die!" and "Mother, save me!" (166). The walkers follow the footsteps of their ancestors through the borderlands—generations of mothers, fathers, and children. The ghosts are symbols, then, of the border's dual position as a landscape that is both wholly alien and intimately familiar.

Urrea highlights the colonial and precontact histories these stories evoke by including the song lyrics of "Stolen at Gunpoint," by Tijuana No!, a Mexican ska and punk band he asserts many of the walkers were familiar with:

> *California*
> *Stolen at gunpoint!*
> *Arizona*
> *Stolen at gunpoint!*
> *Texas*
> *Stolen at gunpoint!*
> *Nuevo México*
> *Stolen at gunpoint!*
> *El Alamo*
> *Stolen at gunpoint!*
> *Aztlán*
> *Stolen at gunpoint!*
> *Puerto Rico*
> *Stolen at gunpoint!*
> *América*
> *Stolen at gunpoint!*
> *We gonna get it back.* (76–77)

The song presents a truncated version of border history, focusing on the displacement of Indigenous peoples. Flooded with defiance, the song declares that Aztlán is the Chicanxs' rightful home. Urrea's inclusion of the song in the story of the Wellton 26 suggests that the coyotes and *pollos* may have seen themselves as "outlaw[s]," braving the "wicked Sonoran heat" to reclaim what is theirs: "Coyote-as-Che." From this angle, Urrea suggests that the walkers are retracing the footsteps of the Aztecs who "walked south, out of the deserts on their way to what would become Mexico City. They apparently walked across the Devil's Highway on their way home" (77). Aztlán provides an alternative pilgrimage, one more closely linked to the desert landscape than the rosaries and Hail Marys Zepeda finds lacking. The Holy Land hinted at through references to Moses, Jesus, and Catholic prayer is realigned as the lost homeland, a place whose materiality has been obscured by border stories and legends.

READING AND WRITING THE LAND

Urrea reveals the materiality of the Sonoran Desert through the seemingly abstract metaphors and stories of the border. Aztlán, *peregrinación*, ghosts, the history and violence of the border—all of these have left their imprints on the land. While Mary Pat Brady contends that "no place exists apart from the social interactions that construct it or the discursive systems that elaborate it" (122), suggesting that meaning is created by humans, Barad argues that "matter and meaning are *mutually* articulated.... Neither has privileged status in determining the other" ("Posthumanist Performativity" 140; emphasis added). These intra-actions are made visible in stories that are written into the land. Particular landmarks represent stories of those who have walked before: "In certain places, boulders form straight lines, arrayed along compass directions on the burning plains.... Cairns that serve as mysterious signposts for messages long forgotten mix with ancient graves. Etchings made in the hardpan with feet or sticks form animals centuries old and only visible from the air" (Urrea 7). Urrea writes that both the walkers and the Border Patrol who hunt them "read the land like a text. They search the manuscript of the ground for irregularities in its narration. They know the plots and the images by heart. They can see where the punctuation goes. They are landscape grammarians, got the Ph.D. in reading dirt" (29). Like Mary Austin in the California desert one hundred years earlier, they look beyond human-made trails and survey for "bug-sign," left when "small creatures begin to scurry about just before dawn" (30). The footprints of both humans and nonhumans "wrote the story" (31). The footprints of the twenty-six border crossers and the footprints of walkers throughout the history of the area recorded narratives. Being able to read the land is a necessary skill, a skill that can make the difference between life and death. If the border crossers can read the land, they can find their way across it and can find the life-giving water hidden in the hills. If the Border Patrol can read the land, they can find the walkers before they walk into anonymity in the United States or die in the desert. Matter and meaning are entangled.

Reading the land also embeds the walkers within a long history of desert walks, a long history of migration. In telling the story of the twenty-nine walkers who attempted to cross the Devil's Highway in May 2001, Urrea returns again and again to images of walking. He writes, "They walked. They walked. There was no other story: they walked" (159). Yet their walking itself connected *many* other stories. The movement of the men's bodies was not an isolated experience. Rather, through walking the men connected their border crossing with the rich and complicated histories of *peregrinación*, Aztlán, and economic migration. Luis D. Léon claims, "The theme of exile and return permeates the Mexican and Chicano imagination, for ethnic Mexicans live in many diasporas: from the mother country in Mexico and from the economic, political, and cultural mainstream" (199). Like religious pilgrims, the border walkers merge the individual with the communal in the movement of their bodies. Walking ties them to complex cultural histories of movement. Yet both determining and overshadowing these stories is the materiality of the land. At least fourteen of the men were not able to follow previous walkers out of the desert; they walked themselves to death.

The US-Mexico border can be represented as a place of romance and adventure, a portrayal that can easily accommodate ideas about religious pilgrimage and Aztlán. As cultural touchstones, these narratives offer a sense of homeland and spiritual distinction, a way of elevating the experience of marginalized and detested border crossers. However, Urrea's insistence on the materiality of the journey undercuts any urge toward romanticization. Instead, these framing narratives are used to highlight the deep historicity and materiality of the men's walk. In a description of the Border Patrol's search for the lost walkers, Urrea writes, "Somebody had to follow the tracks" (31). In the structuring of the narrative, the framing of the border crossers' journey, and the excruciating descriptions of their walking bodies, *The Devil's Highway*, and by extension its readers, becomes that "somebody," matching faltering footsteps to meaning, following as "their narratives wandered like they wandered" (133). The complex history of Chicanxs and Mexicanos in the borderlands brings together cultural memory, place, and the body. Walking in the borderlands provides a physical way for accessing this web of identity.

NOTES

1. In recent years there has been a movement among scholars, writers, and activists to replace *Chicano* as the appellation for Americans with Mexican ancestry (*Chicano* itself replaced the older *Mexican American*). The masculine *Chicano* was first replaced with *Chicano/a* or *Chican@* to include women. More recently still, there has been a critique that *Chicano/a* and *Chican@* retain a limiting gender binary, and the term *Chicanx* has gained traction. Scholars María R. Scharrón-del Río and Alan A. Aja address the debate over the related term *Latinx*, which refers to peoples with ancestry from Latin American countries, while *Chicanx* is more narrowly focused on Mexican ancestry. Advocating the use of *Latinx*, Scharrón-del Río and Aja contend, "Recognizing the intersectionality of our identities as well as our locations within the various systems of privilege and oppression—on a personal and social level—fosters solidarity with all of our Latinx community and is also necessary to engage in liberatory praxis." For the reasons Scharrón-del Río and Aja cite, I use *Chicanx* throughout this chapter except when quoting sources or writing about a specific historical moment when a different identifier was commonly used. See Scharrón-del Río and Aja's article for more about this debate.

2. There is another "Devil's Highway" in the Southwest: US Route 491 (designated US Route 666 until 2003) in the Four Corners region. This other Devil's Highway has its own set of myths and stories that claim the road has a high number of fatal car accidents linked to "the number of the Beast" ("U.S. 666").

3. Kokopelli, the ubiquitous flute player common to kitschy versions of "Southwest" decor, is an important figure for many Native American peoples

in the American Southwest and is thought by some scholars to have originally depicted Mesoamerican long-distance traders known as *pochteca* who traveled north from Mesoamerica (Wesson 114).

4. While the actual number of walkers in the group was probably twenty-nine, they are usually counted as twenty-six, the number of corpses and survivors that were recovered by the Border Patrol. For consistency between my analysis and source materials, I will generally follow this convention while also acknowledging the presence of the three forgotten walkers.

5. At the time of the march to Sacramento, Aztlán had not yet become one of the primary symbols of the Chicano movement—that would happen three years later with the drafting of "El Plan Espiritual de Aztlán" at the First Chicano National Youth Conference in Denver in 1969. However, as the farm workers moved across the land, they walked with a clear sense of their own cultural and familial history and a strong sense of place.

6. It is important to note that there continues to be debate about the appropriateness and usefulness of conceiving Aztlán as synonymous with the American Southwest. Daniel Cooper Alarcón asserts that such an equation limits access to "the political leverage to help Chicanos living elsewhere" (33). He argues that "as long as Chicanos inhabit the Southwest in the mental geography of the dominant culture, it is there that Chicano needs will be addressed, and not in those Chicano communities that exist outside Aztlán, spiritual universality notwithstanding" (33–34). Alarcón goes on to suggest that Aztlán's key value lies in its "multidimensionality," the way in which the idea of Aztlán has become a palimpsest, continuously written over to reflect political and historical concerns (34). He continues, "Conceiving of Aztlán as a palimpsest acknowledges both its exclusionary power and its provisional quality" (35). The concern of Alarcón and other critics about the too strict identification of Aztlán with a particular geographic region is a significant consideration in theorizing and understanding the development of Chicano stereotypes and the limiting effect of attempting to claim a monolithic "Chicano identity." However, Patricia Price argues for the need for critical engagement with "the significance of Aztlán as an explicitly *spatialized* tool of resistance" (63; emphasis in the original). She asserts that "Aztlán as a mythic idea was consciously projected onto the desert terrain of the U.S. Southwest as a way to legitimate, root, and define the presence of Mexican-descended peoples residing in that region" (64). Thus, while it is important to recognize that identifying the story of Aztlán solely with the US-Mexican borderlands excludes the concerns of Chicanx who do not live in the American Southwest, this geographical identification remains a useful concept for understanding narratives of border crossings and the ways in which Chicanx writers draw connections between the experience of walking across the border, pilgrimage, and Aztlán.

7. Rudolfo A. Anaya and Francisco Lomeli reflect this dual positioning in their identification of Aztlán as a geographical place that "signal[s] a unifying point of cohesion through which [Chicanx] c[an] define the foundations for an identity" (ii) as well as a "symbol and archetype. It is a symbol which speaks of origins and ancestors, and it is a symbol of what we imagine ourselves to be. It embodies a human perspective of time and place" (iii).

8. Two of the fourteen dead have never been identified. They were buried in "the potter's field in Tucson nameless, there to lie, forgotten" (Urrea 193). The other twelve were flown home in a jet rented by the governor of Veracruz on May 31, less than two weeks after they walked into the desert. Rita Vargas, the Mexican consul in Calexico, calculated that the flight alone had cost more than sixty-eight thousand dollars. "'What if,' she asked, 'somebody had simply invested that amount in their villages to begin with?'" (qtd. in Urrea 199).

9. See the Vatican's website for a full version of the Apostle's Creed ("Compendium").

10. The Rosary is a form of prayer that involves saying more than fifty "Hail Mary" prayers interspersed with a handful of other ritualized prayers. In order to keep count, the one praying holds a string of beads, with each bead representing one or more specific prayers (Thurston and Shipman). A full version of the Hail Mary is available on the Vatican's website ("Compendium").

11. There are several versions of the *via crucis*. The most common includes fourteen stations: (1) Jesus is condemned to death; (2) Jesus takes up the cross; (3) Jesus falls the first time; (4) Jesus meets Mary, his mother; (5) Simon of Cyrene carries the cross for Jesus; (6) Veronica wipes Jesus's face with her veil; (7) Jesus falls a second time; (8) Jesus meets the women of Jerusalem; (9) Jesus falls the third time; (10) Jesus is stripped of his clothes; (11) Jesus is nailed to the cross; (12) Jesus dies on the cross; (13) Jesus's body is removed from the cross and given to his mother; and (14) Jesus is laid in the tomb ("The Way of the Cross at the Colosseum"). Sometimes there is a fifteenth station—Jesus's resurrection.

5

Walking Between Worlds

Material and Metaphorical Maps in Louise Erdrich's Novels

Focusing on events in a fictional Anishinaabe reservation and the surrounding towns, Louise Erdrich's twelve interlocking North Dakota novels track the complicated family histories of the community and the devastation wrought by federal policies, particularly the General Allotment Act of 1887.[1] The novels are told from the perspectives of dozens of narrators, depict the lives of scores of people across several generations, and are tied together through character, location, and theme. Each novel contributes to a rich tapestry of national and tribal histories, Anishinaabe beliefs and traditions, and federal corruptions and transgressions.[2] Each is also crisscrossed with paths and roads linking peoples and places and the spaces in between. In particular, *Love Medicine*, *Four Souls*, and especially *Tracks* are filled with trails and roads, populated by characters walking to and from town and through the woods. In all three novels, these paths are places of possibility and danger, spaces opened up between worlds. With emphases on material and metaphorical movement, Erdrich's paths and roads act as intersections between precontact and postcontact experience, alternative maps that establish continuity through history and story while simultaneously exposing the lasting impact of colonialism on the physical and symbolic movements of Erdrich's Anishinaabe characters.

As novels, Erdrich's texts may at first seem further withdrawn from the material world than the nonfiction narratives examined in the previous chapters. The North Dakota landscape of Erdrich's novels is deliberately fictionalized, and thus ostensibly closer to the symbolic than the material. Erdrich writes that "the reservation depicted in... [the North

Dakota] novels is an imagined place consisting of landscapes and features similar to many Ojibwe reservations" (*Last Report* 357). However, like the texts discussed in earlier chapters, Erdrich's novels engage in figurative and metaphorical language in ways that illuminate and make knowable the material. Semiotician and ecocritic Timo Maran provocatively asks, "What are the relations between meanings embodied in matter and our representational practices?" (141). Maran draws attention to the translational process through which the agential power of matter is expressed in imaginative modes such as narrative. Ultimately, every representation of the land is a kind of fiction in that the "real" is removed from our grasp through language that alters and distorts in the very act of description. Erdrich's novels, though set in a mindfully fictionalized landscape, engage the material land through representations of movement along paths and trails and through immersion in Anishinaabe storytelling traditions, wherein the relationships among the land and human and nonhuman beings are manifested through narrative and language. In other words, these novels are less concerned with "factual representation" than with Anishinaabe storytelling and its understanding of reciprocity with the land.

In Erdrich's North Dakota novels the material world is positioned as both metaphor—a figurative representation of themes within the lives and experiences of the characters—and as an agent of meaning making itself. The materiality of land is revealed in part by the trails and paths the characters travel. Roads and paths weave through the novels, connecting the reservation with nonreservation towns, schools, and convents, zigzagging through woods and around lakes, clearly demarcated and lost in vegetation. These spaces also mark the margins between worlds, liminal spaces that are not clearly one place or another but somewhere in between. Catherine Rainwater contends that "Erdrich's concern with liminality and marginality pervades all levels of her texts. It affects not only characterization but also thematic and structural features" (406). I would extend this point to suggest that in the novels, movement through liminal spaces—those spaces that are in between places or states or realities—also informs the characters' material experience of land and place. Ecocritic Joni Adamson's concept of "the middle place" is useful here. Adamson defines the middle place as a "contested terrain" where contrasting epistemologies about the long entanglement between humans and the more-than-human world come into contact and conflict (*American Indian Literature* xvii). The roads that the characters traverse represent places that are at once metaphorically and materially marginal, intersections of epistemology, story, history, and lived experience. As Erdrich's characters walk and drive the many paths in these novels—both material and metaphorical—they enter a space where definitions are called into question and paths multiply.

Through her creation of a fictionalized landscape and representation of material realities of Anishinaabe life and history, Erdrich proposes a new way to view and interpret the land and human relationships to it, a new way of mapping place. Erdrich writes against a tradition of Euroamerican mapping that has calcified dominant understandings of place through repeated representations, which are themselves a form of fiction. Dominant mapping traditions have superimposed meaning on land and people that is mistaken as natural and true. Citing Gillian Rose, Kelli Lyon Johnson explains: "Geographical knowledge has been founded on 'a particular form of masculinist rationality' that 'assumes a knower who believes he can separate himself from body, emotions, past and so on, so that he and his thought are autonomous, context free and objective,' in a word, *universal*" (104; emphasis in the original). Understood as scientific and transparent, European and Euroamerican maps appear to be unquestionable truth. Mishuana Goeman extends this idea to encompass not only maps but also other representational practices. She writes, "Colonial spatializing of our lands, bodies, and minds has occurred since contact; maps, travel logs, engravings, newspapers, almanacs, and many other forms of colonial writings formed a systematic practice of confining and defining Native spaces from land to bodies" (296). How space is imagined and represented has far-reaching implications for how land and people are understood and, in colonial contexts, dominated.

Erdrich's novels suggest alternative mappings of the land, maps that are less invested in geographical accuracy than in pre- and postcontact stories of human intra-action and experience; her mapping recenters human, more-than-human, and the land, entities that Euroamerican traditions have subordinated to concerns of abstracted landownership. Spokane poet and scholar Gloria Bird suggests that in Native American literature, issues of marginality are complicated and inverted, as spaces considered "marginal" by Euroamerican ideologies and cartographic traditions—like reservations—are often recognized as "home/center" by Native communities (41). In highlighting "the middle place," spaces that are neither origin nor destination, Erdrich destabilizes notions of peripheries and centers—centering routes and redrawing maps. Travel and movement between spaces are reconfigured to be as important or sometimes more important than the places routes link.

The mapping of Erdrich's fictional reservation is not dissimilar to Mary Austin's mapping of Owens Valley. Austin purposefully obscures the land, creating a map that is difficult if not impossible to follow while still engaging with the material specificity of the desert. In a similar manner, the environs in Erdrich's novels may be fictional, but in their mapping and description the land emerges as fiercely material and present. Geographer Philip E. Steinberg writes that mobility is conventionally seen "against the normative portrayal of the world as timelessly and naturally divided into bordered units: sovereign, territorial states that define the scope of governance and nations" (469). Such borders and limits, however, are not intrinsic to the land but are created through the intra-action of human and nonhuman in creating meaning. Because, as Karen Barad posits, this meaning making is always shifting through the very intra-action that constitutes it, meanings themselves are in a constant state of becoming. "Intra-actions not only reconfigure spacetimematter but reconfigure what is possible," she writes. "Questions of responsibility and accountability present themselves with every possibility; each moment is alive with different possibilities for the world's becoming and different reconfigurations of what may yet be possible" (*Meeting* 182). The literary mapping in Erdrich's novels uses a fictionalized North Dakota landscape to draw attention to the materiality of the land and to the agency and presence of Indigenous people, while simultaneously pushing readers to be active participants in the world's becoming.

These alternative mappings are reflected in and created by storytelling traditions that link the material and the figurative, creating a complexity of meaning within the matrix of the physical world, symbolic representation, and the materiality of language. Anishinaabe/Lakota scholar Patrick LeBeau argues for the specific linking of figurative language and the material land in Anishinaabe storytelling and mapping traditions. "While written in the symbology of mythology," he contends, "the maps of the ancient migration of the Ojibwa have identifiable reference points to the modern landscape" (qtd. in Miner 330). The symbolic and the material are clearly linked through bodily movement, as symbolism gives meaning to physical landscapes at the same moment that those landscapes provide imagery that actively shapes symbolic readings. Anthropologist Christopher Tilley argues, "The centre of our own existence is always our body, as an axis from which spatiality and temporality are oriented.... Structures of bodily experience work their way up to abstract meanings, embodied imagination" (34–35). Tilley suggests that creativity and abstract thought are intimately connected to the material realm of the body and the land. Storytelling, he argues, arises from intra-action with matter. In Erdrich's novels the material land underlies the fiction, forming a firm basis upon which the author inscribes metaphorical and cultural meanings. This is not to suggest that matter is simply a background to or conduit of linguistic artifice. Indeed, as Stacy Alaimo argues, "Nature or the environment cannot serve as a mere resource within an ontology that sweeps us all up in interrelations of material dynamism" (*Bodily Natures* 157). Rather, the intra-action between human and nonhuman is what creates meaning and narrative. The characters and descriptions in Erdrich's novels are created through language, always intra-acting with the material land. As the characters walk along the myriad paths and roads in the novels, their entanglement with the nonhuman world is highlighted and the materiality of the land is made manifest.

THE GENERAL ALLOTMENT ACT AND ANISHINAABE-AKII (ANISHINAABE HOMELAND)

Indigenous experience and knowledge of the land has been and continues to be challenged by federal treaties, policies, and laws. In 1887 the US Congress passed the General Allotment Act, which divided commonly held tribal land into individual parcels on reservations throughout much of the United States. This act and its aftermath serve as major reference points in many of Erdrich's North Dakota novels. One of the intended purposes of the General Allotment (or Dawes) Act was to facilitate assimilation of Indigenous peoples into capitalistic white society through individual landownership. Section 6 of the act reads in part:

> And every Indian born within the territorial limits of the United States to whom allotments shall have been made under the provisions of this act, or under any law or treaty, and every Indian born within the territorial limits of the United States who has voluntarily taken up, within said limits, his residence separate and apart from any tribe of Indians therein, and has adopted the habits of civilized life, is hereby declared to be a citizen of the United States, and is entitled to all the rights, privileges, and immunities of such citizens. ("An Act to Provide for the Allotment")

Proponents and lawmakers believed that transitioning from tribal to individual landownership would encourage Native peoples to adopt dominant values and integrate into white society and, eventually, attain citizenship. Activist and member of the (all-white) Indians Rights Association J. F. Kinney argued in 1888, "The general effect of the Severalty Law is beneficial to the Indians. By taking land in severalty, the Indian becomes individualized. Disintegration follows. Fealty to chiefs is destroyed. Submission to their authority is no longer rendered. The Indian on land of his own, separated from the general mass which belong to all in common, for the first time becomes conscious of his own manhood" (qtd. in Stremlau 280). The proponents of the Dawes Act understood themselves to be operating from a stance of kindness and morality.[3] However, in addition to provisions for distributing tribal land to individual male tribal members, the act also contained multiple sections that outlined the many ways any "extra" land would be available for purchase by US citizens. The Allotment Act led to the loss of millions of acres of land and had a devastating impact on generations of families and communities. Billy J. Stratton and Frances Washburn argue that notions of landownership "did not exist in American Indian cultures who considered land as an organic, communally owned entity, a source of physical survival, but also of spiritual survival.... These are oppositional cultural concepts of land as a commodity within European cultural concepts, and land as place within American Indian cultural concepts" (67–68). Viewing the land as something that can be divided into sections and owned by individuals is directly at odds with Indigenous conceptions of land as inextricable from self and community, land as kin.

In contrast to dominant conceptions of land as inert resource, Anishinaabe oral traditions reveal a much more complex, living land filled with movement. Anishinaabe stories recount the five-hundred-year Great Migration of the Anishinaabeg from the East Coast to Lake Superior as a significant and foundational experience. According to one version of this narrative, the sacred *migis* (cowry) shell appeared to the Anishinaabeg and led them on a journey along inland waters, guiding them to their new homeland.[4] The route itself is "one of the defining elements of Ojibway culture," remaining central to a sacred origin story and also providing "vital clues about the actual physical landscapes through which ancestral Ojibway migrated" (*Tracing the Trail*). This migration story reflects a long tradition of walking, part of a rich oral tradition that includes other migration stories as well as seasonal movement across a large homeland that extends far beyond the artificial boundaries of reservations.[5]

The history of migration and movement across the land infuses Anishinaabe oral traditions. Anishinaabe critic Gerald Vizenor writes, "The sovereignty of motion is mythic, material, and visionary, not mere territoriality, in the sense of colonialism and nationalism. Native transmotion is an original natural unison in the stories of emergence and migration that relates humans to an environment and to the spiritual and political significance of animals and other creations" (*Fugitive Poses* 183). The centrality of motion, Vizenor suggests, is both described by the stories and reinforced by the act of creating and transmitting those stories. Erdrich incorporates this sense of movement and creation in her novels in a landscape that is not inert but filled with life. Adamson explains that this "living, breathing" landscape indicates "the official landscape is not necessarily the real/true, but only the existing reality, which is transformable" (*American Indian Literature* 109).[6] The movement of the narrative, the movement within the narrative, and the physical movements of humans across the land are bound together in storytelling that is ongoing and always becoming.

The importance of movement and land is reinforced by Anishinaabemowin (Anishinaabe language) itself. Like the Diné language, Anishinaabemowin is verb based, emphasizing action, movement, and relationships in the very structure of language. In her memoir *Books and Islands*, Erdrich writes, "Two-thirds of [Anishinaabemowin] words are verbs, and for *each verb*, there can be as many as six thousand forms. This sounds impossible, until you realize that the verb forms not only have to do with the relationships among the people conducting the action, but the precise way the action is conducted and even under what physical conditions" (82–83; emphasis in the original). Anishinaabe linguist Margaret Noori connects this action-oriented language structure to Anishinaabe concepts of the more-than-human world: "In the notably verb-based language of Anishinaabemowin, no single noun equates with the concept of 'nature.' . . . Readers find in older texts a concept of nature that encompasses people's relationship with the land, the trees, the water, and the weather" (36). Noori emphasizes the core questions that undergird traditional Anishinaabe storytelling: "What happened? What did the people and animals do? What was the relationship of the Anishinaabeg to the space and sparks around them? How did the Anishinaabeg discuss the relationships between humans, animals, and forces not seen?" (36–37). Attention to action rather than description stresses not only movement but also materiality, drawing attention to the relationships between humans and nonhumans and to the ways they intra-act in the process of becoming and meaning making.

Throughout *Tracks*, *Four Souls*, and *Love Medicine*, the characters counter the "official" history of the Anishinaabeg as told in history books, colonial writings, and maps with their own sacred stories. Kelli Lyon Johnson argues that Indigenous women authors such as Erdrich respond to attempts to universalize experience "by rejecting the imposition of European (and Euroamerican) knowledge as a paradigm for reading Native texts; by presenting their own Indigenous cultures as sources of knowledge; and by explaining and using those Indigenous knowledges as a means of asserting sovereignty for Native nations in the United States" (104). She goes on to examine Indigenous mapping as a way that these authors accomplish these tasks. If mapping traditions are one way that authors reassert sacred history by replacing the imposition of Euroamerican worldviews through the delimiting of land, the movement along paths and roads throughout Erdrich's North Dakota novels performs a similar act of reclamation.

Euroamerican mapping methods privilege certain kinds of markers such as named roadways and officially recognized and designated landforms, and as a result other ways of recording the land are erased. Maria DePriest notes that according to a recent cartographic study of contemporary maps, reservations are largely represented as open space: "While on some maps, the reservation is excised—it is not there, nor is its absence indicated—on the maps... studied, the reservation is represented merely as a placeholder, a blank, an empty open space" (249). Reservation roads and pathways are not represented on these maps; it is as if they do not exist at all. Mirroring the long-standing stereotype of the "vanishing Indian"—who has been described as being on his last legs almost since first contact with Europeans some five hundred years ago—the reservations themselves are erased from maps, the "official" way Europeans and Euroamericans define and visualize land. Nanapush, one of the narrators of *Tracks*, echoes this myth at the beginning of the novel when he claims, "I guided the last buffalo hunt... saw the last bear shot... trapped the last beaver with a pelt of more than two years' growth... [and] axed the last birch" (2). Yet his subsequent narration challenges readers to reject the story of the doomed Indian. While treaties and federal policies like the Allotment Act have undeniably and tragically ravaged the Anishinaabe land and people, Erdrich's novels offer the possibility of alternative ways of conceiving land and community. In remapping the land through stories involving characters walking along the liminal spaces of roads and trails, Erdrich draws attention to the significance of these actions and spaces and reclaims the land and the people's history.

ROADS AND PATHS—CENTERING THE MARGINS

Throughout her North Dakota novels, Erdrich explores the possibility of alternative maps of Anishinaabe land, culture, and history. *Tracks*, *Four Souls*, and *Love Medicine* are engaged in remapping the land in the wake of the General Allotment Act by following the patterns of Anishinaabe oral traditions, emphasizing movement and land and drawing readers' attention to Anishinaabe histories and stories. In Anishinaabe storytelling traditions, "the story does not exist apart from, but in intense interaction with other aspects of reality.... [S]tory affects not only the world that people *experience*.... [Rather] story affects the fundamental reality in which creation *happens*" (Garroutte and Westcott 73–74; emphasis in the original). Storytelling and the material world are intimately linked, and in Erdrich's novels that link is manifested through the physical movement of characters through space. In highlighting this movement and recentering the marginal spaces it occurs in, the novels suggest a way to remap space and reassert Anishinaabe understandings of the material relationships between human communities and the land.

Taking place between 1912 and 1924, the characters' constant movement to, from, and within the reservation in *Tracks* is closely tied to land loss, most clearly exemplified in the stories of two characters, Nanapush and Fleur Pillager.[7] Nanapush, one of the book's two narrators, sets the stage for his story by noting the impact of colonialism on the community, highlighting treaties, exile, and a dwindling land base. He relates how the "trouble came… from liquor and the dollar bill. We stumbled toward the government bait, never looking down, never noticing how the land was snatched from under us at every step" (4). In his articulation of land loss, Nanapush employs the language of walking over the land, linking a figurative "stumble" with the physical land that is stolen and sold. A few pages later, he asserts, "Starvation makes fools of anyone. In the past, some had sold their allotment land for one hundred poundweight of flour. Others, who were desperate to hold on, now urged that we get together and buy back our land, or at least pay a tax and refuse the lumbering money that would sweep the marks of our boundaries off the map like a pattern of straws" (8). Nanapush highlights not just the land loss itself but also the attendant splintering of the community into factions. The timber interests denude the land of actual trees, while the people are similarly uprooted from land and community. As allotment threatens to "sweep the marks of our boundaries off the map," so too does it endanger kinship bonds, as some "fattened in the shade of the new Agent's storehouse," while others "weakened… as one oak went down, another and another was lost" (9). Linking the weakened and sickened bodies of the Anishinaabeg to the bodies of felled trees, Nanapush underscores the relationship between human and nonhuman that is both psychological and material.

Nanapush presents this connection between human and more-than-human in material bodies moving across the land. In the opening chapter of *Tracks*, Nanapush fills his narration with images of roads and paths that he explicitly connects to historical change and land loss. This movement is multidirectional and overtly communal. Anishinaabe scholar Kimberly Blaeser explains, "The stories of pilgrimage in Native American literature… are seldom the account of individual movement or of a search for a single isolate destiny. More often they are braided accounts that entwine themselves with the destinies of communities, generations, tribal nations, the ecosystem of a region, the spiritual inheritance of a people" (85–86). Nanapush begins the novel with a story of colonialism and mobility, drawing together the desolation of illness and removal with attention to the sacred four directions of the Anishinaabe Medicine Wheel: "For those who survived the spotted sickness from the south, our long flight west to Nadouissioux land where we signed the treaty, and then a wind from the east, bringing exile in a storm of government papers, what descended from the north in 1912 seemed impossible" (1).[8] In this chapter Nanapush goes on to emphasize other kinds of trail walking: his hunting ability (2), his journey on foot with Edgar Pukwan to the Pillager cabin to see if anyone has survived the tuberculosis epidemic that devastated the community (2), their subsequent rescue of Fleur and trek back along the trail to Nanapush's house at the crossroads (4), and the spirits of Nanapush's and Fleur's families as they move through the trees (6). The connections among the trails and the liminal spaces between life and death, between the Anishinaabeg and the US government, and between reservation and nonreservation lands are revealed in these opening pages. Physical movement over the trails conjures the people's forced movement onto reservations and the devastation wrought by colonial policies while simultaneously highlighting traditional movements across the land and the connections between people and the more-than-human world.

In *Tracks* the blank spaces on the map are filled with matter and walking bodies, even as official roads and landmarks are sometimes absent. Late in the novel, Father Damian shows Nanapush, Margaret, Fleur, and Eli a map of the reservation. "We examined the lines and circles of homesteads paid up," Nanapush tells us. "They were colored green. The lands that were gone out of the tribe—to deaths with no heirs, to sales, to the lumber company—were painted a pale and rotten pink. Those in question, a sharper yellow" (173). This "official" mapping of the reservation, based on allotments and individual ownership, is challenged by the physical movement of characters who refuse the assumptions and expectations of the maps. For example, throughout the novel those who traverse forest paths do not always leave footprints or physical traces of their movement. Both Pauline and Nanapush tell readers that there are times when Fleur walks "without leaving tracks" (215). Further, the spirits who roam the woods remain just out of sight. When the death road walked by the spirits is revealed to Pauline and Fleur following the death of Fleur's newborn baby, Pauline, who rejects her Anishinaabe identity,[9] marvels, "I had been everywhere on the reservation, but never before on this road, which was strange because it was so wide and so furiously trodden that the snow was beaten to a rigid ice" (159). Pauline's wonder at the existence of a wide, well-traveled road that she has never seen before further challenges the limiting Euroamerican vision that cannot perceive the Anishinaabe worldview clearly and so attempts to erase it completely. The road, like the Anishinaabeg themselves, has always been there, even if Pauline has been unable (or unwilling) to see it. As Johnson argues, "Non-Native mappings continue to exploit Native lands, to erase Native knowledges, and eliminate Native peoples" (111). In other words, not only does Erdrich insist on remapping the bordered spaces of the physical land, but she also includes an alternative mapping system. The Anishinaabe land is transformed from a blank space on the map to a complexly traveled and peopled land, a three-dimensional map more intricate than any Western map could capture.

In the process of remapping Indigenous movements and spaces, the characters walk along paths and roads not only as a means of traveling from one location to another, but also as a way of asserting purposeful, ceremonial movement. For instance, when Margaret and Nanapush are attacked and shamed by Clarence Morrisey and Boy Lazarre, Fleur responds first by shaving her head in solidarity with Margaret and then by "walking the four streets" of the reservation town, "once in each direction" (119). In doing so, she is echoing Nanapush's invocation of the four directions at the start of the novel and enacting the four sections of the sacred Anishinaabe Medicine Wheel, joining her movement to the four directions, the land, and the four-times-seven sacred teachings.[10] Purposefully walking along the streets, Fleur reveals the connections between the modern roads and traditional belief systems, drawing together two ways of organizing and understanding the world. The four roads become the permeable margin between present and past, modern and ancient. DePriest argues that Fleur "expresses the fluidity of a symbolic and practical system of intersections in which human and non-human, life and death, temporal and spiritual, singular and plural, are linked and sometimes even blended" (255). Just as she is linked to the woods peopled with spirits, so too is she connected to the Anishinaabe traditional beliefs and practices. When she walks the four roads of the town, she draws on these identities and insists on the continual presence of the Anishinaabeg in a land that has never been empty or blank.

Throughout much of the novel, Fleur's connection to the land and her ancestors helps her fend off the grasping hands of the local Bureau of Indian Affairs agent. Nanapush tells us, "The Agent went out [to the Pillager land], then got lost, spent a whole night following the moving lights and lamps of people who would not answer him.... [H]e asked Fleur again for money, and the next thing we heard he was living in the woods and eating roots, gambling with ghosts" (9). The Agent is tricked by the wandering spirits that Fleur apparently calls upon, who continue to move through the land. The spirits of the Pillagers remain "just beyond the edges of... sight, they flickered, thin as needles, shadows piercing shadows" (6). Fleur's spiritual connection to the land and to the lake creature, Misshepeshu, shields her and protects her land from the grasp of the Agent. Fleur's movement along the forest paths echoes this mixing of spheres, as Pauline, the other narrator, reports, "We followed the tracks of her bare feet and saw where they changed, where the claws spread out, the pad broadened and pressed into the dirt" (*Tracks* 12). Here along the paths around the lake, Fleur's bear-clan identity is made material, as she transforms into a bear and leaves physical tracings.[11] Through her connection to the land and traditional worldview, Fleur thrives in her home on the shore of the lake before losing her allotment.

Fleur's movement throughout the novel is determined by her connection to the land, and the ghostly movements of spirits in the woods further tie her to place. Yet as Lawrence William Gross argues, her powerful control begins to fracture, and "her strength temporarily fades," resulting in the loss of her land and her movement along the road to the city (53). Struggling with onerous and ultimately illegal fees and taxes, the characters in *Tracks* attempt to find ways to raise funds to save their land. In the end, they raise enough to save only one allotment, and it is not Fleur's. After staging a final act of rebellion by sawing through the trees and calling up a windstorm so that they fall around and on top of the loggers, Fleur walks away from her land. As land loss is inextricable from material economic conditions, Fleur's decision to cut down the trees herself is a way of asserting her agency and maintaining a link to the land that forms her own body and identity, even as she appears to abandon it.[12]

Just as movement reveals the link between Fleur and traditional teachings, so too does movement reinforce the symbolic and material correlation between Nanapush and the Anishinaabe trickster figure Naanabozho.[13] Throughout *Tracks* Nanapush functions as a trickster and storyteller, shaping and influencing the narrative. In a passage that most clearly reflects Nanapush's spiritual power and traditional role, he facilitates Eli's successful moose hunt. Emphasizing the steps of ceremony, Nanapush uses a piece of coal to blacken his face. He relates that he then "placed my otter bag upon my chest, my rattle near. I began to sing slowly, calling on my helpers, until the words came from my mouth but were not mine, until the rattle started, the song sang itself, and there, in the deep bright drifts, I saw the tracks of Eli's snowshoes clearly."[14] Nanapush's ceremony allows him to access Eli's consciousness, as "the song picked up and stopped him until he understood…that everything around him was perfect for killing moose" (101). With his drum and song, Nanapush changes Eli's pace from "wandering" to "walk[ing] carefully" (101), and he guides Eli's movement through the woods to a successful shot, "my song directed [Eli's bullet] to fly true" (103). Nanapush continues to sing and guide Eli, encouraging him to butcher and transport the meat correctly, avoiding souring the meat and moving too quickly and dying in the cold. Nanapush relates, "I took the drum from beneath my bed and beat out footsteps for Eli to hear and follow. Each time he speeded I slowed him down. I strengthened the rhythm whenever he faltered.… In that way, he returned" (104). The rhythm of the drum merges with the rhythm of Eli's footfalls. As Eli follows the path Nanapush maps for him, he walks along the margin between the physical world and the world of spirits, and the worlds blur and blend. Nanapush's power to direct and control Eli's physical actions recalls Naanabozho's relationship to movement. Louis Owens notes, "Trickster was going along" begins "almost all trickster narratives in the Native American tradition" (228). A master of verbal acrobatics, misdirection, and misunderstandings, Naanabozho in his trickster guise is intimately enmeshed in physical movement, walking from one adventure to the next. Nanapush, too, is a linguistic trickster, and his home at the crossroads and interest in and power over walking and movement indicate his role as a conduit between past and present, people and land.

Tracks ends with the paired movement of Fleur leaving the reservation and her daughter, Lulu, returning home. Both journeys emphasize the liminal, "in between" nature of the road. Fleur, having lost her land to corrupt allotment policies, takes up a handcart and walks away from home. Nanapush recalls Fleur's leaving: "She looked at me, her face alight, and then she set out. I stood in the middle of the path. I watched her until the road bent, traveling south to widen, flatten, and eventually in its course meet with government school, depots, stores, the plotted squares of farms" (224).[15] Nanapush's position "in the middle of the path" allows him an unobstructed view of Fleur's trajectory away from home to nonreservation spaces; this journey reflects the nature of the trail itself, as it flattens and widens to accommodate automobile traffic and larger numbers of travelers. As a symbol of the changing material circumstances of the Anishinaabeg, Fleur's road focuses attention on the material land, tying symbolism securely to materiality.

Fleur's movement away from community is countered several paragraphs later by her daughter Lulu's homing movement. Having attended a boarding school and thus having been absent from the community for several years, Lulu is finally brought home through Nanapush's persistent efforts. In a kind of presaging of Fleur's return home in a fancy white car at the end of *Four Souls* and Lipsha's symbolic returning of June's car at the end of *Love Medicine*, *Tracks* ends with Lulu's emergence from "the rattling green vehicle the government sent." Lulu steps down from the automobile and sees Nanapush and Margaret, her grandmother, across the street. Nanapush reminds her later, "You went up on your toes, and tried to walk, prim as you'd been taught. Halfway across, you could not contain yourself and sprang forward. Lulu. We gave against your rush like creaking oaks, held on, bracing ourselves together in the fierce dry wind" (226). In contrast to the felled trees of the lumber company that force Fleur's departure, Nanapush and Margaret are sturdy oaks that can withstand the storm. Similarly, Lulu's resilience and refusal of the behavioral mandates of the government school are represented by her shift "halfway across" the street from reserved walking to a springing run. In between the government car and Nanapush's wagon, in between constrained and "natural" energy, at the end of the novel Lulu crosses the road back to her people and returns home.

As characters linked to traditional lifeways, Fleur and Nanapush draw attention to the complexity of the roads and paths the people walk daily. Rather than simply utilitarian routes from one place to another, these spaces become limens, or borders, where multiple possibilities are manifest. For Nanapush and Fleur, movement over roads and paths incorporates both opportunity and memory, tracing alternative maps of pasts, presents, and futures for the Anishinaabeg.

The story of Fleur's movement away from the reservation at the end of *Tracks* is picked up in the beginning of *Four Souls*. The opening scene of that book, in a chapter called "The Roads," is a retelling of Fleur's final scene in *Tracks*, describing her walk away from home in what we learn is her vengeful search for John James Mauser, the white man who bought the land that was taken from her. Narrated again by Nanapush, the description of her journey closely mirrors his description of her departure at the end of *Tracks*: "Fleur took the small roads, the rutted paths through the woods traversing slough edge and heavy underbrush, trackless, unmapped, unknown and always bearing east.... She crossed fields and skirted lakes, pulled her cart over farmland and pasture...kept walking until she came to the iron road" (*Four Souls* 1). Fleur's movement away from the reservation and the allotment land she has lost takes her deep into the margin. The language Erdrich uses here to describe the land emphasizes its place outside of reservation and town: "trackless, unmapped, unknown." And Fleur's movement is along literal boundaries of the "slough edge" and lakeshores. The chapter goes on to follow Fleur along the "iron road," the "path she had been looking for," where she "wore her makizinan to shreds," eating dogs, mud hens, and muskrats, until finally reaching her destination in the city (2). Her journey is symbolically away from home and into the unknown. It is also inescapably material, with long, difficult miles on "rutted paths" and "iron road" that destroy her *makizinan* (moccasins), as well as a physical isolation that requires her to rely on her resourcefulness and ability to draw on traditional knowledge to live off the land. Her intra-action with place, the ways her body marks her relationship with the more-than-human, communicates a profound sense of entanglement that transcends the "merely" symbolic. Fleur's movement away from the reservation is not a rejection of that land but rather an act to reclaim it; paradoxically, she must walk away from her home in order to return to it.

Once Fleur reaches the city, her physical movement becomes radically limited. Arriving at Mauser's home, she is hired as a washerwoman before slowly becoming indispensable to him as a healer. Eventually, Mauser annuls his marriage to his first wife and marries Fleur. Fleur's revenge plot necessitates that while she is in Mauser's home, she lives according to Euro-american conceptions of proper womanhood, including restriction to the domestic sphere. When she first arrives, she is given new shoes and a uniform: "A black dress. An apron, with pinstripes, small gussets, a bow to be tied just so at the small of her back" (15). Later, after she marries Mauser, she "began to appear at certain functions in dramatic, daring, and yet somehow decently reserved exquisite gowns" (61). First a maid and then a wife, Fleur's clothing signals the ways her movement is monitored and contained.

However, always joined to the land and its rhythms, even in her voluntary domestic captivity Fleur is connected to the more-than-human world through movement in the home. Nanapush tells us that Mauser's house is constructed on traditional Anishinaabe lands using indigenous building materials. The house is built on "a favorite spot [of the Anishinaabe] for making camp in those original years before settlement" (4). It is constructed of brownstone quarried "from an island in the deep cold northern lake called Gichi gami" and oak trees harvested "to the north, near yet another lake" (5–6). Other materials are likewise gathered from the land: "Copper. Miskwaabik. Soapstone. Slate for the roof shingles.... The walls were raised and fast against them a tawny insulation of woven lake reeds was pressed tight" (6). Polly Elizabeth, Fleur's friend and Mauser's sister-in-law, remarks, "All of the materials, the fabric, all the raw stuff of our opulent shelter were taken from Fleur's people" (67). As she walks within the house that Mauser built from elements of her homeland, Fleur tells him, "I am the sound that the wind used to make in a thousand needles of pine. I am the quiet at the root. When I walk through your hallway I walk through myself. When I touch the walls of your house I touch my own face" (45). Fleur's entanglement with the land is reflected in both how she conceives of her physical movement within Mauser's house as well as how the house itself is imbued with the moving, living spirit of the land. Her trans-corporeality draws attention to the complexity of agency in the material self. While Fleur is making decisions and driving her revenge plot forward, her movement, her very body, is intimately linked to the elements of the house. Her agency is not hers alone; it is inextricable from the land.

By the time Fleur travels back to the reservation at the end of the novel after several years in the city, she moves in a very different way: in a "white car" and a "whiter suit," she "took the roads" (182, 184). Nanapush reflects on the changes represented by Fleur's movement, commenting:

> Once we were a people who left no tracks. Now we are different. We print ourselves deeply on the earth. We build roads. The ruts and skids of our wheels bite deep and the bush recedes.... I have left my own tracks, too. I have left behind these words. But even as I write them down I know they are merely footsteps in snow. They will be gone by spring.... Even our bones nourish change.... [E]ven such people as we, the Anishinaabeg, can sometimes die, or change, or change and become. (210)

Presenting change in terms of both material and metaphorical meaning, Nanapush draws attention to the dramatic shifts in life and experience brought about by colonialism. Summer Harrison argues, "Nanapush links stories with the material world and specifically with the political context of land use. He draws attention not only to how roads, cars, and buildings affect the earth but also to the historical narratives of progress that legitimize their impact. The deep printing of modern technology disrupts both the local woodlands and the communal identity of a 'people who [once] left no tracks'" (39). Nanapush's meditation on change is rooted firmly in the material: the land itself and human material technology. The material realities are both constitutive of and understood through more abstracted and symbolic change to individual and communal identity and relationships, represented by Fleur's white suit and car. However, that change has *always* been part of Anishinaabe culture and has *always* been a defining aspect of their relationship to place; it is not new. Through time and material change, walking and driving in the marginal spaces tie the people to the historical movement of the Anishinaabeg and present the possibility of adaptation. The spaces, in other words, refuse stereotypes of stasis and insist on the historical reality of cultural as well as physical movement and change.

Continuing the community's story two generations later, *Love Medicine* maintains the emphasis on movement, bookended with stories of roads and travel. The novel opens with Margaret's adopted granddaughter June's journey home to the reservation: "June Kashpaw was walking down the clogged main street of oil boomtown Williston, North Dakota, killing time before the noon bus arrived that would take her home" (1). Right away, the "oil boomtown" is both contrasted with "home" and connected to it by the street June walks along. Rather than boarding the bus and going home, however, June ends up outside of town in the truck of a passed-out mud engineer early Easter Sunday morning. Getting out of his vehicle, she strikes out on foot across the snow-covered fields. As her "feet grew numb... her heart clenched and her skin turned crackling cold," her body dies and her spirit continues to walk. This first chapter ends with the rich imagery of June's spirit as she "walked over [the snow] like water and came home" (7). The symbolism in this opening story set on Easter Sunday is strongly Christian, as, like Jesus, June walks on water and, emerging from the cracked eggshell of her body, continues past her physical death. However, beyond the Christian imagery, the emphasis on homeward movement links June to Anishinaabe migration stories.[16] Michif artist and historian Dylan A. T. Miner asserts that for the Anishinaabeg, stories are a method of returning home to a more integrated and balanced cultural and personal identity. He writes, "To decolonize, one must migrate home through stories.... These stories, as a form of strengthening the earth, serve as cartographic devices that lead us through the landscape of an ever-urbanizing Anishinaabewaki" (330).

Linked to modern colonial impacts such as urbanization and drilling and fracking for oil, the Allotment Act continues to materially affect the community. Albertine, Nector's granddaughter and one of many narrators, tells the story of how land had been allotted to Rushes Bear (Margaret from *Tracks*) and her children, except for Nector and Eli, who were too young to register for an allotment. Her ten older children received allotments, "but because there was no room for them in the North Dakota wheatlands, most were deeded parcels far off, in Montana, and had to move there or sell. The older children left" (18).[17] The loss of these children (who never return) as a direct result of the Allotment Act haunts the narrative through multiple references to other characters and narrators finding their way home: Nector and Lulu return home from boarding school, Marie returns from the convent, June's spirit walks home, and Gerry repeatedly dreams of returning home. Albertine articulates the pull of the land in her narration of her own homing movement:

> All along the highway that early summer the land was beautiful.... Tattered silver windbreaks bounded flat, plowed fields that the government had paid to lie fallow.... Driving north, I could see the earth lifting. The wind was hot and smelled of tar and the moving dust....
>
> I always knew [the reservation] was coming a long way off. Even in the distance you sense hills from their opposites—pits, dried sloughs, ditches of cattails, potholes. And then the water. There would be water in the hills when there wasn't any on the plains, because the hollows saved it, collected runoff from the low slopes, and the dense trees held it, too. I thought of water in the roots of trees, brown and bark smelling, cold....
>
> The policy of allotment was a joke. As I was driving toward the land.... I saw as usual how much of the reservation was sold to whites and lost forever. Just three miles, and I was driving down the rutted dirt road, home. (11–12)

Albertine contrasts the harsh, sterile sights and smells of the highway (tar, potholes, fallow fields) with the rich, comforting sights and smells of home ("bark smelling water," tree roots, hills). The materiality of the land is directly involved in her relationship to place; "home" is not an abstract concept but materially determined through the intra-action of people, place, and nonhuman nature. Her movement home counters the devastation of being reminded, "as usual," of the loss of land to allotment policies. Albertine draws readers' attention to the impact of allotment policies while also refusing to allow those policies to have final control over the meaning of the routes the people travel. As she drives home she is involved in the ongoing becoming of place and identity, land and meaning.

The end of *Love Medicine* echoes these images of homeward movement, this time with June's son, Lipsha, poised to drive June's car over a bridge spanning "the boundary river" (366). "I got inside," he narrates. "The morning was clear. A good road led on. So there was nothing to do but cross the water, and bring her home" (367). Like the story that opens the novel, this passage at its close emphasizes repeated images of walking or crossing over water and moving homeward. The journey that June began on that snowy Easter morning is completed when Lipsha drives the car bought with her life insurance money back to the reservation, the "her" in "bring her home" signaling both the car and June herself. Yet, significantly, the book does not end with a cessation of movement or with the car reaching the reservation. We do not follow June and Lipsha home; we only see them en route, crossing over symbolic boundaries of snow and bridge.

The water June and Lipsha travel across and that Albertine mentions ties their journeys even more closely to Anishinaabe lands and traditions. Critic Melissa K. Nelson (Anishinaabeg/Métis/Norwegian) writes, "Being people of the Great Lakes and the Mississippi headwaters, Anishinaabeg people are water people. There are many important Anishinaabeg stories about the significance of water. According to traditional teachings, water or *niibi* is a primary sacred element in life and therefore must be cherished as an essential relative, elder, and teacher" (217). She continues, "The Ojibwe natural world is characterized by lakes and rivers—great and small—slough, creeks, ice and snow. Travel was traditionally done by birch-bark canoe along the immense waterways traversing Anishinaabe-akii (Ojibwe homeland)" (217–18). Similarly, Erdrich writes in *Books and Islands*, "[The] people were the lake, and the lake was them. At one time, everyone who lived near the lake was essentially made of the lake" (34). June's and Lipsha's journeys home over water connect their movement thematically and geographically to traditional movement and recall their bodily relation to the water and land. Journey locates their story within the symbolic and material identity of the Anishinaabeg and the Anishinaabe land.

While all three novels end with a version of homecoming—Lulu in *Tracks*, Fleur in *Four Souls*, and June and Lipsha in *Love Medicine*—these endings should not be read as resolutions to the conflicted movement that swirls through the novels. The stories of these characters do not end with these homecomings but continue in subsequent novels. The characters are continually pulled back to the liminal spaces of paths and roads, spaces of conflict and power. Karen Barad argues that our very understanding of the margins or borders of bodies—human or nonhuman—is fallacious. "Bodies do not simply take their place in the world," she writes. "They are not simply situated in or located in, particular environments. Rather, 'environments' and 'bodies' are intra-actively co-constituted. Bodies ('human,' 'environmental,' or otherwise) are integral 'parts' of, or dynamic reconfigurings of, what is" (*Meeting* 170). In other words, bodies are intimately and inextricably connected to the rest of the material world, a world that is never static but always becoming. Read through this lens, the characters' bodily movements on roads and paths resist any attempt to understand movement as only or even primarily symbol and metaphor for the characters' individual and cultural development. Instead, the materiality of the characters and the roads they walk and drive on is pushed to the forefront. Beginning and ending with characters' movements to, from, and within their homeland, the novels remap space and demonstrate how meaning is intimately tied to the intra-action among human and nonhuman matter and accentuate the ways movement underlies these material relationships.

STORY ROUTES

The mobility in Erdrich's novels joins the figurative with the material, drawing multiple meanings together with the physical land. In addition, the representations of physical movement and the textual movement impact readers as well, keeping them off-balance. Kathleen Sands suggests that Erdrich's readers are "forced to shift position, turn, ponder, and finally integrate the story into a coherent whole" (12). Erdrich grapples with colonial and cultural histories that offer conflicting maps of the land and the people. In so doing, she draws our attention to the shifting grounds of "story," "materiality," and "identity" by allowing multiple community narrators to tell their own versions of their stories. What emerges is a land continually made and remade through intra-action among human, nonhuman, and the language of storytelling.

Roads, trails, and paths map the movement of these stories; as we follow characters along their travels, we encounter diverse stories that range from traditional narratives to modern trickster tales to colonial and postcolonial histories. If we pay attention to the ground they walk, we can see these spaces as palimpsests, where different and even conflicting versions clash, interact, and merge. Pauline reveals this multiplicity in her description of walking the death road with Fleur: "We glided west, following the fall of night in a constant dusk. We passed dark and vast seas of moving buffalo and not one torn field, but only earth, as it was before.... There were no fences, no poles, no lines, no tracks. The road we walked was the only sign of humans" (159). In her description of the death road and its apparent existence in a precontact time, Pauline draws together traditional belief systems and nonnative systems, while maintaining an emphasis on the land itself. By marking both what *is* and what *is not* there, Pauline in effect peels back a layer of the palimpsest to reveal a new map. The death road, like the other trails and paths in the novels, functions as an overlapping margin between worlds and between worldviews. Yet in spite, or perhaps because, of the contrasting narratives, the earth remains a constant. The death road shows both what existed prior to modern development and also what remains, regardless of that development. This is not to claim, of course, that the land has not been irrevocably changed, but rather that it has always been an agential part of the intra-action through which meaning is created and re-created. The land of Erdrich's North Dakota novels is alive with trails and paths, with people moving along ancient migration tracks, traditional hunting trails, ceremonial spokes of the Medicine Wheel, trade routes, and modern roads and highways. Her characters' continual movement along, through, and around these spaces acknowledges and defies the impact of colonialism on the physical, spiritual, and communal lives of the Anishinaabeg.

In *Books and Islands*, Erdrich explains the deeply material connection between land and people. "As the [Anishinaabeg] lived off fish, animals, the lake's water and water plants for medicine," she writes, "they were literally cell by cell composed of the lake and the lake's islands.... Their origins are familiar. The cosmology is in the surrounding landscape, in the stars, in the shapes of the rocks and islands, and in the mazinapikiniganan, the paintings that the people made on the sides of the rocks" (34). Erdrich describes the intrinsically intra-active relationship among human, nonhuman, and land. The connection is cellular. Scholar Simon Estok makes a similar point, arguing, "The human body is the expressive site upon which material agencies flow and are reworked.... Our bodies are, in other words, the narrative agents that reveal both our exposure to and our participation in this complex of relationships" (131). Erdrich's characters move through the land in ways that remind readers of their connection to place, a connection that goes beyond historical emplacement or personal preference to a level of integration that cannot be severed.

NOTES

1. A prior version of this chapter, which has been heavily revised, appeared in *Critical Insights: Louise Erdrich*, edited by P. Jane Hafen (Salem Press, 2012).

2. The North Dakota novels that connect through location or character (or both) that have been published to date are *Love Medicine* (1984), *The Beet Queen* (1986), *Tracks* (1988), *The Bingo Palace* (1994), *Tales of Burning Love* (1997), *The Last Report on the Miracles at Little No Horse* (2001), *The Master Butchers Singing Club* (2003), *Four Souls* (2004), *The Painted Drum* (2005), *The Plague of Doves* (2008), *The Round House* (2012), and *LaRose* (2016).

3. The language Kinney employs here is strikingly similar to James Carleton's call to restrict the Diné to a reservation and Richard Pratt's description of the function of Indian education, both discussed in chapter 2. All three men were steeped in the ideology of assimilation, believing that the solution to the "Indian problem" was to eradicate Indigenous worldviews.

4. *Anishinaabe* (pl. *Anishinaabeg*) is a phonetic transcription from the oral tradition of the name the people use for themselves, meaning "the original people." More specifically, *Anishinaabe* designates the Three Fires of the Ojibwe/Ojibway/Ojibwa, the Potawatomi/Bodewadmi, and the Ottawa/Odawa. The Ojibwe were considered the eldest brother, the Odawa the middle brother, and the Potawatomi the youngest brother (Dickmann and Leefers 73). *Ojibwe/Ojibway/Ojibwa* and *Chippewa* are different spellings for the same name, though the former versions are perhaps more accurate representations. *Anishinaabe* and *Ojibwe/Ojibway/Ojibwa* all appear in this chapter as they are used by different authors. In my own writing, however, I use *Anishinaabe* to reflect the people's self-designation.

5. Today the Anishinaabeg live on reserves in Ontario and Manitoba and on reservations in Minnesota, Wisconsin, Michigan, and North Dakota, as well as in off-reservation towns and cities all over the country and the world (Vizenor, *People* 32). John Nichols notes that "Ojibwe and the other languages grouped together in the Algonquian language family resemble each other so closely in sound patterns, grammar, and vocabulary that at one time they must have been a single language.... At the time of the European invasion of North America, the languages of the Algonquian family were spoken by Indians along the Atlantic coast from what is now North Carolina to Newfoundland, inland across Canada to the Great Plains, and in the region of the Great Lakes, perhaps ranging as far south as Alabama and Georgia" (qtd. in Vizenor, *People* 16).

6. Rob Nixon's explanation of "official" and "vernacular" landscapes is useful here: "A vernacular landscape is shaped by the affective, historically textured

maps that communities have devised over generations, maps replete with names and routes, maps alive to significant ecological and surface geological features.... By contrast, an official landscape—whether governmental, NGO, corporate, or some combination of those—is typically oblivious to such earlier maps: instead, it writes the land in a bureaucratic, externalizing, and extraction-driven manner that is often pitilessly instrumental" (17).

7. Maria DePriest notes, "Tracking the moments when land becomes property, [*Tracks*] moves implacably from 1912 to 1924, just at the time when the consequences of the Allotment Act of 1887 and its several amendments were the most devastating for the tribe" (251).

8. See chapter 1, note 16, for a brief explanation of the term *nadouissioux*.

9. Pauline tells the readers early on in *Tracks*, "I wanted to be like my mother, who showed her half-white. I wanted to be like my grandfather, pure Canadian. That was because even as a child I saw that to hang back was to perish. I saw through the eyes of the world outside us" (14).

10. Anishinaabe elder Lillian Pitawanakwat explains that the teachings of the Medicine Wheel "are vast. There are seven teachings within each direction on the Ojibwe wheel, and all these have sub-teachings to them, such as where all the medicines like sweetgrass came from, and what they mean." The Medicine Wheel is visually represented as a circle divided into four quadrants that represent the four cardinal points and the four seasons, as well as sacred colors, animals, plants, and stories. Also contained in the Medicine Wheel are the Seven Grandfather Teachings ("Honesty, Humility, Courage, Wisdom, Respect, Generosity and Love") and the Seven Stages of Life ("The Good Life, The Fast Life, The Wandering Life, the stages of Truth, Planning, and Doing, and The Elder Life").

11. In her reading of this passage, Joni Adamson argues that "Pauline accuses Fleur of wielding the malign powers of a bearwalking sorcerer, or one who transforms herself into a bear in order to use her power for self-aggrandizement.... Fleur, Pauline lets it be known, has gotten herself into some half-forgotten medicine that causes her to mess with evil." Adamson goes on to explain that it is not Fleur's link to the natural world that is intrinsically evil, but rather Pauline's representation of it as a sign of sorcery. Pauline, Adamson argues, is on a "mission to 'close the door' on her people and community," something she does by rejecting the Anishinaabe world, where "gods walk among humans, the boundaries between humans and nature are permeable, and everything in the natural world is connected to everything else" (*American Indian Literature* 106).

12. We learn in *Four Souls* that cutting down the trees and walking away from the lake are the first step in Fleur's elaborate plan to reclaim her land.

13. Nancy Peterson lays out some of the connections between the two: "Episodes in the story of Naanabozho parallel episodes in Nanapush's story. Both share the ability to come back to life after death or near death; both are noted for their keen ability to track people; both avenge wrongs committed on family members; both are powerful storytellers" (990). The connection is also marked by the location of trickster's home on the crossroads (Barbara Babcock notes that the crossroads is a location common to trickster figures in Native American stories [162]) and by trickster's ability to survive (Nanapush is the last surviving member of his family and at fifty is considered an elder because so few elders have survived the sickness that claimed his family [Erdrich, *Tracks* 2]). Andrew Wiget argues that traditional trickster narratives "shift the burden of meaning from the cognitive sphere to the moral one.... Instead of asking, What is Truth in the matter—an unanswerable question...—one must ask, What is right?" (92–93). The circling, contradictory trickster narratives expose the limitations of "official" historical accounts and suggest that cultural survival rests not in the certainty of factual truth but on the shifting ground of interpretation, adaptation, and ethics. Nanapush's role in *Tracks* keeps the other characters off-balance. In one moment, he is telling a story with the sole purpose of causing Pauline to lose control of her bladder, and in the next he is enacting sacred ceremonies. Such a contrast is not a contradiction but rather a clear sign of trickster's vibrant character, both creator and fool, wise elder and prankster.

14. Victoria Brehm argues that Nanapush's ceremony reflects his initiation to the sacred medicine society of the Anishinaabeg, Midéwiwin, or Midé: "In the center of *Tracks* Nanapush begins a 'medicine' hunt, in which he guides Eli to a moose by lying down and holding his otter skin bag to his chest. Such a bag signifies that Nanapush has been initiated into the first degree of the Midéwiwin" (705n56).

15. Nanapush's description of Fleur's journey echoes Frederick Jackson Turner's controversial "frontier thesis": "Stand at Cumberland Gap and watch the procession of civilization, marching single file—the buffalo following the trail to the salt springs, the Indian, the fur trader and hunter, the cattle-raiser, the pioneer farmer."

16. Louis Owens contends that June's role of "permanent traveler" is evidence of her "infinit[e] dislocate[ion] with no family/community/tribe to expect her return" (195). In my reading, however, her movement connects her closely with her "family/tribe/community"; rather than a sign of alienation, her movement is a sign of her ultimate connection to people and place.

17. The General Allotment Act did not provide a provision for deeding land off reservation or on other reservations, and the historical record does not

indicate that such an interpretation was at all common. The Allotment Act deeded reservation land to male tribal members who lived on the reservation, and in the event that there was not enough land to provide lots of the sizes specified in the act, "the lands embraced in such reservation or reservations shall be allotted to each individual of each of said classes pro rata" ("An Act to Provide for the Allotment"). In other words, the reservation land would be divided into smaller parcels to account for all the tribal members who were eligible for allotments. The act also specified that tribal members not living on a reservation could be deeded allotments on federal lands.

Epilogue

Walking for Survival

In 2015 a group of young Diné, mostly women, organized a walk commemorating the 150th anniversary of the Long Walk and protesting fracking and other environmental hazards on Diné land. Called Nihígaal bee Iiná, or Our Journey for Existence, the walk took them across Diné Bikéyah, with the four sacred mountains as focal points. "We are journeying back to our original selves including our responsibility as women to protect the land and take care of it," explains Laura Red Elk, one of the organizers (Johnston). "Everything we do is a prayer to return to our original selves," Red Elk continues. "The mountains were our original naat'áanii [leaders] before IRA governments or the tribal council. Since our government is failing to protect us, we are returning to our original leadership by letting the mountains determine how we walk on the land" (Johnston). The links between walking, stories, and the American land are, and always have been, implicated in the material realities of culture and politics. Nihígaal bee Iiná reflects the ongoing ethical dimensions of moving on foot across the land, an ethics of walking that enters into a much longer history of movement.

It is not a new idea to suggest that the trails and paths rubbed into the American soil by the feet of walkers are central to understanding American histories. In 1890 Frederick Jackson Turner wrote, "The buffalo trail became the Indian trail, and this became the trader's 'trace;' the trails widened to roads, and the roads into turnpikes, and these in turn were transformed into railroads." He goes on to argue that as the paths were transformed, so too were the people, becoming less "European" and more "American." For Turner, walking creates American identity, an identity contained in the story of Euroamericans moving from east to west and writing over

Indigenous histories by obscuring ancient pathways. However, when we broaden our perspective, it becomes immediately apparent that the footpaths and trails crisscrossing the American land tell the stories of many different peoples. Just as Chicanx, Indigenous, and Euroamerican writers engage the rich trope of walking to connect to complex cultural stories and to communicate a variety of ideas, so too do the traces of their peregrinations reveal a multifaceted story about the relationships among self, culture, story, and land. The writers and walkers I have discussed in this book complicate the idea that walking in America narratives is a smooth line from east to west. Rather, the paths carved into the American land travel in all directions—from east to west and west to east, from north to south and south to north, and in cyclical patterns of departure and return.

The literal paths the walkers follow become a trope in literary articulations of travel. In *Wanderlust: A History of Walking*, Rebecca Solnit writes, "The history of walking is an unwritten, secret history whose fragments can be found in a thousand unemphatic passages in books, as well as in songs, streets, and almost everyone's adventures" (3). While walking may not have an obvious or forceful presence in American literatures, representations of walking and the stories of walkers are, in fact, central images in American literatures from many different cultural contexts. Writing about walking is a way writers tap into many cultural stories and beliefs about bodily movement. Walking can indicate the passage of life and time, bodily and psychological suffering, and change from one place to another or from one mentality to another. Representations of walking play a crucial role in Euroamerican, Chicanx, and Indigenous religious and secular stories, and references to walking can prompt readers to access those more complex cultural inheritances. Thus, when Mary White Rowlandson writes about wandering in the wilderness, her Puritan audience will immediately recall biblical stories of the Hebrews. Or when Urrea mentions Aztlán, his readers connect walking across the border with the legendary migration of the Aztecs. Or when Louise Erdrich depicts Fleur's footsteps transforming into the tracks of a bear, readers are alerted to Anishinaabe clan identities and stories. As a neglected literary trope, walking provides a rich site for investigating American literature from a cross-cultural context.

Yet these texts also suggest that there is something else to be gleaned, something beyond literary and cultural allusions. That "something else" is the act of walking itself. Yes, American authors tap into the vast array of allusions and ideas contained in walking. However, walking in these texts is not *only* a literary device. These texts tell the tales of people who literally walked, people who moved their bodies by placing one foot in front of the other. Their blisters may serve as a metaphor for mental suffering, but they are also a real result of walking for long distances. This intrusion of the "real" into the metaphorical is perhaps most poignant in Urrea's retelling of the journey of the twenty-six border crossers. Though their deaths may serve as symbols for the inhumanity of US border policies, they are not only symbols. Those men—some of whom remain unnamed and unclaimed—actually lost their lives.

Solnit suggests, "If the body is the register of the real, then reading with one's feet is real in a way that reading with one's eyes is not" (70). Walking serves as a nexus—a point where complex metaphor meets the real, where the stories that are told about American histories and identities come up against the traces of the people whose lives and experiences are often obscured by those very stories. To truly understand American identity, we must attend to the intersection of language, body, and the material land—an intersection we can locate in walking.

The materiality of the land and of human and nonhuman bodies intra-acts with social, economic, political, cultural, and discursive systems in the ongoing creation of the world. Walking acts as a connecting node, alerting readers to the complexity of forces acting on and with us. The literatures of the United States are literatures in motion, moving across the American land. Contained in the tangle of physical traces and textual representations lie the stories of the United States. While one branch of those stories—the Euroamerican man striding forth in the act of material and intellectual colonialism—has become the dominant representation of walking in America, there are many other kinds of American walking that reveal the complexity of American stories and experiences.

Movement in the twenty-first century is accelerating at a dizzying rate, as highway speed limits are increased, high-speed trains whisk people between places, and private companies invest in space travel. But the basic unit of human movement, the footstep, still possesses both symbolic and material power. Our walking bodies hold a vast history of human intra-action with the more-than-human world. Following the physical and literary trails of American walking reveals the complexity of these intra-actions and focuses attention on the ethical implications of human entanglement with the material world.

> The earthen dance floor beneath them,
> the stars and the moon above them.
> That rhythm, that rhythm
> it makes them one. (Zepeda 13–16)

Works Cited

"An Act to Provide for the Allotment of Lands in Severalty to Indians on the Various Reservations, and to Extend the Protection of the Laws of the United States and the Territories over the Indians, and for Other Purposes." Avalon Project, Yale Law School, 2008, avalon.law.yale.edu/19th_century/dawes.asp. Accessed 13 May 2016.

Adamson, Joni. *American Indian Literature, Environmental Justice, and Ecocriticism: The Middle Place*. U of Arizona P, 2001.

———. "The Ancient Future: Diasporic Residency and Food-Based Knowledges in the Work of American Indigenous and Pacific Austronesian Writers." *Canadian Review of Comparative Literature*, vol. 42, no. 1, Mar. 2015, pp. 5–17.

———. "Seeking the Corn Mother: Transnational Indigenous Organizing and Food Sovereignty in Native North American Literature." *Indigenous Rights in the Age of the U.N. Declaration*, edited by Elvira Pulitano, Cambridge UP, 2012, pp. 228–49.

———. "Source of Life: *Avatar*, *Amazonia*, and an Ecology of Selves." Iovino and Opperman, pp. 253–88.

Adamson, Joni, and Salma Monani, eds. *Ecocriticism and Indigenous Studies: Conversations from Earth to Cosmos*. Routledge, 2017.

Alaimo, Stacy. *Bodily Natures: Science, Environment, and the Material Self*. Indiana UP, 2010.

———. "Trans-corporeal Feminisms and the Ethical Space of Nature." Alaimo and Hekman, pp. 237–64.

———. *Undomesticated Ground: Recasting Nature as Feminist Space*. Cornell UP, 2000.

Alaimo, Stacy, and Susan Hekman, eds. *Material Feminisms*. Indiana UP, 2008.

Alarcón, Daniel Cooper. *The Aztec Palimpsest: Mexico in the Modern Imagination*. U of Arizona P, 1997.

Algeo, Matthew. *Pedestrianism: When Watching People Walk Was America's Favorite Spectator Sport*. Chicago Review Press, 2014.

Allen, Paula Gunn. *The Sacred Hoop: Recovering the Feminine in American Indian Traditions*. Beacon Press, 1986.

Amato, Joseph A. *On Foot: A History of Walking*. New York UP, 2004.

Ammons, Elizabeth. *Conflicting Stories: American Women Writers at the Turn of the Twentieth Century*. Oxford UP, 1991.

Anaya, Rudolfo A., and Francisco Lomeli, eds. *Aztlán: Essays on the Chicano Homeland*. U of New Mexico P, 1989.

Anderson, Gary Clayton, and Alan R. Woolworth. *Through Dakota Eyes: Narrative Accounts of the Minnesota Indian War of 1862*. Minnesota Historical Society P, 1988.

Andrews, William L., et al., eds. *Journeys in New Worlds: Early American Women's Narratives*. U of Wisconsin P, 1990.

Annerino, John. *Dead in Their Tracks: Crossing America's Desert Borderlands*. Four Walls Eight Windows, 1999.

Anzaldúa, Gloria. *Borderlands/La Frontera: The New Mestiza*. Aunt Lute Books, 1987.

Arthur, Claudeen, Sam Bingham, and Janet Bingham, eds. *Between Sacred Mountains: Navajo Stories and Lessons from the Land*. Sun Tracks: An American Indian Literary Series, vol. 2, U of Arizona P, 1984.

Austin, Mary. *The American Rhythm*. Harcourt Brace, 1923.

———. *Earth Horizon: Autobiography*. U of New Mexico P, 1932.

———. *Everyman's Genius*. Bobbs-Merrill, 1925.

———. *Land of Little Rain*. 1903. *Stories from the Country of Lost Borders*, 3–149.

———. "Non-English Writings II: Aboriginal." *The Cambridge History of American Literature*, edited by William Peterfield Trent, et al., G. P. Putnam's Sons, 1921, pp. 610–34.

———. *Stories from the Country of Lost Borders*, edited by Marjorie Pryse, Rutgers UP, 1987.

———. "The Walking Woman." *Lost Borders*. 1909. *Stories from the Country of Lost Borders*, pp. 255–62.

Babcock, Barbara. "'A Tolerated Margin of Mess': The Trickster and His Tales Reconsidered." *Critical Essays on Native American Literature*, edited by Andrew Wiget, G. K. Hall, 1985, pp. 153–85.

Bailey, L. R. *The Long Walk: A History of the Navajo Wars, 1846–1868*. Westernlore P, 1964.

Banner, Stuart. *How the Indians Lost Their Land: Law and Power on the Frontier*. Belknap P of Harvard UP, 2005.

Barad, Karen. *Meeting the Universe Halfway: Quantum Physics and the Entanglement of Matter and Meaning*. Duke UP, 2007.

———. "Posthumanist Performativity: Toward an Understanding of How Matter Comes to Matter." Alaimo and Hekman, pp. 120–54.

Begay, Dugal Tsosie. "Family Narrative." Roessel, pp. 213–17.

Begay, Hosteen Tso. "Family Narrative." Roessel, pp. 262–66.

Benally, Chahadineli. "Family Narrative." Roessel, pp. 57–74.

Bennett, Jane. *Vibrant Matter: A Political Ecology of Things*. Duke UP, 2010.

Bercovitch, Sacvan. *The Puritan Origins of the American Self*. Yale UP, 1975.

Beyale, John Sr. "Family Narrative." Diné of the Eastern Region, pp. 41–43.

Bierhorst, John. *Four Masterworks of American Indian Literature*. Farrar, Straus and Giroux, 1974.

Bighorse, Tiana. *Bighorse the Warrior*. Edited by Noël Bennett, U of Arizona P, 1998.

Bird, Gloria. "Searching for Evidence of Colonialism at Work: A Reading of Louise Erdrich's *Tracks*." *Wicazo Sa Review*, vol. 8, no. 2, Autumn 1992, pp. 40–47.

Blackbird, Chelsea, and Barney Nelson, eds. *Mary Austin's Southwest: An Anthology of Her Literary Criticism*. U of Utah P, 2005.

Blackhawk, Ned. *Violence over the Land: Indians and Empires in the Early American West*. Harvard UP, 2008.

Blaeser, Kimberly M. "Sacred Journey Cycles: Pilgrimage as Re-turning and Re-telling in American Indigenous Literatures." *Religion & Literature*, vol. 35, nos. 2–3, Summer–Autumn 2003, pp. 83–104.

Blend, Benay. "Mary Austin and the Western Conservation Movement, 1900–1927." *Journal of the Southwest*, vol. 30, Spring 1988, pp. 12–34.

Bogost, Ian. *Alien Phenomenology; or, What's It Like to Be a Thing?* U of Minnesota P, 2012.

Bonnevin, Joëlle. "From *Tracks* to *Four Souls* by Louise Erdrich: Fleur Pillager's Loss and Recovery of Her Land and Heritage." *Thy Truth Then Be Thy Dowry: Questions of Inheritance in American Women's Literature*, edited by Stéphanie Durrans, Cambridge Scholars, 2014, pp. 169–84.

Brady, Mary Pat. *Extinct Lands, Temporal Geographies: Chicana Literature and the Urgency of Space*. Duke UP, 2004.

Brehm, Victoria. "The Metamorphoses of an Ojibwa Manido." *American Literature*, vol. 68, no. 4, Dec. 1996, pp. 677–706.

Breitwieser, Mitchell Robert. *American Puritanism and the Defense of Mourning: Religion, Grief, and Ethnology in Mary White Rowlandson's Captivity Narrative*. U of Wisconsin P, 1990.

Breu, Christopher. *Insistence of the Material: Literature in the Age of Biopolitics*. U of Minnesota P, 2014.

Brooks, Lisa. *The Common Pot: The Recovery of Native Space in the Northeast*. U of Minnesota P, 2008.

Buell, Lawrence. *The Environmental Imagination: Thoreau, Nature Writing, and the Formation of American Culture*. Belknap P of Harvard UP, 1995.

Burnham, Michelle. *Captivity and Sentiment: Cultural Exchange in American Literature, 1682–1861*. UP of New England, 1997.

———. "The Journey Between: Liminality and Dialogism in Mary White Rowlandson's Captivity Narrative." *Early American Literature*, vol. 28, 1993, pp. 60–75.

Buske, Frank E. "In Search of John Muir." *John Muir in Historical Perspective*, edited by Sally M. Miller, Peter Lang, 1999, pp. 1–8.

Cajete, Gregory. *Native Science: Natural Laws of Interdependence*. Clear Light, 2000.

Carew-Miller, Anna. "Between Worlds, Crossing Borders: Mary Austin, Liminality, and the Dilemma of Women's Creativity." Graulich and Klimasmith, pp. 105–27.

Castiglia, Christopher. *Bound and Determined: Captivity, Culture-Crossing, and White Womanhood from Mary Rowlandson to Patty Hearst*. U of Chicago P, 1996.

Charley, Florence. "Family Narrative." Roessel, pp. 148–50.

Chávez, César. "Sacramento March Letter, March 1966." *The Words of César Chávez*, edited by Richard J. Jensen and John C. Hammerback, Texas A&M UP, 2002, pp. 15–16.

Chávez, John. "The Chicano Homeland." *The Multicultural Southwest: A Reader*, edited by A. Gabriel Meléndez et al., U of A Press, 2001, pp. 11–21.

Chedgzoy, Kate. *Women's Writing in the British Atlantic World: Memory, Place and History, 1550–1700*. Cambridge UP, 2007.

Cheek, Lawrence. *The Navajo Long Walk*. Rio Nuevo, 2004.

Clifford, James. *Routes: Travel and Translation in the Late Twentieth Century*. Harvard UP, 1997.

Cohen, Deborah. *Braceros: Migrant Citizens and Transnational Subjects in the Postwar United States and Mexico*. U of North Carolina P, 2011.

Cohen, Michael P. *The Pathless Way: John Muir and American Wilderness*. U of Wisconsin P, 1984.

"Compendium of the Catechism of the Catholic Church." *Vatican: The Holy See*, 2005, Libreria Editrice Vaticana, www.vatican.va/archive/compendium_ccc/documents/archive_2005_compendium-ccc_en.html. Accessed 22 Mar. 2016.

Conley, Robert J. *The Cherokee Nation: A History*. U of New Mexico P, 2005.

Cornelius, Wayne A. "Death at the Border: Efficacy and Unintended Consequences of US Immigration Control Policy." *Population and Development Review*, vol. 27, no. 4, 2001, pp. 661–85.

Crèvecœur, J. Hector St. John de. "From *Letters from an American Farmer*." Finch and Elder, pp. 52–59.

Cutter, Martha J. *Unruly Tongue: Identity and Voice in American Women's Writing, 1850–1930*. UP of Mississippi, 1999.

Denejolie, Mose. "Family Narrative." Roessel, pp. 241–44.

DePriest, Maria. "Once upon a Time, Today: Hearing Fleur's Voice in *Tracks*." *Journal of Narrative Theory*, vol. 38, no. 2, Summer 2008, pp. 249–68.

Derounian-Stodola, and Kathryn Zabelle. *The War in Words: Reading the Dakota Conflict Through the Captivity Literature*. U of Nebraska P, 2009.

Derounian-Stodola, Kathryn Zabelle, and James Arthur Levernier. *The Indian Captivity Narrative, 1550–1900*. Twayne's United States Author Series. Twayne, 1993.

Dickmann, Donald I., and Larry A. Leefers. *The Forests of Michigan*. U of Michigan P, 2003.

Dietrich, Deborah J. "Mary Rowlandson's Great Declension." *Women's Studies*, vol. 24, 1995, pp. 427–39.

Diné of the Eastern Region of the Navajo Reservation. *Oral History Stories of the Long Walk: Hwéeldi Baa Hané*. GPO, 1991.

Dodge, Robert V. *Which Chosen People? Manifest Destiny Meets the Sioux as Seen by Frank Fiske, Frontier Photographer*. Algora, 2013.

Doerfler, Jill, Niigaawewidam James Sinclair, and Heidi Kiiwetinepinesiik Stark, eds. *Centering Anishinaabeg Studies: Understanding the World Through Stories*. East Michigan State UP, 2013.

Domosh, Mona, and Joni Seager. *Putting Women in Place: Feminist Geographers Making Sense of the World*. Guilford P, 2001.

Downing, David. "'Streams of Scriptural Comfort': Mary Rowlandson's Typological Use of the Bible." *Early American Literature*, vol. 15, 1980–81, pp. 252–59.

Ebersole, Gary L. *Captured by Texts: Puritan to Postmodern Images of Indian Captivity*. UP of Virginia, 1995.

Emerson, Ralph Waldo. *Emerson's Prose and Poetry*, edited by Joel Porte and Saundra Morris, W. W. Norton, 2001.

Erdrich, Louise. *Books and Islands in Ojibwe Country*. National Geographic Society, 2003.

———. *Four Souls*. Harper Perennial, 2004.

———. *The Last Report on the Miracles at Little No Horse*. HarperCollins, 2001.

———. *Love Medicine*. Harper Flamingo, 1984.

———. *Tracks*. Harper Perennial, 1988.

Estok, Simon. "Painful Material Realities, Tragedy, Ecophobia." Iovino and Opperman, pp. 130–40.

Evers, Larry. "By This Song I Walk: Navajo Song." *Words and Place: Native Literature from the American Southwest*, parentseyes.arizona.edu/wordsandplace/natonabah_intro.html. Accessed 10 Nov. 2015.

———. "Words and Place: A Reading of *House Made of Dawn*." *Critical Essays on Native American Literature*, edited by Andrew Wiget, G. K. Hall, 1985, pp. 211–30.

Faery, Rebecca Blevins. *Cartographies of Desire: Captivity, Race, and Sex in the Shaping of an American Nation*. U of Oklahoma P, 1999.
Farella, John R. *The Main Stalk: A Synthesis of Navajo Philosophy*. U of Arizona P, 1984.
Finch, Robert, and John Elder, eds. *The Norton Book of Nature Writing*. College Edition. W. W. Norton, 2002.
Fink, Augusta. *I-Mary: A Biography of Mary Austin*. U of Arizona P, 1983.
Fox, Steve. "Roads to Heaven: Pilgrimage in the Southwest." *The Multicultural Southwest: A Reader*, edited by A. Gabriel Meléndez et al., U of Arizona P, 2001, pp. 242–52.
Friedman, Susan Stanford. *Mappings: Feminism and the Cultural Geographies of Encounter*. Princeton UP, 1998.
Garroutte, Eva Marie, and Kathleen Delores Westcott. "The Story Is a Living Being: Companionship with Stories in Anishinaabeg Studies." Doerfler, Sinclair, and Stark, pp. 61–80.
Gevalt, Geoffrey. "N.H. Pair Ends Bicen Trek Across U.S." *Portland Press Herald*, vol. 26, July 1976, pp. A1+.
Glancy, Diane. *Pushing the Bear: A Novel of the Trail of Tears*. Harcourt, 1996.
———. *The West Pole*. U of Minnesota P, 1997.
Goeman, Mishuana. "(Re)Mapping Indigenous Presence on the Land in Native Women's Literature." *American Quarterly*, vol. 60, no. 2, June 2008, pp. 295–302.
Gómez, Reid. "The Storyteller's Escape: Sovereignty and Worldview." *Reading Native American Women: Critical/Creative Representations*, edited by Inés Hernández-Avila, AltaMira P, 2005, pp. 145–69.
Gorman, Eli. "Family Narrative." Roessel, pp. 197–209.
Gorman, Howard. "Family Narrative." Roessel, pp. 23–42.
Gould, Janice. "American Indian Women's Poetry: Strategies of Rage and Hope." *Signs: Journal of Women in Culture and Society*, vol. 20, no. 4, 1995, pp. 797–817.
Graulich, Melody. "Walking Off an Illness? Don't Go West, Young Man: The Construction of Masculinity in *Cactus Thorn*." Graulich and Klimasmith, pp. 267–82.
———, ed. *Western Trails: A Collection of Short Stories by Mary Austin*. U of Nevada P, 1987.
Graulich, Melody, and Elizabeth Klimasmith, eds. *Exploring Lost Borders: Critical Essays on Mary Austin*. U of Nevada P, 1999.
Gray, Tom. "The Treaty of Guadalupe Hidalgo." *National Archives*, www.archives.gov/education/lessons/guadalupe-hidalgo. Accessed 16 Jan. 2017.
Gross, Lawrence William. "The Trickster and World Maintenance: An Anishinaabe Reading of Louise Erdrich's *Tracks*." *Studies in American Indian Literatures*, vol. 17, no. 3, Fall 2005, pp. 48–66.

Harrison, Summer. "The Politics of Metafiction in Louise Erdrich's *Four Souls*." *Studies in American Indian Literature*, vol. 23, no. 1, Spring 2011, pp. 38–69.

Hart, Tara. "Serving Suspended Sentences: Mary Austin's Compositions and Explanations." Graulich and Klimasmith, pp. 87–103.

Heilbrun, Carolyn. *Writing a Woman's Life*. Ballantine Press, 1988.

Henwood, Dawn. "Mary Rowlandson and the Psalms: The Textuality of Survival." *Early American Literature*, vol. 32, 1997, pp. 169–86.

Heyne, Eric, ed. *Desert, Garden, Margin, Range: Literature on the American Frontier*. Twayne, 1992.

Holmes-Rodman, Paula Elizabeth. "'They Told What Happened on the Road': Narrative and the Construction of Experiential Knowledge on the Pilgrimage to Chimayo, New Mexico." *Intersecting Journeys: The Anthropology of Pilgrimage and Tourism*, edited by Ellen Badone and Sharon R. Roseman, U of Illinois P, 2004, pp. 24–51.

Homestead Act. Pub. L. 37-64 12 STAT 392. 20 May 1862. *Our Documents*, www.ourdocuments.gov/doc.php?doc=31&page=transcript. Accessed 15 May 2016.

Hoyer, Mark T. *Dancing Ghosts: Native American and Christian Syncretism in Mary Austin's Work*. U of Nevada P, 1998.

Indian Removal Act of 1830. *Cal Humanities: Teaching Democracy Webinar Series*, 18 July 2012, www.calhum.org/files/uploads/program_related/TD-Indian-Removal-Act-1830.pdf. Accessed 15 Jan. 2017.

Iovino, Serenella, and Serpil Opperman, eds. *Material Ecocriticism*. Indiana UP, 2014.

Iverson, Peter. *Diné: A History of the Navajos*. U of New Mexico P, 2002.

Jacobson, David. *Place and Belonging in America*. Johns Hopkins UP, 2002.

Jaycox, Faith. "Regeneration Through Liberation: Mary Austin's 'The Walking Woman' and Western Narrative Formula." *Legacy*, vol. 6, no. 1, Spring 1989, pp. 5–12.

Johnson, Kelli Lyon. "Writing Deeper Maps: Mapmaking, Local Indigenous Knowledges, and Literary Nationalism in Native Women's Writing." *Studies in American Indian Literatures*, vol. 19, no. 4, Winter 2007, pp. 103–20.

Johnston, Lyla. "Young Navajos State 200 Mile Journey for Existence." *Idle No More*, 25 Jan. 2015, www.idlenomore.ca/young_navajos_stage_200_mile_journey_for_existence. Accessed 23 June 2016.

Justice, Daniel Heath. *Our Fire Survives the Storm: A Cherokee Literary History*. U of Minnesota P, 2006.

Kelley, Klara Bonsack, and Harris Francis. *Navajo Sacred Places*. Indiana UP, 1994.

Kellogg, J. H. *Plain Facts for Young and Old*. Segner & Condit, 1881, Project Gutenberg, www.gutenberg.org/files/19924/19924-h/19924-h.htm. Accessed 5 July 2016.

Kestler, Frances Row, ed. *The Indian Captivity Narrative: A Woman's View*. Garland, 1990.

Kimmerer, Robin Wall. *Braiding Sweetgrass: Indigenous Wisdom, Scientific Knowledge, and the Teachings of Plants*. Milkweed Editions, 2013.

Klah, Hasteen. *Navajo Creation Myth: The Story of the Emergence*. Recorded by Mary C. Wheelwright, Museum of Navajo Ceremonial Art, 1942.

Kolodny, Annette. *The Land Before Her: Fantasy and Experience of the American Frontiers, 1630–1860*. U of North Carolina P, 1984.

———. "Letting Go Our Grand Obsessions: Notes Toward a New Literary History of the American Frontiers." *American Literature*, vol. 64, no. 1, Mar. 1992, pp. 1–18.

LaDuke, Winona, and Sean Aaron Cruz. *The Militarization of Indian Country*. Makwa Enewed, 2013.

Lang, Amy Schrager. "Introduction: Mary White Rowlandson." Andrews et al., pp. 13–26.

Langan, Celeste. *Romantic Vagrancy: Wordsworth and the Simulation of Freedom*. Cambridge UP, 1995.

Lape, Noreen Groover. *West of the Border: The Multicultural Literature of the Western American Frontiers*. Ohio UP, 2000.

Leal, Luis. "In Search of Aztlán." *Aztlán: Essays on the Chicano Homeland*, edited by Rudolfo A. Anaya and Francisco A. Lomelí, Academia/El Norte, 1989, pp. 6–13.

Léon, Luis D. *La Llorona's Children: Religion, Life, and Death in the U.S.-Mexican Borderlands*. U of California P, 2004.

Lewis, Corey Lee. *Reading the Trail: Exploring the Literature and Natural History of the California Crest*. U of Nevada P, 2005.

Lewis, R. W. B. *The American Adam: Innocence, Tragedy and Tradition in the Nineteenth Century*. U of Chicago P, 1955.

Limerick, Patricia Nelson. *The Legacy of Conquest: The Unbroken Past of the American West*. W. W. Norton, 1987.

Logan, Lisa. "Mary Rowlandson's Captivity and the 'Place' of the Woman Subject." *Early American Literature*, vol. 28, 1993, pp. 255–77.

Maran, Timo. "Semiotization of Matter: A Hybrid Zone Between Biosemiotics and Material Ecocriticism." Iovino and Opperman, pp. 141–56.

Marks, Paula Mitchell. *In a Barren Land: American Indian Dispossession and Survival*. William Morrow, 1998.

Marmon, Lee, and Tom Corbett. *Laguna Pueblo: A Photographic History*. U of New Mexico P, 2015.

McKenna, Theresa. *Migrant Song: Politics and Process in Contemporary Chicano Literature*. U of Texas P, 1997.

McKusick, James C. *Green Writing: Romanticism and Ecology*. St. Martin's P, 2000.

McPherson, Robert S. *Sacred Land, Sacred View*. Charles Redd Center for Western Studies, Brigham Young U, 1992.

Metcalfe, Dale. "Singing Like the Indians Do: Mary Austin's Poetry." Graulich and Klimasmith, pp. 65–85.

Miles, John David. "Captured by Genre: Mary Rowlandson's Western Imagination on the Nineteenth-Century Frontier." *Before the West Was West: Critical Essays on Pre-1800 Literature of the American Frontiers*, edited by Amy T. Hamilton and Tom J. Hillard, U of Nebraska P, 2014, pp. 102–29.

Miller, Perry. *Errand into the Wilderness*. Harvard UP, 1984.

Miner, Dylan A. T. "Stories as *Mshkiki*: Reflections on the Healing and Migratory Practices of *Minwaajimo*." Doerfler, Sinclair, and Stark, pp. 317–40.

Mitchell, Tezbah. "Family Narrative." Roessel, pp. 246–52.

Mogen, David, Mark Busby, and Paul Bryant, eds. *The Frontier Experience and the American Dream: Essays on American Literature*. Texas A&M UP, 1989.

Mooney, James. *James Mooney's History, Myths, and Sacred Formulas of the Cherokees*. Bright Mountain Books, 1992.

Morris, Irwin. *From the Glittering World: A Navajo Story*. U of Oklahoma P, 1997.

Muir, John. *My First Summer in the Sierra*. 1911. Houghton Mifflin, 1998.

———. *A Thousand-Mile Walk to the Gulf*, edited by William Frederic Badè, Houghton Mifflin, 1916.

Natonabah, Andrew. "By This Song I Walk: Navajo Song." *Words and Place: Native Literature from the American Southwest*, parentseyes.arizona.edu/wordsandplace/natonabah.html. Accessed 10 Nov. 2015.

Nelson, Ernest. "Family Narrative." Roessel, pp. 171–75.

Nelson, Melissa K. "The Hydromythology of the Anishinaabeg: Will Mishipizhu Survive Climate Change, or Is He Creating It?" Doerfler, Sinclair, and Stark, pp. 213–36.

Newcomb, Steven. "Convoluted U.S. 'Logic' About the Western Shoshone Nation and Its Territory." *Indian Country Today*, 23 Apr. 2014, indiancountrymedianetwork.com/news/opinions/convoluted-us-logic-about-the-western-shoshone-nation-and-its-territory/. Accessed 19 Jan. 2016.

Nixon, Rob. *Slow Violence and the Environmentalism of the Poor*. Harvard UP, 2011.

Noori, Margaret. "*Beshaabiiag G'gikenmaaigowag*: Comets of Knowledge." Doerfler, Sinclair, and Stark, pp. 35–60.

O'Grady, John P. *Pilgrims to the Wild*. U of Utah P, 1993.

Oliver-Rotger, Maria Antònia. "Ethnographies of Transnational Migration in Rubén Martínez's 'Crossing Over.'" *MELUS*, vol. 31, no. 2, Summer 2006, pp. 181–205.

Ortiz, Simon. "Towards a National Indian Literature: Cultural Authenticity in Nationalism." *Multi-ethnic Literature of the U.S.*, vol. 8, no. 2, Summer 1981, pp. 7–12.

Owens, Louis. *Other Destinies: Understanding the American Indian Novel.* U of Oklahoma Press, 1992.

Paes de Barros, Deborah. *Fast Cars and Bad Girls: Nomadic Subjects and Women's Road Stories*. Peter Lang, 2004.

Pavlik, Steve. "The Role of Bears and Bear Ceremonialism in Navajo Orthodox Traditional Lifeway." *Social Science Journal*, vol. 34, no. 1, 1997, pp. 475–84.

Peterson, Nancy J. "History, Postmodernism, and Louise Erdrich's *Tracks*." PMLA, vol. 109, no. 5, Oct. 1994, pp. 982–94.

Pettee, Karen. Letter to the author. 15 Mar. 1976.

Pinxten, Rik, Ingrid Van Dooren, and Frank Harvey. *Anthropology of Space: Explorations into the Natural Philosophy of Semantics of the Navajo.* U of Pennsylvania P, 1983.

Pioche, Harry. "Family Narrative." Diné of the Eastern Region, p. 95.

Pitawanakwat, Lillian. "Ojibwe/Powawatomi (Anishinabe) Teaching." *Four Directions Teachings*, 2006, www.fourdirectionsteachings.com/transcripts/ojibwe.pdf. Accessed 9 June 2011.

Pratt, Mary Louise. *Imperial Eyes: Travel Writing and Transculturation.* Routledge, 1992.

Pratt, Richard H. "The Advantages of Mingling Indians with Whites." *Americanizing the American Indians: Writings by the "Friends of the Indian," 1880–1900*, edited by Francis Paul Prucha, Harvard UP, 1973, pp. 260–71.

Price, Patricia L. *Dry Place: Landscapes of Belonging and Exclusion*. Minneapolis: U of Minnesota P, 2004.

Rader, Dean, and Janice Gould. "Introduction: Generations and Emanations." *Speak to Me Words: Essays on Contemporary American Indian Poetry*, U of Arizona P, 2003, www.uapress.arizona.edu/catalogs/dlg_show_excerpt.php?id=1508. Accessed 26 Jan. 2017.

Rainwater, Catherine. "Reading Between Worlds: Narrativity in the Fiction of Louise Erdrich." *American Literature*, vol. 62, no. 3, 1990, pp. 405–33.

Riley, Glenda. *Women and Indians on the Frontier, 1825–1915*. U of New Mexico P, 1984.

Roberts, David. *A Newer World: Kit Carson, John C. Fremont and the Claiming of the American West*. Simon and Schuster, 2000.

Roessel, Ruth, ed. *Navajo Stories of the Long Walk Period*. Navajo Community College P, 1973.

Rowlandson, Mary White. "A True History of the Captivity and Restoration of Mrs. Mary Rowlandson." 1682. Andrews et al., pp. 27–65.

Salisbury, Neal. "Introduction: Mary Rowlandson and Her Removes." *The Sovereignty and Goodness of God, Together with the Faithfulness of His Promises Displayed: Being a Narrative of the Captivity and Restoration of Mrs. Mary Rowlandson and Related Documents*. Bedford/St. Martin's, 1997, pp. 1–60.

Samuels, Shirley. "Sentimentalism and Domestic Fiction." *Oxford Bibliographies*, 29 Aug. 2012, www.oxfordbibliographies.com/view/document/obo-9780199827251/obo-9780199827251-0015.xml. Accessed 22 Sept. 2015.

Sandoval, Charley. "Family Narrative." Roessel, pp. 142–43.

Sands, Kathleen M. "Louise Erdrich's Love Medicine." *Studies in American Indian Literatures*, vol. 9, no. 1, 1985, pp. 12–24.

Scharrón–del Río, María R., and Alan A. Aja. "The Case for Latinx: Why Intersectionality Is Not a Choice." *Latino Rebels*, 5 Dec. 2015, www.latinorebels.com/2015/12/05/the-case-for-latinx-why-intersectionality-is-not-a-choice/. Accessed 24 Jan. 2017.

Scheick, William J. "Mary Austin's Disfigurement of the Southwest in *The Land of Little Rain*." *Western American Literature*, vol. 27, no. 1, Spring 1992, pp. 37–46.

Schlenz, Mark. "Waters of Paradise: Utopia and Hydrology in *The Land of Little Rain*." Graulich and Klimasmith, pp. 183–201.

Schultz, Duane. *Over the Earth I Come: The Great Sioux Uprising of 1862*. St. Martin's Press, 1992.

Shapiro, Karl, and Robert Beum. *A Prosody Handbook*. Harper and Row, 1965.

Silko, Leslie Marmon. *Yellow Woman and a Beauty of the Spirit: Essays on Native American Life Today*. Simon and Schuster, 1996.

Slotkin, Richard. *Regeneration Through Violence: The Mythology of the American Frontier, 1600–1860*. U of Oklahoma P, 1973.

Slovic, Scott. *Seeking Awareness in American Nature Writing: Henry Thoreau, Annie Dillard, Edward Abbey, Wendell Berry, Barry Lopez*. U of Utah P, 1992.

Smith, Henry Nash. *Virgin Land: The American West as Symbol and Myth*. Harvard UP, 1950.

Smith, Reggie. "Pair Salute Bicentennial America with Sore Feet." *Los Angeles Times*, 25 July 1976, p. F1.

Solnit, Rebecca. *Wanderlust: A History of Walking*. Viking, 2000.

Stegner, Wallace. *The American West as Living Space*. U of Michigan P, 1987.

Steinberg, Philip E. "Sovereignty, Territory, and the Mapping of Mobility: A View from the Outside." *Annals of the Association of American Geographers*, vol. 99, no. 3, July 2009, pp. 467–95.

Stineman, Esther Lanigan. *Mary Austin: Song of a Maverick*. Yale UP, 1989.

Stout, Janis. *The Journey Narrative in American Literature: Patterns and Departures*. Greenwood Press, 1983.

Stratton, Billy J. *Buried in the Shades of Night: Contested Voices, Indian Captivity, and the Legacy of King Philip's War*. U of Arizona P, 2013.

Stratton, Billy J., and Frances Washburn. "The Peoplehood Matrix: A New Theory for American Indian Literature." *Wicazo Sa Review*, vol. 23, no. 1, Spring 2008, pp. 51–72.

Stratton, Rev. Royal B. "Captivity of the Oatman Girls" [1857]. *The Indian Captivity Narrative: A Woman's View*, edited by Frances Roe Kestler, Garland, 1990, pp. 304–43.

Stremlau, Rose. "'To Domesticate and Civilize Wild Indians': Allotment and the Campaign to Reform Indian Families, 1875–1887." *Journal of Family History*, vol. 30, no. 3, July 2005, pp. 265–86.

Strong, Pauline Turner. *Captive Selves, Captivating Others: The Politics and Poetics of Colonial American Captivity Narratives*. Westview Press, 1999.

Tapahonso, Luci. "Come into the Shade." *Open Spaces, City Places: Contemporary Writers on the Changing Southwest*, edited by Judy Nolte Temple, U of Arizona P, 1994, pp. 73–85.

———. *Sáanii Dahataał: Poems and Stories*. U of Arizona P, 1993.

Tarble, Helen M. "The Story of My Capture and Escape During the Minnesota Indian Massacre of 1862" [1904]. *The Garland Library of Narrative of North American Indian Captivities*, edited by Wilcomb E. Washburn, vol. 105, Garland, 1976.

Thoreau, Henry David. "Walking." Finch and Elder, pp. 180–205.

———. *A Year in Thoreau's Journal: 1851*. Penguin Classics, 1993.

Thurston, Herbert, and Andrew J. Shipman. "The Rosary." *The Catholic Encyclopedia*, vol. 13, Robert Appleton, 1912, www.newadvent.org/cathen/13184b.htm. Accessed 2 Apr. 2008.

Tilley, Christopher. *Metaphor and Material Culture*. Blackwell, 1999.

Timbisha Shoshone Tribe. 2003. Timbisha Shoshone Tribe, 6 Dec. 2007, timbisha.com. Accessed 15 Feb. 2016.

Tohe, Laura. "Grounded in Spiritual Geography: Restoring *Naabaahi* in *Enemy Slayer, Navajo Oratorio*." Adamson and Monani, pp. 82–97.

———. "Hwéeldi Bééhániih: Remembering the Long Walk." *Wicazo Sa Review*, vol. 22, no. 1, Spring 2007, pp. 77–82.

———. "In Dinétah." *Sister Nations: Native American Women Writers on Community*. Minnesota Historical Society, 2002, pp. 100–104.

———. *No Parole Today*. West End Press, 1999.

Toohey, Michelle Campbell. "Mary Austin's *The Land of Little Rain*: Remembering the Coyote." Graulich and Klimasmith, pp. 203–20.

Toulouse, Teresa A. *The Captive's Position: Female Narrative, Male Identity, and Royal Authority in Colonial New England*. U of Pennsylvania P, 2007.

Tracing the Trail: The Pictured Rocks Segment of the Anishnaabeg Migration Route. National Park Service and Alex K. Ruuska, Northern Michigan U, nmuanthro.net. Accessed 5 May 2011.

Trafzer, Clifford E. *The Kit Carson Campaign: The Last Great Navajo War*. U of Oklahoma P, 1982.

Turner, Frederick Jackson. "The Frontier in American History." *American Studies at the University of Virginia*, Sept. 1997, xroads.virginia.edu/~HYPER/TURNER/home.html. Accessed 24 May 2016.

Turner, Victor, and Edith Turner. *Image and Pilgrimage in Christian Culture: Anthropological Perspectives*. Columbia UP, 1978.

Urrea, Luis Alberto. *The Devil's Highway: A True Story*. Back Bay Books, 2004.

"U.S. 666: 'Beast of a Highway'?" *Highway History: U.S. Department of Transportation Federal Highway Administration*, 18 Nov. 2015, fhwa.dot.gov/infrastructure/us666.cfm. Accessed 10 Mar. 2016.

Vásquez, Mary S. "Food for the Journey: Walking the Border with Rubén Martinez and Luis Alberto Urrea." *Monographic Review/Revista Monográfica*, vol. 21, 2005, pp. 180–93.

Viehmann, Martha L. "A Rain Song for America: Mary Austin, American Indians and American Literature and Culture." *Western American Literature*, vol. 39, no. 1, 2004, pp. 4–35.

Vizenor, Gerald. *Fugitive Poses: Native American Indian Scenes of Absence and Presence*. U of Nebraska P, 1998.

———, ed. *Narrative Chance: Postmodern Discourse on Native American Indian Literatures*. U of New Mexico P, 1989.

———. *The People Named the Chippewa: Narrative Histories*. U of Minnesota P, 1984.

Wakefield, Sarah. *Six Weeks in the Sioux Tepees: A Narrative of Indian Captivity* [1864]. Edited by June Namias, U of Oklahoma P, 1997.

"The Way of the Cross at the Colosseum." *Vatican: The Holy See*, 2004, Libreria Editrice Vaticana, vatican.va/news_services/liturgy/2004/documents/ns_lit_doc_20040409_via-crucis_en.html. Accessed 22 Mar. 2016.

Webster, Anthony K. *Explorations in Navajo Poetry and Poetics*. U of New Mexico P, 2009.

Wesley, Marilyn C. *Secret Journeys: The Trope of Women's Travel in American Literature*. State U of New York P, 1999.

Wesson, Cameron B. *Historical Dictionary of Early North America*. Scarecrow Press, 2005.

Wheeler, Rita. "Family Narrative." Roessel, pp. 75–85.

Whitman, Walt. *Leaves of Grass*. 1892. Signet Classics, 1962.

Wiget, Andrew. "His Life in His Tail: The Native American Trickster and the Literature of Possibility." *Redefining American Literary History*, edited by A. LaVonne Brown Ruoff and Jerry W. Ward Jr., MLA, 1990, pp. 83–96.

Work, James. "The Moral in Austin's *The Land of Little Rain*." *Women and Western American Literature*, edited by Helen Winter Stauffer and Susan J. Rosowski, Whitson, 1982, pp. 297–309.

Worth, Sol, and John Adair. *Through Navajo Eyes: An Exploration in Film Communication and Anthropology*. 1972. U of New Mexico P, 1997.

Wyatt, David. *The Fall into Eden: Landscape and Imagination in California*. Cambridge UP, 1986.

Wyman, Leland C. *Blessingway*. U of Arizona P, 1970.

———. *The Mountainway of the Navajo*. U of Arizona P, 1975.

Zahne, Herbert. "Family Narrative." Roessel, pp. 232–35.

Zapf, Hubert. "Creative Matter and Creative Mind: Cultural Ecology and Literary Creativity." Iovino and Opperman, pp. 51–66.

Zepeda, Ofelia. "Waila Music." *Ocean Power: Poems from the Desert*. U of Arizona P, 1995, pp. 48–49.

Zolla, Elémire. *The Writer and the Shaman: A Morphology of the American Indian*. Translated by Raymond Rosenthal, Harcourt Brace Jovanovich, 1973.

Index

About the Author

AMY T. HAMILTON is an associate professor of English at Northern Michigan University. She earned her BA at Pomona College and her MA and PhD at the University of Arizona. Her work includes essays on American Indian women writers, Euroamerican captivity narratives, and US Southwest-border literatures. She is the author of the critical collection, *Before the West Was West: Critical Essays on Pre-1800 Literature of the American Frontiers*, coedited with Tom J. Hillard.